special photography

MICHAEL FARRELL

CONRAN OCTOPUS

the
complete
WOODWORKER'S
companion

ROGER HOLMES

First published in 1996 by
Conran Octopus Limited
37 Shelton Street
London
WC2H 9HN

'Tea Table' by Stemmer & Sharp, made in solid maple

British Library Cataloguing-in-Publication Data
A catalogue record for this book is available from the British Library.

ISBN 1 85029 780 0

Commissioning Editor: Denny Hemming
Project Editor: Catriona Woodburn
Editorial Assistant: Helen Green
Copy Editor: Janet Swarbrick
Index: Hilary Bird

Art Editor: Alistair Plumb
Illustrator: Paul Bryant
Special 'step' photography: Michael Farrell
Picture Researchers: Helen Fickling, Claire Limpus

Production Controller: Clare Coles

Printed in China

A note on names and numbers

As an American trained in Britain, I bring a mid-Atlantic vocabulary to this
book. While differences between American and British woodworking
terminology have lessened, some remain, and I have tried to use terms
familiar to British readers in this edition. In some instances, however, I have
chosen a less common term, such as 'dado', whose meaning is more
precise than the familiar 'housing' or 'groove'. I have tried to define all the
important terms in the book by description or context, and to use them
consistently throughout.

I write a mid-Atlantic English, but work in old-fashioned imperial feet and
inches, and the metric measurements you find here are conversions. Where
generic measurements are given, as in descriptions of tools or standard
sizes of material, the metic measures provided are rounded equivalents of
imperial sizes. For project parts and other precise measurements, and on
drawings, only the metric measure is given, and it is an exact conversion
from the imperial. As there is no need to make a trestle upright exactly
57mm (the conversion from 2 ¼ in.), I encourage you to make slight changes
(to 55mm, for instance), which will make work easier while not altering the
proportions of the piece.

CONTENTS

INTRODUCTION

*T*wenty five years ago I decided to become a furniture maker. Enthralled with the thought of making useful, beautiful things with my own hands, I rented a small building and set up shop. Having stumbled across a collection of turn-of-the-century British magazines illustrating the handsome, forthright furniture of the Arts and Crafts Movement, I knew exactly what kind of things I wanted to make.

Unfortunately, I had no idea how to go about making the traditional joints that I saw in the English examples that so inspired me. For a year I struggled in my little shop, a period of many trials and even more errors. Finally, frustrated but determined, I decided to go to the source. I wrote to Alan Peters, an English craftsman whose name I'd seen in a book, and much to my surprise and delight, he offered me a spot in his shop.

The genius of the system of apprenticeship was evident from the first day. There is no better way to learn a craft than by first-hand observation and hands-on instruction from a master. I discovered, for example, that I had been working with dull tools – having never seen a truly sharp chisel or plane iron before, I had no way of knowing that mine were not up to snuff. Mine wasn't a true apprenticeship – I was too old for that – but the skills I learned during my time with Peters provided a sound foundation, the basis for years of enjoyable and successful woodworking.

Today, apprenticeships and student-ships are still rare, but a beginning woodworker will find more possibilities for instruction than I did – books, videos, weekend workshops, even degree courses at colleges. Yet many enthusiastic beginners, eager to explore and master tools and techniques that

**Opposite: The American Shakers'
concentration on function produced
furniture of simple elegance.**

**Right: Erik De Graaff's Abingdon
folding chair in red oak and
rubber is constructed using lap
and finger joints to create a form
that is sculptural and simple.**

fascinate them, still find themselves in my predicament, searching libraries and bookshops for solid instruction in the basics: how to saw, how to plane, how to chisel, how to sharpen tools (and know when they are sharp); how to cut mortises, tenons, dados, dovetails and assemble them into functional, attractive solid-wood furniture.

This book is my answer to those questions, my attempt to help others acquire the woodworking skills that have given me so much pleasure.

Solid yew and sycamore were used for this cabinet by Stephen Hounslow.

What is in this book

Woodworking encompasses a sizeable collection of individual crafts: cabinetmaker, joiner, carpenter, chair maker, wood turner, and finisher, to name a few. The range of tools, techniques, joints, and constructions employed to work wood can be at once fascinating and overwhelming to a beginner. Fortunately, it is possible to make a great many useful and attractive wooden things with a surprisingly small number of hand and machine tools, fundamental skills and basic joints, and it is these that are included in this book.

While gaining the skill to cut a crisp mortise, tenon, or dovetail can be the source of considerable satisfaction on its own, few people want to spend their time in the shop cutting sample joints. So here you'll find tools, techniques, and joints presented as part of the larger process of making useful things. The book is divided into five sections. The first two cover tools, materials and basic wood preparation. The next two present essential woodworking joints in the context of simple designs that embody constructions used in a wide range of furnishings. You can make the designs as shown in the dimensioned drawings or alter them to suit your needs or fancy. Or you can apply the techniques to projects of your own or someone else's design. Throughout the book, photos of work by contemporary makers demonstrate some of the possibilities of the constructions and techniques, including some intended to inspire you to explore methods not covered here. The final section introduces several basic finishing methods for protecting wood surfaces and enhancing their appearance.

The techniques covered involve both hand and machine tools. Some rely completely on hand tools, some on machines, many combine both. They are skilled operations, both simple and complex, all requiring a certain amount of practice to master. I have avoided methods that rely on elaborate jigs or complicated gadgets. A maker whose skills reside in his hands and head requires fewer tools and can tackle a far wider range of projects than the maker whose skill resides in an array of jigs and fixtures. Today, when even modest home workshops bristle with high-quality machinery, it is worth remembering the value of hand work. Some craftsmen enjoy the connection to centuries-old traditions; others take pride in being able to manipulate hand tools accurately and efficiently. Even if you prefer to work on machines, the experience of the hand-tool techniques your machines have replaced can make you a better woodworker, and may open up a whole new area of interest and enjoyment.

For similar reasons of practicality and pleasure, this is a book about working solid wood. Despite the introduction of plywood, particle board, and similar man-made materials, the basic repertoire of joinery and construction in use today would be largely familiar to a medieval craftsman. If you use man-made materials, you can apply many of the techniques in this book to them. But while we may appreciate the convenience of large sheets of plywood, most woodworkers prefer solid wood, with its variety of colours, textures and working qualities. The tactile pleasure of peeling a long paper-thin shaving off a slab of solid wood can't be matched by any operation on man-made boards.

As in other crafts, there is seldom a single correct path to woodworking success. My hope is that readers of this book will gain from it not only a solid foundation of skills and practical knowledge, but the confidence and inspiration to explore the wider world of woodworking that lies beyond these pages.

This English elm trestle table, made by Illingworth & Partridge, has a top 76mm thick.

This beech cabinet incorporates knock-down carcass joints for easy transport.

TOOLS AND MATERIALS

Good tools, well-chosen materials, an interesting project, and a comfortable place to work – it is hard to do good work (and even harder to have fun) without these elements. For many woodworkers, the attraction of the craft itself resides in them. Some enjoy the character and feel of fine old tools, others the diverse beauty and intriguing qualities of wood. The challenge of design motivates some (and frustrates others). And many woodworkers find respite from daily cares in the comfortable clutter of the workshop. Whatever your feelings toward them, you'll find useful practical advice about each in this section.

Opposite: There is great pleasure to be found in using good tools well, and the time and effort spent acquiring hand-tool skills is repaid with hours of enjoyment in the workshop that lead to successful woodworking.

1

DESIGN AND CRAFTSMANSHIP

Most woodworkers are enthusiastic craftsmen and reluctant designers. We all want the things we make – whether rustic chairs or elaborate break-front china cabinets – to be well made. We also want them to be handsome and well suited to their purpose. But while most woodworkers derive satisfaction from acquiring and improving skills with hand tools and machines, many find the design process daunting.

Part of the reason for this state of affairs is that craft skills, the manipulation of tools and shaping of materials, are physical and appear accessible to anyone willing to put in the practice. Seeing someone ride a bike, we surmise that if we make the same movements, we can ride a bike, too. Design, on the other hand, takes place largely in the mind. The physical skills of drawing and modelling are needed to bring a design to life, but the ideas guiding the hand, and the process by which they are formulated, are only hinted at in what we see. With the essence of the process hidden from view, the casual observer too often assumes design to be the province of the artistically gifted, assuming: 'I can't draw, so I won't be able to design'.

DESIGN
Design is not so mysterious or inaccessible. In fact, most people regularly practise it. When you are deciding which knick-knacks go where on the mantle, or figuring out how to lay eight place settings comfortably at a table for six, or arranging the flowers in the centre of the table, you are designing. Designing in wood is frequently no more complicated than these everyday examples. Most of us do not need to think too hard to come up with a bookshelf for a child's room or a cupboard for the back hall. The process is so simple you may never have thought of it as design. First you identify the problem – books are overrunning a child's room. You consider possible solutions: stack them neatly on the floor, put them in a box, build a bookcase. Choosing the

Opposite: A desk and stool combination in ash by Illingworth & Partridge.

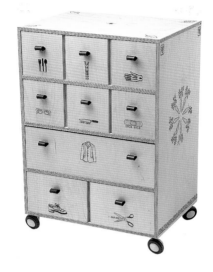

Designs applied with a rubber stamp add character to a simple plywood chest of drawers designed for The Holding Company.

bookcase, you count and measure the books, determine the space available in the room, how high the child can reach, and so on. Answering these practical questions determines how many, how deep, how wide, and how far apart the shelves must be. These dimensions in turn impose restrictions of size and strength on the materials you can use. Selecting suitable material, you are off to the workshop. You may not even have a drawing, just a few dimensions on a piece of paper and a picture in your mind of how the finished bookshelf will look.

Though the scale and complexity of the designs are much different, the process by which Chippendale designed a bookcase was probably much the same. If you strip away the elaborate embellishment – fretwork, carvings, mouldings – you will find his bookcase is also a stack of shelves whose dimensions are determined (at least in part) by the practical task of supporting books within a given space.

Of course it would be silly to carry this comparison much further. Clearly, what separates Chippendale from the rest of us is his marvellous talent for embellishment, along with a flair for materials and, perhaps most important, a superb sense of proportion that orchestrates all the elements.

The design process, then, is accessible to everyone and can be employed even by beginners to produce simple, practical solutions. Producing distinctive, imaginative designs, or solutions to complex problems, however, requires either a flair for it (some people are gifted) or a great deal of hard work, practice, and experience.

For those of us who are not particularly gifted there are several ways to approach design. The simplest is to let someone else do it for us. Many people are quite happy to work from existing plans and enjoy the challenge of craftsmanship. There are enough published plans of superb historical pieces to fill years of workshop time. The selection of contemporary plans is also broad, although the quality varies considerably.

If you are interested in developing design skills (and producing attractive pieces while you are at it), start by 'borrowing' from designs that you like. Design is a bit like language, the larger your vocabulary and the more comfortable you are using it, the more you can say. Furniture comes in a relatively few basic forms but a vast number of 'expressions' within each form. It was easy, for example, to work out the practical necessities of our little bookcase. Rendering those necessities in pleasing proportion, perhaps in a distinctive form, or with some sort of decorative embellishment requires that you have a considerable design 'vocabulary' to draw on as you cast about for an 'expression' that pleases you.

Build your vocabulary by collecting pictures of work you like. Buy books, subscribe to magazines, visit museums and craft galleries. At first, you may just try to copy an admired design or even work from a published plan. Don't be embarrassed to copy – for centuries artists and sculptors learned their crafts that way. But as you copy, question and analyse. Picture the doors with wider rails; the legs square instead of tapered; a more robust curve to the top; and so on. Would such changes improve or detract from the piece? Why?

As you gain experience, you will use borrowed designs less as sources of 'parts' to be assembled and more as inspiration. Even after you have gained a personal design vocabulary, borrowed design may remain a fundamental part of your design process – many accomplished designers 'adapt' details, proportions, and good ideas from other designers and historical pieces.

Some practical design suggestions

Designers work in widely varying ways. Some spend hours at the drafting table finalizing every detail. Others scratch out a few rough sketches, then head for the workshop where they complete the design in three dimensions, mocking up part or all of the piece full scale with scrap material. In time, you will find the method that suits you. It is useful for beginners to work out designs as completely as possible on paper. Draw plan and elevation views to scale. Make full-scale drawings of details and joints. This process helps ensure that you think everything out beforehand, producing fewer disasters in the workshop.

Proportion and scale – the relationship of the parts of a piece to the whole and of the piece to its surroundings – are at the root of most successful designs. Mocking up designs in three dimensions, full scale if possible, is the best way to develop an eye for these elusive qualities. A mock-up allows you to shave 6mm off a door rail and see the effect from a variety of angles. It allows you to play with the effects of light and shade on panels, overhangs, chamfers, and other features. Not every piece deserves a mock-up, but for those special pieces, a mock-up will repay the extra time and expense.

At every stage in the design process, evaluate the project not only for looks and function, but think about how you are going to make it. If there is no visual or functional reason for making the carcass sides 2mm thicker than the drawer fronts, make them the same thickness – it will save you time at the planer. The same applies to widths and lengths, specification of hardware and so on. In general, the fewer differences there are between parts, the easier the work of building will be.

CRAFTSMANSHIP

Becoming a craftsman is not unlike becoming a musician. A beginner concentrates on his instrument while reading the score note by note. The accomplished musician, master of his instrument, concentrates on making music. He knows the score intimately, beginning to end, and is conscious not of the individual notes but of the harmony or melody that sings from his horn or his strings.

The craftsman's results are rather more concrete than a musician's, but his performance is no less artful. His tools are extensions of his hands, instruments of his intentions. He is as little conscious of 'technique' as the horn player is of his fingering. Years of practice have made this second nature. Before he begins a project, he knows where he is going and how he will get there. Each stage of the process is efficiently organized, as is each individual task. In short, an accomplished craftsman wastes neither time nor motion.

We may never be the equal of those journeyman cabinetmakers of the past who honed their skills on a daily basis for many years in small workshops specializing in furniture of the highest quality. Nevertheless, learning to think like a craftsman is a big step on the road to becoming one. Weekend woodworkers or professionals, we can all benefit from an organized approach to our work. From conceiving the design to buffing the final finish, from placing tools on a bench to arranging your entire workshop, thinking like a craftsman will improve your work.

The Shakers' credo of simplicity is reflected in the form of this day bed, which relies on joinery that is traditional, if not necessarily simple itself.

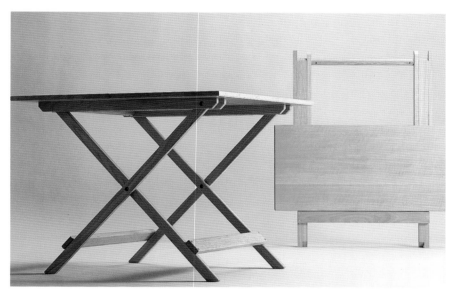

Robert Williams used simple mechanical fastenings and no traditional joinery for this oak folding table.

Learning to relish routine

Even the most complicated woodworking projects can be broken down into a hierarchy of discrete steps, the most basic of which comprise a surprisingly small number of manual skills – sawing, paring off wood with edge tools, and boring holes. Whether for a table, a chair or a chest of drawers, the stages of construction and the individual techniques involved in them are all much the same. The craftsman makes a virtue of woodworking's routine, repetitious nature. By doing the same job in the same way, time after time, you save time and, if your technique is sound, motion. Unless you are prone to daydreaming, you cut down on mistakes, too.

When cutting dovetails, for example, some craftsmen work their way across the board making all the right-to-left slanting cuts first, then work back the other way, cutting those slanting from left to right. It is not the only way or necessarily the best way to do it, but because they do it that way every time, they have become good at it. They do it without thinking (but not without concentrating), accurately and quickly.

Extending your routines beyond the actual sawing or planing extends your efficiency. Always stack project parts, for example, according to function – all the door rails together, drawer fronts together, boards for carcass sides and so on – then group these by the thickness of the rough-sawn boards. As you stack and restack after each operation, orient the parts so the grain will not tear as you plane and thickness the parts. You can quickly work through a stack arranged according to grain direction. This kind of orderliness may sound excessive, but it makes a difference. You will develop a satisfying – and efficient – rhythm for these repetitive tasks.

Joinery

Joinery is often an important visual as well as a structural consideration, and many factors can influence your decision to dovetail a carcass rather than join it with a tongue and groove. But once decided, think about how the process of making the joints might be rationalized. If there are several different components to be dadoed, can you standardize their sizes or their configuration to realize savings of time or material? Can you reduce the number of different-sized mortise-and-tenon joints from six to three? If so, you will eliminate three mortise-gauge set-ups, three drill-press set-ups, three table-saw set-ups and so on. These decisions often have a cascading effect that can save a great deal of time or eliminate complexity where errors can creep in.

As you move through the project, cutting joints and shaping the parts, use jigs and fixtures wherever possible. These can be simple blocks of wood clamped on a fence for a stop, or elaborate contraptions that hold parts for shaping. Jigs increase speed and accuracy, and reduce the risk of error.

Cutting lists and rods

Cutting lists are a good way to organize your work. (We have provided one for each project in this book.) At a glance, you can see the dimensions, material and, if you wish, the joinery for any part. Use the cutting list as a final check on your design. Examine it to determine which parts might be made the same thickness or width, which might be made of the same material, and so on. Those with computers can run up handy cutting-list forms.

In addition to working drawings and cutting lists, an invaluable aid to efficient working is the rod. Sometimes called a 'story stick', this is a narrow piece of wood on which the lengths and widths of all the major parts have been accurately set out full size. Rather than measure each drawer side in a stack with a rule and risk marking some at 550mm and others 545mm, you mark them directly off the rod. It also saves time. When selecting and cutting material to rough and then final dimensions, you need not return to the plan or cutting list to check every measurement. It is surprising how much information you can get on a 75mm-wide piece of plywood. It helps to paint the rod white and, if the piece is complicated, use different coloured pencils or pens (sharp pointed) to indicate different parts.

Organizing your workshop

A poorly organized workshop can take the fun out of woodworking. It is amazing how much time can be wasted searching for a box of screws or an infrequently used tool. Having to search for a frequently used tool can ruin your whole day.

There is not a right or wrong way to set up a workshop. Your workshop

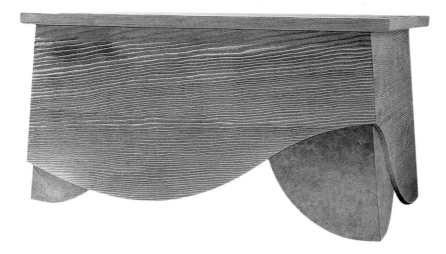

should reflect the way you work. Take time to consider the kinds of things you make, how often you make them and the processes involved. Position benches, fixed machines, hand tools and storage according to the way projects most often make their way through the workshop. Put your timber racks, for instance, where they are easy to restock (accessible to outside door or driveway), perhaps close to the tablesaw or bandsaw that you use to rough cut parts. Place the planer and thicknesser nearby, with a work table or room for a rolling trolley to hold the parts you are working on.

It is often helpful to identify 'work triangles', or groupings (in a variety of actual shapes) of machines, benches, hand tools and so on that are frequently used together. The bandsaw-planer-thicknesser arrangement above can speed the rough-cutting and the dimensioning of parts. A tablesaw, work-bench and hand tool rack may take care of most of your joint-cutting needs. With a little thought any workshop can be made a more productive and pleasant place to work.

WORKSHOP SAFETY

Woodworking is an inherently dangerous activity. Hand tools are sharp, machines are powerful and noisy, materials are heavy, dust and fumes are irritating or worse. Nevertheless, working safely is not difficult. It requires vigilance, consistency, and above all, common sense. The following discussion offers general advice on working safely.

Hand tools

Hand tools can be the source of a great many nicks, scratches, and the occasional nasty gash. Take a few simple precautions and hand tools will cause few problems.

- Sharp tools not only work better than dull ones, in most instances they're also safer, requiring less force and allowing better control.
- Carry chisels with the cutting edge toward the floor.
- If you drop an edge tool or it rolls off the bench, don't try to catch it before it hits the floor. Better a chipped tool than a stitched finger.
- Keep work areas clear of tools not in use. A cluttered benchtop is a disaster waiting to happen.

Machines

Woodworking machines may be involved in fewer accidents than hand tools (counting every nick and hammered thumb), but they can cause a lot more damage. The tablesaw is not inherently the most dangerous stationary machine in a workshop (the spindle moulder is probably that), but it is involved in more serious accidents than any other because it is used far more often. Seemingly safer machines, such as the drill press, thickness planer, even the bench grinder, can be dangerous if you are careless. Remember: most workshop accidents are likely to be the operator's, not the machine's, fault.

Airline pilots are required to go through a rigorous systems check each time they prepare for take-off. Woodworkers can benefit from the same routine when using machinery. Here are some check-lists and rules of thumb you might keep in mind before you turn on the machine.

Before you turn on the machine

- Is the task within the capabilities of the machine and the operator? If you are uncertain, take the time to construct a jig, or switch to another machine or hand tool.
- Organize your work. Think through each of the steps of the operation beforehand. Arrange the work area so that you know exactly where the pieces are coming from and where they are going after you have made the cut.
- Clear all unnecessary items off the machine and out of the area where you will be walking and standing.
- Make sure the machine will remain stationary during a cut. If it is on castors, immobilize them with brakes or wedges.
- If you are sharing a small workshop with other workers or visitors, check to see where everyone is before starting a cut.
- Make sure that everyone in the workshop (children particularly) understands that they are never to interrupt someone who is running a machine.

When the machine is running

- Give it your undivided attention.
- During the cut, keep your eyes on the sawblade or cutterhead – you are far less likely to run your hand into the blade if you are looking at it.
- Stand to the side of the blade or cutterhead, not directly in line with it – if something does kick back, you are more likely to avoid injury.
- Do not attempt to either pick up or push aside small or narrow pieces of waste which accumulate near a blade while the saw is running.

- Do not reach across a moving blade.
- At the completion of a cut, do not try to 'catch' pieces about to drop off the side or back of the table. Better a bruised board than a mangled hand. Plan ahead for a helper, outfeed rollers or extension tables to support the work.

On guard

Most woodworking machines come with guards of one sort or another to protect the operator from moving parts or flying debris. The best practice is to install and use the guards as directed by the manufacturer. You shouldn't even think about using most machines without one. Many woodworkers, however, have problems with tablesaw guards, so a few words here may be helpful. (Please note that to help you see exactly what is going on, we have removed guards from some machines while taking photographs.)

Standard-issue guards supplied with many tablesaws too often interfere with operations regularly performed on the machine. Typically, these guards consist of a metal or clear plastic cage attached to a metal plate directly behind the blade and bolted to the saw table or the arbour yoke. In addition to supporting the cage, the plate, which is the thickness of a saw blade, serves as a riving knife, preventing the sawkerf from closing and binding on the blade. Some blade guards and riving knives are also fitted with anti-kickback pawls, small wing-shaped pieces of metal, whose notched ends ride up on the material as it passes by, preventing it from being withdrawn or thrown back in the direction of the operator.

While these guards can operate somewhat clumsily for basic ripping and crosscutting, they do not make it impossible. (In some, the cage rides on the workpiece, and the effort to force it up over the piece's leading edge can be annoying and, worse, distracting.) But the riving knife makes any cut that does not go through the thickness of the wood impossible. After unbolting these guards a few times to cut a tongue, groove or tenon, they tend to stay off.

Several manufacturers offer a type of guard that overcomes many of these problems. Suspended over the table by a long tubular arm, with an independent riving knife that can be quickly depressed beneath the table, the guard poses no obstructions to dadoing and similar operations. If you need unobstructed airspace above the blade, the cage and arm can be swung out of the way. Unfortunately, these improved guards can be expensive.

So, what to do? Use guards even when it costs you a little time to put them on and take them off. If you can afford it, invest in an improved guard – and use it. If you must use the saw without a guard, work even more carefully and conservatively than you normally would. Use push sticks, keep your eyes on the blade at all times and your hands well away as the cut proceeds. Don't exceed the capacity of the machine. If you have removed the riving knife and a kerf begins to close causing the wood to bind on the saw, turn the saw off immediately, insert a wedge to reopen the kerf or remove and recut the board.

Eye and ear protection

A piece of sawdust in the eye half-way through a cut can break your concentration, not to mention damage your eye. Wear eye protection whenever the task creates flying sawdust: tablesaws and routers are particular offenders.

Prolonged exposure to the whine of high-speed blades and cutterheads may damage your hearing. Too many woodworkers suffer high-frequency hearing loss that can be attributed to router noise. Even noise that will not damage hearing can affect concentration, so it is a good idea to wear ear plugs or ear 'muffs'.

Protecting lungs and skin

Sawdust from some woods and fumes from solvents and finishes can cause respiratory damage or allergic reactions. To be on the safe side, wear a lightweight dust mask when you're likely to breathe in much dust (sanding, routing, prolonged sessions at a machine) or when you are working with non-toxic finishes. For greater protection, invest in an industrial respirator fitted with replaceable vapour cartridges and dust filters. Makers of paints, finishes and solvents can tell you which cartridge is needed to filter the product's vapours. Where skin rashes are possible, cover your body or, better yet, choose another wood.

Repetition

A craftsman makes the most of repetition and routine. You get into a groove when doing a skilled operation – cutting dovetails or tenons, planing edges for joints. But remember that repetition can lead to carelessness, particularly with machinery. Guard against this by taking a breather every 15 minutes or so, not long enough to break your rhythm, but enough to keep you from getting mesmerized.

No-brainers

Never work when you have been drinking alcohol or have taken drugs that impair your judgement or reflexes. (Anti-histamines, for example, have this effect on some people.)

Never push yourself to the limit. Quit work or don't start if you are tired or upset. Numerous accidents occur because people try to do just a little bit more at the end of the day.

Eye and ear protectors are essential for many machine operations. In addition, wear a dust mask or respirator to protect against respiratory damage.

2

WOOD

Of all the raw materials worked by craftsmen and women, wood is easily the most varied. There are thousands of species of trees, and hundreds of them have been used for woodworking. The wood milled from these trees exhibits a staggering range of characteristics. Colours run from the clean white of holly through the yellows of satinwood or ramin, the reds of mahogany and cherry, to jet black ebony. Add in similarly varied texture, figure, hardness, density and strength, and wood presents unlimited possibilities. Throughout this book photographs speak eloquently of the inherent beauty of wood. Here, we'll concentrate on the practical considerations of choosing wood.

A BRIEF ANATOMY OF WOOD

The visual characteristics and the working qualities of wood relate directly to its structure. The cells of a tree are long and thin. Rather like drinking straws, they are more-or-less hollow and hold and conduct fluids, primarily water. It is relatively easy to separate a bundle of drinking straws along their length, much more difficult to break them cleanly across their length. So it is with wood fibres: makers of ladderback and Windsor chairs take advantage of the ease with which fibres of certain woods separate when green (undried), splitting chair parts from the log faster than they could saw them from a board.

Trees grow from the centre out, adding cells around their circumference. Most trees add more cells during certain times of year than others, producing the growth rings that we see on tree stumps. In temperate climates, the rings can be markedly different colours and widths. Tropical trees tend to grow more uniformly throughout the year, producing more subtle distinctions.

Over the years, wood closer to the tree's centre, called heartwood, ceases to conduct nutrient fluids while accumulating other materials that often change the wood's colour and composition. In some woods the distinction between heartwood and the outer sap-

wood is considerable. Walnut, for example has rich reddish brown heartwood and almost white sapwood.

When a tree is sawn into boards, the angle at which the saw cuts the growth rings has a considerable effect on two critical qualities: the look of the boards' surfaces and the boards' stability.

Figure

The fastest and most common way to produce boards from a tree is to saw it 'through and through'. This happens when the saw intersects the growth rings near the centre of the tree at nearly right angles. These boards are often called 'radial-sawn' or 'quarter-sawn'. (True quartersawing involves quartering the tree trunk and cutting boards from each quarter more-or-less on a radius.) If the growth rings are distinct, this produces roughly parallel lines on the board's wide faces. Moving from the centre, the angle of the saw to the growth lines becomes more tangential. Growth rings on these faces produce oval or V-shaped patterns.

These surface patterns, called figure, are one of the delights of wood. Due to the idiosyncracies and vagaries of growth, trees exhibit a range of often breathtaking figure – curly, rippled, wavy, mottled and tiny localized swirls of 'bird's-eye' figure. Stretched or compressed fibres at the juncture of the trunk and a heavy branch can produce a spectacular 'crotch' figure.

Stability

Growing trees are very wet – hardwoods can be as much as 40% to 50% water by weight. When the tree is cut, water evaporates until the amount in the tree is in balance with the amount of water in the surrounding air. When water in the cell walls evaporates, the wood shrinks. Left to dry in the hot sun, a board can twist itself up as the outer fibres rapidly shrink while the inner remain moist. Reputable sawmills take great care to control evaporation and shrinkage by drying wood in covered and ventilated sheds or in artificially climate-controlled kilns.

Opposite: Restacked as logs after sawing, these boards are air drying.

SAWING AND FIGURE
Log sawn through and through

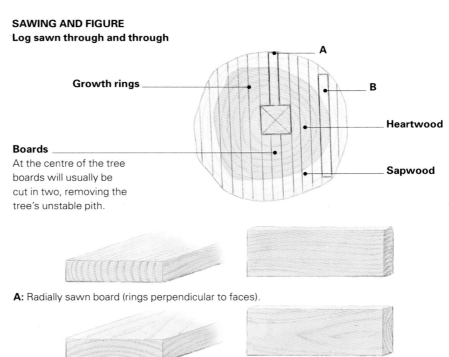

Growth rings

A

B

Heartwood

Boards
At the centre of the tree boards will usually be cut in two, removing the tree's unstable pith.

Sapwood

A: Radially sawn board (rings perpendicular to faces).

B: Flat-sawn board (rings tangential to faces).

The gain and loss of moisture unleashes strong forces as wood dries, as shown on the weathered butt end of this cedar log from Morocco.

The most important thing to know about all wood, air-dried or kiln-dried, is that it will continue indefinitely to gain and lose moisture and to shrink and swell as a result. That's why every year the drawers in your grandmother's 100-year-old bureau are likely to stick during humid conditions and rattle around in their openings when the house dries out during a hot spell. To work successfully with solid wood, you must learn to anticipate and accommodate the inevitable expansion and contraction of the wood with appropriate joints and construction.

CHOOSING THE RIGHT WOOD

It is a truism to say that the best material for a project is the one most suited to the purpose. However it does point up the importance of having a clear sense of purpose when selecting wood. Rosewood and rock maple are both strong, hard, durable woods, but you would only consider using one of them for a workbench.

Depending on purpose, the relative importance of a wood's strength, durability, working properties, stability, appearance and price will vary. A rosewood workbench might perform beautifully and last forever, but you would have a hard time working the brittle wood, even if you could afford enough to make a bench.

The majority of woods are so strong and durable that these two criteria are usually important only for large unsupported spans (shelves, for example) or surfaces such as tabletops subject to marring in use. Working properties of wood vary considerably from species to species and from tree to tree within the species. Some woodworkers prefer hard to soft wood, or buttery to brittle, others the reverse. Given sharp tools, most commercially available hardwoods and softwoods are workable. Some put up a struggle. Silica deposits in the heartwood or just plain

SAWING AND WOOD MOVEMENT

Flat-sawn (Dry, unrestrained.)

Greater shrinkage parallel to the growth rings (see drawing at right) causes flat-sawn boards to cup when they are dried without stacking or restraint.

Flat-sawn (Green.)

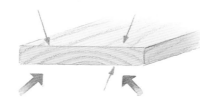

In all boards, expansion and contraction is greatest parallel to the growth rings (large arrows), least perpendicular to them (small arrows). Forces at oblique angles to the faces and edges of a flat-sawn board cause it to cup.

Radial-sawn (Green or dry.)

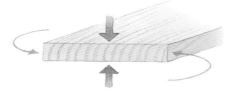

Movement parallel to the rings (thickness) is minimal because the distance is so small. Shrinkage forces are at right angles to the faces and the edges, so drying leaves the board relatively flat.

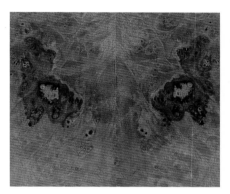
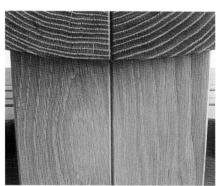

Arrested just in time, fungi produced the decorative decay shown on the maple doors (top left). A profusion of growth buds produced the burr elm veneered to this tabletop (top centre). Thin cross-sections of yew make a striking drawer front (above). Veneer makes possible mirror image patterns like the one shown bottom left. Sensitively matched for grain and pattern 'ordinary' woods (like the oak at bottom right) can also be eye-catching.

hardness will dull tools rapidly; interlocking grain tears easily; large open pores don't hold detail. But difficult woods very often have redeeming qualities that override their drawbacks. Rosewood, bubinga and vertical grain fir, respectively, fit the previous descriptions and all are worth the trouble for certain projects.

The stability of wood, the amount it expands or contracts due to changes in the level of humidity – its movement – varies from species to species. It also varies from board to board depending on the orientation of the growth rings to the board's faces. For most purposes, the movement of a board along its length and through its thickness is negligible, but noticeable and problematic across its width.

Movement is greater tangential, or parallel, to the growth rings than perpendicular to them. A radial-sawn board will shrink less across its width than a flat-sawn board of the same species. Because of the orientation of their rings, flat-sawn boards are also more likely to cup across their width, so

sawmills stack timber with small battens between boards to allow air flow for drying, and the weight of the stack restrains the tendency of the boards to cup.

Were stability the deciding factor, radial-sawn boards would always be the best choice. However, because of the figure produced in part by the ring orientation, flat-sawn boards are often the most attractive. Fortunately for many uses, movement differences between the two types of board are not significant enough to override other considerations, such as appearance. Where stability is a major concern, as it is for drawer sides, radially sawn boards are the best choice. But remember, no matter how it is cut, solid wood will move, so you must make sure your construction allows for it.

WHERE TO BUY WOOD

Finding a dependable supplier of good quality wood is, for committed woodworkers, on a par with locating a good family doctor or car mechanic. There are several likely sources.

Timber yards

You may not have to look any further than your town's timber yard for supplies of basic domestic hardwoods – oak, ash, maple, birch, cherry, walnut, sometimes even a regional favourite. A good timber yard can be a real joy to the woodworker. The selection may not be very broad or deep, but convenience and a personal touch can mean a lot – particularly if you are allowed to pick through the piles. Being able to rummage through several dozen boards to find four with matching grain and colour for that special tabletop can more than make up for any possible shortcomings in the inventory.

Sadly, the supply of old-fashioned timber yards has dwindled under an onslaught of mass-market home improvement centres. Where the concentration of woodworkers is high enough, a new type of speciality supplier is appearing. There you may find domestic and exotic species, sold by the board or the truckload, as well as a range of veneer and plywood unavailable at even the best local timber yards.

The straight-grained olive ash Matthew Burt used in this folding table suits the simple but elegant lines of this design much better than a highly figured wood.

Cabinetmakers

If you come up empty handed at the local timber yard, check out the professional craftsmen in your area. Keep in mind that they sell you wood as a favour – they earn their living making things out of wood, not selling it – and you are likely to find them very helpful. Although small workshops may not work with a wide range of material, they will probably have common domestic hardwoods and cabinet-grade plywood. If you are looking for larger quantities of material or something special, the shop may be willing to add your order to one of the regular orders they place with their wholesaler.

Sawmills

There are still a surprising number of small sawmills. Not all will be keen to sell in small quantities or to allow you to pick through the piles. But some will. You may not find a wide selection of species at a small mill; most deal exclusively with local hardwoods and softwoods. But you should be able to buy at good prices. And, if you get to know the operator, you might be able to get some custom sawing done. In some places it is common practice to keep together boards cut from a single log. Buying whole logs makes it much easier to match grain and colour for a piece of furniture or even an entire dining set. In addition, you can specify board thicknesses and, if the sawyer's

equipment and inclination permit, you can specify how you want it cut. Custom sawing is not cheap, but it can give you something you cannot get anywhere else.

Wholesale

Useful as local suppliers can be, there may come a time when your favourite timber yard or sawmill cannot supply what you want and you have to look farther afield. Although wholesale timber dealers are primarily set up to handle large orders, many will accommodate smaller purchases. Probably the best way to locate wholesalers in your region is to ask around at local sawmills and cabinet workshops. If you only need small quantities, perhaps you can go in with the workshop on an order, or alternatively get together with a group of woodworking friends and place a joint order. Sales policies differ among wholesalers, so it will take a phone call or two to sort things out. Be straightforward with the salespeople – do not claim to be a business if you are not – they are usually sympathetic and will try to work something out for you.

Mail-order

These days you can buy just about anything, including timber, through the mail. Mail-order is the most expensive way to buy wood, but if you cannot find what you need any other way, or you are looking for a small quantity of an unusual wood, mail-order may be worth the price. (See 'Sources of Supply' for mail-order suppliers.)

BUYING WOOD

When buying timber it is helpful to know something of the terms used in wood measurement, grading, surface preparation and seasoning.

Standard sizes

Most places sell hardwoods in imperial (sometimes metric) sizes. The lengths start at about 6ft (180cm) and increase in 1-2ft (30–60cm) increments. Widths start from about 4in (10cm) for temperate hardwoods (such as ash, oak and maple) and 6in (15cm) for other hardwoods; maximum widths can reach about 12in (30cm). Timber is usually sold in sawn straight-edged boards in the following thicknesses: 1in

(25mm), 1½in (40mm), 2in (50mm), 3in (75mm) or 4in (100mm), depending on the species.

Softwoods are generally sold in metric units. They are not usually kiln dried unless specified and so are prone to bowing and twisting. They are sold either rough-sawn or planed in lengths starting at 6ft (180cm), increasing in roughly 12in (30cm) increments. Board widths are up to about 9in (23cm). If the timber is sawn you get the specified dimension, if it is planed the nominal or finished size is usually ³⁄₁₆in (5mm) less than the specified size. Board thicknesses range from about ½in (15mm) to 2in (50mm).

Length and width
Hardwood timber is often sold 'random length and width', all boards being within specified limits. Assume, for example, you're buying random length and width cherry guaranteed to be at least 6in (15cm) wide and 8ft (250cm) long. The boards you receive might all be 6in (15cm) wide and 10ft (300cm) long, or they might contain widths between 6in (15cm) and, say, 15in (38cm) and come in a range of lengths over 8ft (250cm). If specific lengths and widths are important to your project, you can specify them, though it will probably cost a bit more.

Grading
Some familiarity with the system of grading wood is useful if you're buying boards sight unseen, say from a distant supplier. The standards for imported wood set by the timber standards institutes and associations of the countries of origin, identify a range of grades that differ, basically, in the number of defects allowed on the board's faces. Many suppliers put together the top two grades into a single category of first and second grade wood. If you are buying small quantities or need wide, blemish-free surfaces, stick with these

A pile of logs awaits processing at a mill. Though the practice is increasingly rare, buying wood in the log allows you to specify thicknesses, lengths and widths to the sawyer.

two. Either of the next two grades can be a good deal for projects requiring narrower finished pieces or if you are willing to glue-up wide pieces from several narrow ones. You can save money on lower grades if your projects will allow for more defects.

Surface preparation
Most timber yards sell boards that have been surface planed on the two wide faces. This PBS or P2F (planed both sides or planed two faces) stock is easier to evaluate than rough-sawn boards as defects and blemishes are obvious. Planing the edges in addition to the faces produces PAR (planed parallel but not square) boards and PSE (planed square edged) boards of uniform width as well as thickness. Other terms you may come across are PAR nosed one edge and PAR rounded (one edge).

Wholesalers generally offer rough-sawn timber, though they will surface plane faces and edges for an additional charge. Pushing a board through a thicknesser cleans its faces, but rarely flattens it. Flattening and thicknessing your own roughsawn boards with a

handplane or machines allows you to get the greatest thickness out of the material and ensures the flat parts necessary for quality work.

Seasoning
Except for timber bought directly from a sawmill, the timber you buy will almost certainly be seasoned, either in a dry kiln or the open air. If you buy from a reputable supplier, you can count on most of it being properly dried, which is just as well because drying defects are sometimes impossible to detect until you start to work the boards.

If you buy from a sawmill, it is prudent to stack and air dry the boards, even if the mill has done so already. Regardless of who seasons the wood, remember that if placed in a moist environment seasoned wood will absorb water vapour and swell; so to avoid problems, stack wood in your warm, dry workshop for at least a week or two before beginning a project.

How much to buy
All projects entail waste. How much depends on the design, the specific

wood, the grade, and how stingy you are with money and material. As a rule of thumb buy between 25% and 50% more wood than the total of the finished parts. Wholesale suppliers can often provide estimates of waste for common uses. The projects later in the book will provide experience of working out how much to buy.

The more wood you can buy, the more likely you will be to find boards that match for a top, or that provide nice straight grain for stiles, or a gentle curve for a stretcher. If you have the space and the money, keep your eyes open for handsome boards or good deals and stockpile material for future use.

Storing wood

When you store wood, raise the stack off the ground or floor with sturdy bearers. If the wood is not well-seasoned, ventilate the stack by separating the boards with 2cm-square battens spaced every 45cm to 60cm and extending across the faces. Align the battens directly above each other and above the bottom bearers so the weight is distributed straight down to the floor or ground. It is a good idea to ventilate seasoned wood in this way too. If you store wood outdoors, make sure it is well protected from rain, snow, and also direct sunlight.

MAN-MADE BOARDS

Most woodworkers prefer solid wood. It looks good to the eye, feels good to the touch and there's that special thrill in putting a tool to it, regardless of whether the tool is powered by hand or machine.

The further our chosen material gets from the tree, however, the less satisfying is our relationship with it. Split it from the log or saw it into boards and almost everyone is happy. Peel it off in thin sheets as veneer, and grumbles begin. Grind it up and press it into particleboard, and the objections become more widespread.

Much as purists may hate to admit it, however, 'sheet stock', such as plywood, has several distinct advantages over solid wood. Commonly available in standard widths, it can save time spent flattening, surfacing, and

Narrow wooden 'stickers', or battens, separate boards to increase air flow during air or kiln drying.

gluing-up solid-wood shelving, tabletops and carcass sides. It is stable, moving hardly at all in any direction with changes in humidity. Man-made materials also permit constructions that would self-destruct if subjected to the expansion and contraction of solid wood. Used in conjunction with fine veneers, it conserves valuable, sometimes rare material and allows you to form patterns with grain that would be impossible in solid wood. Surfaced with melamine or formica, sheet materials are excellent for kitchen and bathroom fittings.

Although this book focuses on solid-wood techniques, plywood carcass backs and drawer bottoms can be used where appropriate. You can also substitute plywood or particleboard for solid wood in a number of projects, sometimes without altering the construction (panels in frame-and-panel pieces, for instance), sometimes by using a different joint (a carcass with tongue-and-groove corners instead of dovetails).

A large range of sheet materials is widely available, but for most uses, veneer-core hardwood plywood is recommended. Widely available, it usu-

ally comprises two paper-thin face veneers laid on a stack of thicker veneers of cheaper hardwood or softwood, depending on the quality and the mill. Of better quality, and greater expense, some hardwood ply is made entirely of veneers roughly 2mm thick. There are no voids in any layer, and therefore no gaps on edges, regardless of where you cut it.

Particleboard suitable for cabinetwork and furniture is distinguished from its construction-grade relations by having finer particles overall. Like plywood, the sheets are layered – a core of coarser material is sandwiched between two smoothly sanded faces of very fine particles. On a good-quality 20mm board, each face layer might be as much as 3mm thick.

Ordinary particleboard is unpleasant to work and can be difficult to join adequately, so it is not recommended to beginners. A superior particleboard, called medium density fibreboard (MDF for short), is easier to work and joint. It consists of fine 'particles' that are distributed uniformly from the face through the core, not layered. The result is a material something like butter – cut through it and the edge you expose will look very much like the faces.

If you wish to use sheet materials, top quality plywood and MDF are often worth the extra cost. Their faces and edges are smooth and uniform with no veneer voids or coarse flaky core particles to deal with. Because of their cohesiveness, they are superior to hardwood plywood and particleboard, respectively, for joinery. From simple rebates, to biscuit joinery, to mechanical fasteners, these materials will outperform others in their class. MDF and top quality plywood splinter and chip less when sawed; the edges can be run through the planer, and they even handplane reasonably well.

As you might expect, plywoods are very strong, able to support their own weight and a load better than most hardwoods. MDF and its particleboard cousins do not bear weight well. Solid white oak, for example, will support more than six times the weight of high-density particleboard and almost four times the weight of MDF before

Ron Arad makes use of cherry veneer to create a sculptural form that would be almost impossible to construct in solid wood.

breaking. Problems are less likely to arise in cabinet construction where the spans are supported or reinforced by partitions, face frames and so on, than in tabletops or shelving. Veneered MDF or particleboard is, of course, stronger.

Regardless of their individual advantages, all sheet materials share a common drawback – their edges. Exposing layers of variously coloured strata, plywood edges look like geological samples, down to occasional tunnel-like voids in the plies. Particleboard edges can be crumbly; MDF edges are nondescript. Sheet materials usually need some sort of edging to match surface veneers or adjacent solid wood. If painted, they usually need to be filled and smoothed, if not lipped, to produce a uniform surface.

Edgings include pre-glued wood tape applied with a hot iron; veneer or thicker solid-wood strips are glued with clamps. Wider strips produce a 'banded' or framed look; a V-groove between the strip and panel masks the joint. Tongues can help align lippings during assembly. You can work them on narrow lippings, producing a T-shaped cross-section that fits into a groove cut in the edge. Loose tongues of thin plywood work well for wider lippings. Solid-wood face frames can be added to assembled cabinets to cover edges and stiffen the construction.

WOOD FOR BEGINNERS

If you are just starting out, you are probably eager to have a go at one of those wonderful woods you have encountered in a museum or magazine. English oak, French walnut, quilted maple, Sitka spruce, sugar pine, Douglas fir – exploring the special qualities of each at the workbench and in designs is one of the most exciting parts of woodworking.

But beginners make a large number of mistakes. Even when you don't make mistakes, your results may be a little rough. Premier woods come at a premium price, and some are difficult to work. It makes sense to make mistakes in less valuable, less expensive material. And if your goal is to master skills and techniques, why not do so with cooperative, easy-to-work wood?

Start out with a relatively inexpensive, relatively soft, evenly grained wood, such as soft maple, pine or basswood. (Almost all the step-by-step projects in this book are made of pine.) Eastern or Northern white pine is a less expensive option than Ponderosa or sugar pine, though you will have to include or work around solid knots. A locally or regionally available wood may be a suitable option.

If you can, buy roughsawn boards, which give you more room to manoeuvre when flattening them. If only PBS or P2F boards are available, buy one size up – if you want 20mm carcass sides, buy 32mm PBS boards, which you can flatten and then finish at the desired thickness.

With an inexpensive, easy-to-work wood, do not be afraid to make mistakes. Remember, every mistake is a lesson learned, and rough work smooths out with practice. When you have mastered basic skills and techniques, then break out that special stash of walnut and build an heirloom.

3

WORKSHOP AND WORKBENCH

Talk to woodworkers about their workshops and it is usually not long before you are hearing about the workshops they would like to have, rather than the ones they actually work in. Most of us have little choice when it comes to a workshop, we must make do with half of the garage, a corner of a damp basement, a steamy attic, or an old garden shed. But superb woodworking has long been done in humbler surroundings. A basement can be lightened up and dried out by painting the walls white and installing a portable dehumidifier. Spend some time and a little money insulating the garage or garden shed; add a window on the north side or a skylight; commandeer the spare bedroom or even a walk-in wardrobe for woodworking. Any place you can put a workbench can be a workshop, and if you organize it well, as discussed in chapter 1, it will be efficient.

If all these home remedies fail, explore the possibility of renting space with woodworking friends, perhaps sharing machinery expenses. At the very least, you can enrol in adult education woodworking courses at your local college and use their workshop as your own to practise your skills.

Because situations vary so drastically, workshop location and layout is largely a matter of the use of available space. One rule, however, is universally important. Make sure your shop has an adequate and safe electrical supply. If you spend money on nothing else, hire an electrician to examine your proposed set-up and do whatever it takes to make the shop electrically safe.

THE WORKBENCH

This may well be the most important tool in your workshop, the stage upon which dozens of other tools play their roles in the transformation of rough planks to finished projects. So central is the workbench to so many that we may cease to notice it much, to stop even considering it as a tool. But nothing brings home the value of a good workbench more than being without one.

While cabinetmaker's benches may vary in size, materials, types and placement of vices, the good ones all have at least three features in common. A good bench should be sturdy, able to stand up to daily pounding, as well as frequent burial beneath heavy piles of wood. Taking into account the lateral stresses imposed by hand-planing, resistance to racking is essential.

Weight is equally important. It is frustrating to find yourself pushing your bench around the workshop like a trolley as you attempt to plane a board. Even when the bench is bolted to the floor to keep it in place, weight is still necessary, particularly in the top, to absorb shock and dampen vibration.

The least obvious of the three essentials is a comfortable working height. A single day spent bending over a bench-top that is 8cm too low will provide ample evidence. The correct height, of course, is personal, depending upon how tall you are and the kind of work that you do most often at the bench.

A traditional cabinetmaker's bench is a pleasure to work on. Made of beech, maple, or similar hard, durable wood, its top might be 250cm or more long, 50cm wide, and 75mm thick, supported by a sturdy trestle base. To hold the work there should be two vices – a 'face' vice at the left end, opening perpendicular to the length of the bench; and a 'tail' vice at the right end, opening parallel to the length of the bench. The whole thing might weigh over 135kg.

Traditional cabinetmaker's benches are available, but they are very expensive and you can build your own for a fraction of the price. In addition to saving money, you can make the bench just the right height. The simple bench presented in this chapter is easy to make and should serve you well for years. It is recommended to anyone, particularly to those who are starting

Opposite: A sturdy workbench in a comfortable, organized workshop makes woodworking a pleasure.

Below: Traditional cabinetmaker's benches come in a variety of styles. The best provide ample weight and one or more vice-like devices to hold wood.

Tools can quickly overwhelm an untidy shop. Here, well organized racks and shelves put tools within arm's reach of the bench and keep clutter at bay.

out. Remember that the dimensions can be changed to suit your needs.

The top and underframe of this bench can be inexpensive pine. While not as dense or hard as traditional bench woods, pine is serviceable – when the top gets too scarred, it is easy to plane down. The top is small and if you have material and space, consider making it at least 30cm longer. A worktop need not be as wide as this, particularly if you add a tool tray along the back edge. Add the cross braces to the legs to counter racking stresses.

A good way to determine benchtop height is to stand holding the palm of your hand parallel to the floor and measure the distance from the floor to your palm.

All the techniques needed to build this bench are covered in this book. Consult the chapters in 'Basic Wood Preparation', for how to dimension the parts and how to edge-join boards to make a top. The trestle base is constructed of several mortise-and-tenon joints, all covered in 'Frame Construction'. Blind tenons join the rails to the legs; through tenons join legs to the top cleats. The remaining joints are assembled without glue, making the bench easy to knock-down and transport. The stretcher is positioned by a stub tenon and bolted in place. Lag bolt the top to the cleats. The cross brace is half-lapped and screwed together, then lap-jointed and screwed to the back legs.

If you are building your first bench, you may well face a classic conundrum – you need a bench to build a bench. To expedite matters, a local workshop may dimension the parts, even join up the top for you. If you do not feel up to cutting mortise and tenons, you can bolt the base together. Rebuild it properly when you have gained some experience and confidence cutting joints with the aid of your new bench.

Vices

Traditional cabinetmaker's benches have two vices, a face vice (or sometimes an L-shaped shoulder vice) and a tail vice. For this bench, invest in a good-quality steel face vice with jaws at least 180mm wide, 75mm deep, and opening 200mm. A 'quick-action' vice has a release on the screw mechanism, which allows you to slide the jaw on its guides rather than wind it out, which is a very handy feature.

Mount the vice between the front legs of the base, as close to the left leg as possible. Left-handers may want to reverse this orientation. You can mount the back jaw of the vice directly on the edge, or for a neater job, rout a recess so the jaw finishes flush with the edge. Wooden jaws cover both vice jaws to protect your work and tools from being marked by the cast iron. The wooden jaws are held in place with machine screws provided by the manufacturer for the purpose.

Although a tail vice can be used for a variety of tasks, the majority of the tasks carried out with it will probably involve holding boards between stops for planing. So, instead of the difficult-to-make tail vice, fit a long stop on one end of this bench. Butt a board against the stop, plane toward the stop and the board will not move.

FACE VICE

For a neat job, recess the back jaw of the face vice into the edge of the benchtop. Then screw wooden jaws to the cast-iron jaws to protect your work and tools.

END STOP

A combination of the end stop and turned wooden pegs that slip into holes bored in the benchtop hold a board in place for planing across the grain.

A HOMEMADE WORKBENCH

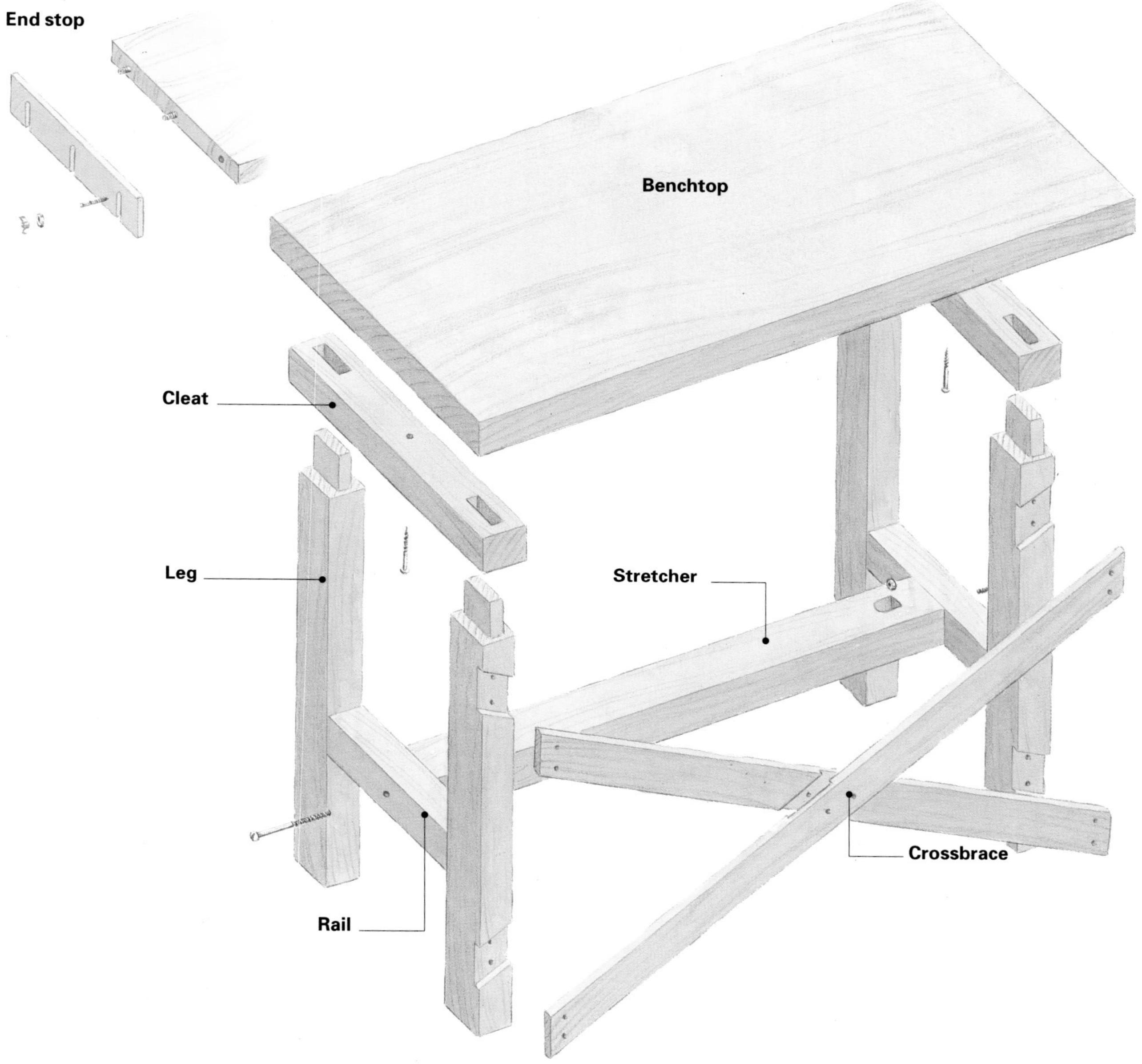

End stop

Benchtop

Cleat

Leg

Stretcher

Rail

Crossbrace

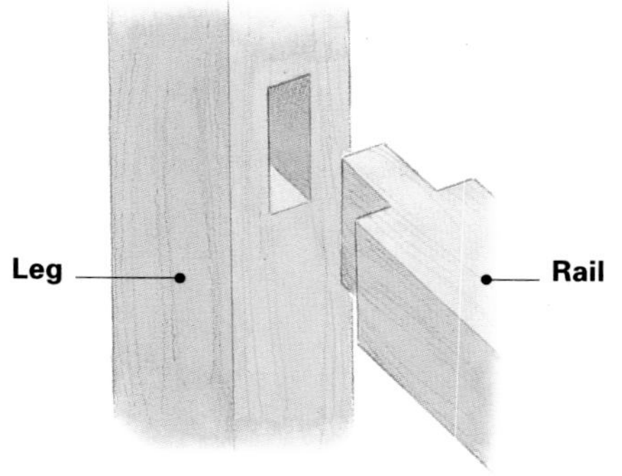

Leg

Rail

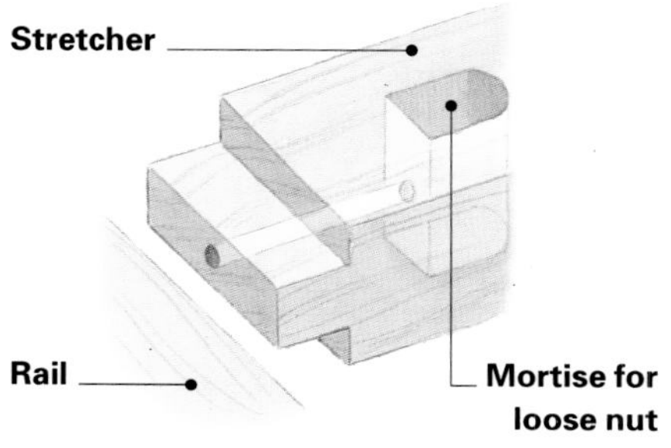

Stretcher

Rail

Mortise for loose nut

Assemble the joint, and bore the hole for
the bolt through the rail into the mortise.

SHOOTING BOARD

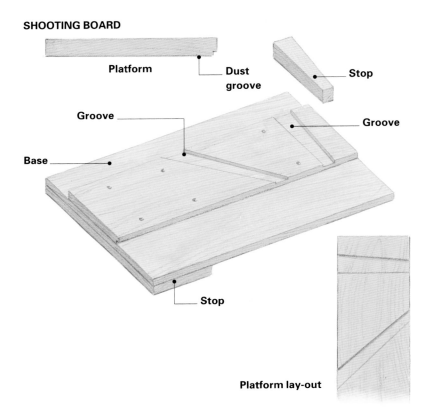

Platform

Dust groove

Stop

Groove

Groove

Base

Stop

Platform lay-out

BENCH HOOK

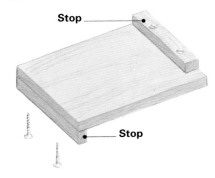

Stop

Stop

The stop is fixed to the end of the bench by three hanger bolts. The wood threads on one end secure the bolt in the end grain of the benchtop, while machine threads at the other end accommodate a wing nut. Plywood works best for the stop, as solid wood tends to split along the grain under planing pressure. Position the bolts and the slots in the stop to allow the stop to be lowered below the surface of the benchtop when not in use.

Working with the stop is easy. Large tabletops as well as small box sides as thin as 3mm can be planed against it. Because the stop contacts only the end of the board, the work can slide sideways when planing at an angle across it. To hold work in place for angled planing, bore a series of holes in the benchtop and turn wooden peg-stops to fit them. They handle the sideways pressure nicely.

Even if your bench has a tail vice, set up some sort of end stop. For many planing tasks, it is quicker than using the tail vice.

BENCH ACCESSORIES
Like many tools, a workbench can be enhanced by accessories. All sorts of bench-mounted bells and whistles have appeared on the market, from router tables to dozens of speciality vices. Some of these are very useful, but two traditional bench accessories that come in very handy need not be purchased and can be easily made in the home workshop.

Bench hook
The bench hook, which is one of the simplest accessories to make, is an excellent partner to the vice. It is indispensable for backsawing tenon shoulders, cutting pieces to length, and other precise crosscutting tasks on relatively small stock. (Large boards should be supported on saw-horses for crosscutting.) The bench hook accomplishes the task far quicker and puts the work in a much more comfortable position (unobstructed by jaws or benchtop) than clamping the board in the face vice.

A bench hook is simply a board fitted with two stops: one at the top, one at the bottom. As you push the work against the top stop, the bottom stop bears against the front edge of the bench. In essence, your hand and the top stop comprise a primitive but effective vice. (Slip a shim of the same thickness as the bench hook under a long piece to support its weight at the far end.)

A bench hook can be cobbled together from wood scraps and nails. After several years' use, the nails may begin to work loose, so add a few screws to hold the stops in place. You can, of course, alter the size, materials and construction to suit your needs and preferences. Do not make the hook too small; let a comfortable sawing distance from the front edge of the bench govern its length.

Shooting board
Although not essential, a shooting board is well worth having. With it, you can square up drawer sides, box sides and other relatively small parts whose ends must be at exact right angles to their edges and faces. With the 45° stop in place, you can trim frame mitres for a gap-free fit.

Unlike the bench hook, the shooting board is a fairly precise tool, and should be carefully constructed. The baseboard shown here is plywood and the platform is made from solid cherry, but because of its dimensional stability, a hardwood plywood would have been a better choice for all parts. Hardwood serves well for the wedge-

shaped stops, which need truing every now and then.

Make the board large enough to support your favourite bench plane. The one shown here accommodates a long try plane. Whatever plane you use, make sure that its sides (at least the one that will run on the platform) are at right angles to the sole. Because of the board's length, add a block in front of the bottom stop to position the top stops at a convenient distance from the edge of the bench.

Some people make a longer version of this board for planing the edges of boards, but others prefer to 'shoot' edges with the stock clamped in the face vice, trusting their hands to plane the edge at right angles to the face.

Lighting is particularly important in a workshop. Natural light, as shown here, is comforting. Remember though, that a bank of large, south-facing windows can turn the workshop into a greenhouse on a sunny day. For close-up work, good artificial light saves a lot of eye strain.

BENCH HOOK AND SHOOTING BOARD

1 Very simple to make and to use, a bench hook is handy for all sorts of precise crosscutting, such as cutting the shoulders on a tenon.

2–3 With the 90°stop in place, a shooting board trims the ends of drawer sides or other small parts dead square. Shifting to the 45°stop, you can true a mitre for

a small door or picture frame. You will find that subtle changes in hand pressure on the plane or workpiece are necessary to get best results.

4

TOOLS

The number and variety of woodworking tools is at once fascinating and daunting. A stroll down the aisles of a local hardware store presents dozens of possible purchases. Page through a mail-order catalogue catering specifically to woodworkers and you find hundreds more. A beginner surveying this vast array has reason to be at least a little anxious. How many tools do I need? Can I afford them?

The most important thing to know about tools is that a few of them used skilfully can be more than the equal of a workshop full of expensive equipment. Remember that most of the exquisite woodworking we admire in museums was made by people who could pack all their tools into a box the size of a blanket chest.

The basic woodworking 'kit' shown and discussed in this chapter includes everything you will need for the techniques and projects in this book, and for a lot of other work as well. In order to help you navigate your way, the list has been pared to a minimum, though a few optional but very useful entries are also included. Hammers, screwdrivers, wrenches and other common tools which you are already likely to have around the house are not included.

Even reduced to essentials, a woodworking tool kit is an expensive proposition. Purchased new, the hand and machine tools on our basic list would cost thousands. You can trim expenses by buying used tools, which can be far less costly. Serviceable hand saws, planes and clamps turn up regularly at second-hand sales and flea markets; machinery is often listed in newspaper classified ads.

Whether it is new or used, buy the best tool you can afford. A good tool will last many years, some a lifetime. Buy from a reputable supplier, local or mail-order, and you are not likely to go wrong. (See 'Sources of Supply' for a listing.)

HAND TOOLS

Much of the attraction of woodworking resides in hand tools and the tasks they perform. The best of them are admirable creations in their own right – small wonder so many woodworkers become *de facto* tool collectors.

Saws

A minimal tool kit would contain just three saws, and rely on machines for many sawing tasks. The crosscut handsaw is used mostly to cut rough timber to approximate length prior to planing and thicknessing. (One or more pairs of sturdy sawhorses are useful for this and other tasks in the workshop.) Joints are cut with a backsaw, waste removed with the coping saw.

Like horse buyers, prospective handsaw purchasers need to pay close attention to teeth. The type and size of a saw's teeth largely determine its use. Handsaw teeth are filed in two shapes depending on whether they are to cut across the grain of the wood or along it. Crosscut saw teeth form points, which score the wood as they cut across the grain; this prevents the wood fibres from tearing. Ripsaw teeth are like a row of tiny chisels. They chop out the

Opposite: Well organized tools greatly increase the efficiency and pleasure of woodworking.

SAWS

Coping saw

Backsaw (e.g. tenon or dovetail saw)

Handsaw

wood as they cut along the grain, where there is little danger of tearout. Both types of tooth are 'set', bent alternately to either side of the blade. Because the wood removed as the saw cuts (called the 'kerf') is wider than the saw blade, the blade is less likely to bind in the cut.

SAW TEETH

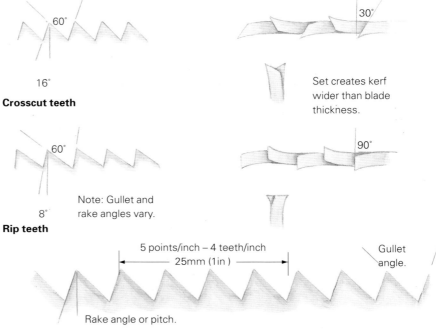

60°

16°

Crosscut teeth

60°

8°

Rip teeth

Note: Gullet and rake angles vary.

30°

Set creates kerf wider than blade thickness.

90°

5 points/inch – 4 teeth/inch
25mm (1in)

Gullet angle.

Rake angle or pitch.

Teeth nomenclature

PLANES

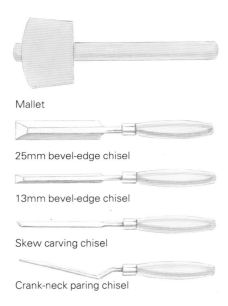

Spokeshave

Shoulder plane

Block plane

Smoothing plane

Try plane

CHISELS

Mallet

25mm bevel-edge chisel

13mm bevel-edge chisel

Skew carving chisel

Crank-neck paring chisel

For rough work, saws have large teeth set to cut a wide kerf. Finer work, such as cutting joints, requires more teeth with less set. Manufacturers indicate either the number of teeth per inch or the number of points per inch. A 10-point crosscut saw and a 15-point tenon saw are good for beginnners.

Planes

Planes are easily the most varied woodworking tool, but many have been supplanted by machines, so our minimal tool kit contains just three: a bench plane, a block plane and a shoulder plane.

Bench planes are workshop workhorses. They strip off thick shavings to flatten rough boards; they true edges flat and square for gluing into wide panels; they curl up thin wisps of wood in the final preparation of surfaces for finishing.

Bench planes are usually grouped into three categories according to length. Smoothing planes put a fine finish on exposed surfaces and are about 8in to 11in (20-28cm) long with cutting irons from 1½in to 2½in (40-65mm) wide. Jack planes, used to rough-plane boards to dimension, are 12in to 18in (30-45cm) long, with irons between 2in and 2½in (50-65mm). (The longer jack planes are sometimes called fore planes.) Try or jointer planes, the longest planes at 22in or 24in (55cm or 60cm) long, with irons of 2⅜in or 2½in (60mm or 65mm) width, are ideal for flattening surfaces and planing edges straight.

Many modern woodworkers continue this pattern of use. But machines have taken over several of these tasks, and a single bench plane can handle what remains. Try out various planes, if you can, and choose one whose size and balance is comfortable for you. Metal bench planes are good for beginners, as the wooden versions can be a little fussier to adjust and maintain.

Two other planes in the kit are more specialized. The block plane is a sort of miniature bench plane, only 6in (15cm) long with a blade 1⅝in (40mm) wide. It is handy for chamfering edges, and when working vertically or in the cramped confines of an assembled carcass. A shoulder plane (sometimes called a trimming plane) is little more

than a rectangular block of steel, its sides perfectly square to its sole, fitted with a cutting iron that extends the full width of the sole. It is indispensable for trimming tenon shoulders and cheeks, and cleaning up machine-cut rebates. A small shoulder plane, about 6in (15cm) long and 1⅛in (30mm) wide, is more comfortable to use and more versatile than large models.

Two optional tools are a spokeshave and scraper blade. The spokeshave is, effectively, a plane with a very short sole, handy for forming or cleaning up curved surfaces such as the edge of a round tabletop or the sweep of a cabriole chair leg. Metal spokeshaves come with flat bottoms, for convex surfaces, or rounded bottoms for concave. Their blades resemble and are sharpened like plane irons. The scraper blade is simply a smallish piece of hardened steel, usually rectangular, 6in or 8in (15cm or 20cm) long, 2in (50mm) or more wide, and ½2in (1mm) or so thick. A slight burr of steel formed by burnishing its long edges raises a fine shaving during the final surface preparation.

Chisels

Every woodworker needs a good set of chisels. Bevel-edged cabinetmaker's chisels are sturdy enough to be driven with a mallet and are also well suited for finer, more accurate paring cuts made with hand power alone. The bevelled face of the blade reduces weight, is comfortable in the hand and allows the chisel to be used in tight spots, such as cleaning out the acute angles of a dovetail.

A basic set would include chisels from ⅛in to 1in (3-25mm) in ⅛in (3mm) increments (the ⅞in is optional). Additional widths of ³⁄₁₆in (5mm) and ⁵⁄₁₆in (8mm) come in handy, but can be difficult to find. Bevel-edge chisels are usually 9in to 11in (23-28cm) long, including the handle, though some woodworkers prefer a shorter type, called butt chisels, which range up to about 9in (23cm) long.

A paring chisel with an offset, or 'cranked', handle allows you to work with the blade flat on the wood surface even in the centre of wide panels. One or two narrower chisels whose cutting edges are ground at a skewed angle are indispensable for cleaning up the sockets of half-blind dovetails. A ¼in (6mm) skew carving chisel works well, or grind bevel-edge chisels to suit.

The quality and temper of the steel is by far the most important factor in choosing a chisel. The steel must be hard enough to hold a keen edge; but tempered too hard, the edge becomes brittle, and will break down quickly. Because it is difficult to check tool steel against standard industry hardness scales, you will need to rely on the reputation of the manufacturer or supplier.

Finally, you will need a mallet. A relatively lightweight (about 340g) mallet packs enough punch and isn't tiring to use. You can make one yourself of any hard, dense wood.

Boring tools

Whether it is clearing waste from mortises, drilling pilot holes for screws, or making holes for shelf fittings, not much time goes by in the workshop without needing to bore a hole.

Despite the low cost of electric hand drills and powered drill presses, the brace is still a valuable part of a woodworker's tool kit. A good general purpose brace is about 14in (35cm) long, offset about 5in (12cm) to give a 10in (25cm) diameter sweep.

Braces are most often used with auger bits, spirals of steel with a screw point and pairs of spurs and cutters at the business end. Auger bits are commonly available in diameters of ¼in (6mm) to 1in (25mm) graduated in 1⁄16in (2mm) increments. For larger holes, buy an expansion bit, which can be adjusted to cut holes from ⅝in to 3in (15-75mm), depending on the kind you buy. It can be difficult (or impossible) to force through hard woods at large settings. More accurate, and more expensive, expansion bits are made for drill press use.

For smaller-diameter holes, hand-powered hand drills or electric hand drills both grip twist bits in a centred three-jaw chuck. Look for an electric drill with a ⅜in or ½in (9mm or 13mm) capacity chuck; higher amperage motors are less likely to burn out under a load.

Two types of twist bits are useful. Spur-point twist bits, available in 1⁄16in (2mm) increments between ⅛in and ½in (3mm-13mm), have a small point and pairs of spurs and cutters that function like those on auger bits to cut clean, accurately sized holes in wood. High-speed steel twist bits are designed to cut metal, and have tapered noses, with no spurs. They are handy for boring pilot holes for screws, as well as for making jigs, fixtures or fittings out of metal or other materials. For making larger diameter holes with an electric drill, try inexpensive flat bits; pricier Forstner bits make cleaner, more accurate holes but must be used on a drill press.

Rounding out the boring tools are countersinks in one or two different pitches for creating tapered seats for flathead screws or for chamfering shelf-support holes.

Measuring and layout tools

Accurate results depend on accurate measuring and layout. You will need a tape measure (10ft/3m minimum). A 12in (30cm) precision steel rule doubles as a measuring tool and a short straight edge. Three squares will ensure that surfaces are exactly at right angles to each other when you mark joints and set up tools. A try square with a 7in (18cm) blade is the most accurate. A combination square with a 12in (30cm) blade and 90° and 45° faces on an adjustable head is the most versatile. A carpenter's framing square, with blades 18in and 24in (45 and 60cm) is essential for squaring lines across wide surfaces.

For laying out angles other than 90° or 45°, the most convenient tool is a sliding bevel. The 8in (20cm) steel blade can be adjusted in the metal or wooden stock to angles as low as about 15° up to 180°.

Most joints require layout lines running parallel to a board's edge, face, or end. Marking gauges do the job more efficiently and accurately than squares or straight edges. The gauge consists of a beam, about ¾in (20mm) square and 8in to 9in (20-23cm) long, and a fence about 1in (25mm) thick, 2in (50mm) wide, and 3in (75mm) long.

In the simplest marking gauge, a single sharpened pin near the end of the beam makes the line. A combination mortise and marking gauge has a single

MEASURING AND LAYOUT

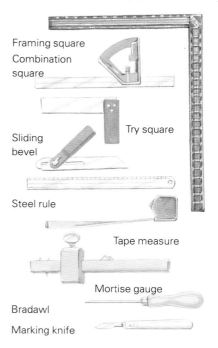

Framing square
Combination square
Try square
Sliding bevel
Steel rule
Tape measure
Mortise gauge
Bradawl
Marking knife

BORING TOOLS

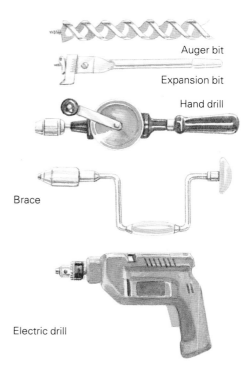

Auger bit
Expansion bit
Hand drill
Brace
Electric drill

CLAMPS

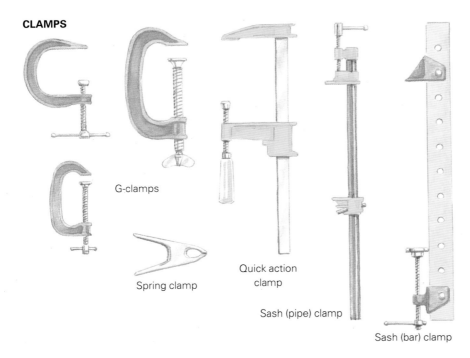

G-clamps

Spring clamp

Quick action clamp

Sash (pipe) clamp

Sash (bar) clamp

pin on one side of the beam and, on the other side, two pins for marking the double parallel lines of mortise and tenon cheeks. One pin is fixed, the other is attached to a piece of brass that slides in a groove along the beam's length.

Two additional gauges, both modifications of a single-pin gauge, are useful. On one, a pencil point replaces the pin; make your own by boring a hole for the pencil in a gauge beam. In the second, a pin of slightly larger diameter is sharpened to a knife edge, which scores a much cleaner line across grain than a pin-point. Commercially made versions, called cutting gauges, have a small knife held in the beam by a set screw or small wedge.

For laying out tenon shoulders and marking dovetail pins, a thin-bladed knife produces a much finer, more accurate line than a pencil. To position auger bits and other drill bits accurately, use a bradawl.

Clamps

A woodworking truism is that you can never have enough clamps (The older term 'cramp' is still widely used). Fortunately, you can handle most clamping tasks with just two kinds of clamp. Sash clamps serve where the

job requires a wide span but little depth, such as gluing edge-joined table-tops, pulling together larger mortise-and-tenon constructions, and assembling carcasses. Quick-action clamps cover a multitude of uses for smaller projects, and for projects where a deep throat is required.

Sturdy, commercially made sash clamps are good, but expensive. For the cost of a single 4ft (100cm) 'I-bar' clamp, you can make two 4ft 'pipe' clamps by fitting a pair of cast-iron jaws on standard ¾in (19mm) black pipe available at hardware stores or plumbing supply shops. Save money by purchasing pipe in a range of lengths and interchanging the jaws according to the job being done. Four pipes each of 3ft, 4ft and 5ft lengths will serve most needs. Lengths from 3ft to 10ft come in handy on occasion.

With one fixed jaw and one that slides along a rectangular steel bar, quick-action clamps are rather like small versions of sash clamps. In addition to serving a wide range of assembly needs, they are invaluable for securing work to a machine or to the workbench and for use with all sorts of jigs. They are generally less expensive than the heavy-duty cast-

iron G-clamps, quick-action clamps are also more convenient because you can quickly slide one jaw snug to the work rather than twisting a long length of G-clamp screw into position. Quick-action clamps come in a range of sizes and weights. A 1ft (30cm) light-duty clamp (2½in/65mm throat depth, ¼in/6mm thick bar) is a good size for most jobs.

While sash clamps and quick-action clamps do the lion's share of the work in a workshop, a supply of small G-clamps and spring clamps, clothes peg-like gadgets, will be useful for setting stop blocks on fences and other jig-rigging tasks.

POWER TOOLS

Power tools have emancipated wood-workers from a great deal of workshop drudgery. The hours spent pushing hand saws and planes to reduce a pile of rough boards to proper length, width and thickness can be shrunk to minutes with a tablesaw, surfacer and thick-nesser. The tedious task of cutting dadoes with tenon, chisel and hand router plane is quickly and accurately done with an electric router.

Machinery takes up space. If you have little to spare, take a look at the smaller, well-made machines that have recently appeared on the market, or consider machines that combine several functions. If your budget is cramped too, buy second-hand machines.

Tablesaw

It is hard to imagine a machine more central to the basic tasks of a small workshop than the tablesaw. With it, you can cut solid wood and all manner of man-made sheet stock to length and width. You can plough grooves and dadoes, fashion tenons, finger joints and dovetails. Devoted tablesaw woodworkers, armed with jigs and fixtures can make the tool perform astonishing feats.

A tablesaw is, in essence, just a circular saw blade protruding through a narrow slot in a tabletop. Almost all cuts are made using two simple fixtures that come with the machine. A fence, aligned parallel to the face of the blade, guides and supports boards being ripped (that is, cut lengthways, with the grain). This 'rip fence' is stationary, and you push the wood along it into the spinning blade. To make cuts across the grain, you hold the board against a fence set at the desired angle to the the blade. Here, however, the fence (called a 'mitre fence') moves, carrying the wood held against it into the blade.

Tablesaws differ widely in size, complexity and quality. When you shop for a saw, look for capacity, stability and accuracy. A good home-shop machine will take a 9in or 10in (23 or 25cm) blade, have a 1½ HP to 3 HP motor, a cast-iron table with heavy sheet metal base, carefully machined working surfaces, and durable fences capable of taking and holding fine adjustments.

It is easy to get confused by the numerous different styles of tablesaw blades available. A general-purpose combination blade with tungsten-carbide teeth designed to rip and crosscut is sufficient for everything in this book. (Look for an 'ATB/R' blade; the acronym describes the configuration of the teeth: 'alternate top bevel with raker.') If you can afford it, buy two combination blades, so you won't lose time while one is being sharpened.

For cutting grooves, or removing waste from tenon cheeks, a set of dado (or grooving) blades comes in very handy. Most sets consist of two outer blades whose teeth resemble those of a combination blade. Between these fit 'chipper' blades with from two to six teeth. Placed in various configurations, the blades make cuts between ¼in and $^{13}/_{16}$in (6-20mm) wide.

Surfacer

Compared to the tablesaw, a surfacer is a very limited machine. But without a surfacer (and its companion, the thicknesser), there is a lot of back-breaking work, flattening, straightening and thicknessing boards with a handplane.

A surfacer is, essentially, a large upside-down plane: the infeed and outfeed tables are the plane's sole and the rotating cutterhead its blade. Instead of pushing the plane across the wood, you push the wood across the cutterhead.

The width of the cutterhead limits the width of board you can flatten. A 6in (15cm) surfacer is barely adequate, and requires that solid-wood tabletops and carcass sides be joined up of pieces no

TABLESAW

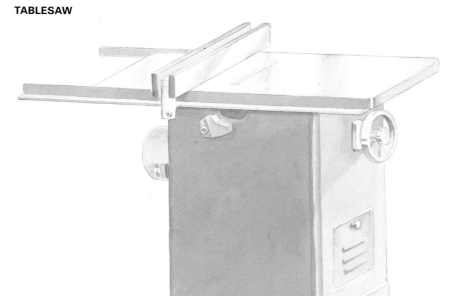

SURFACER

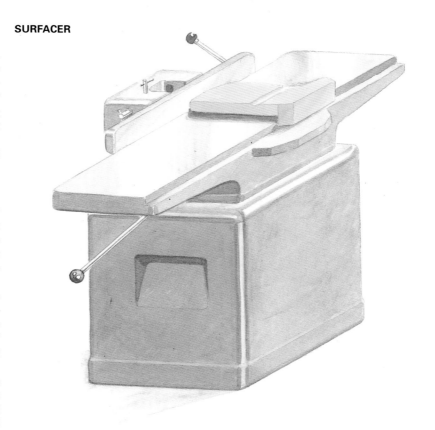

THICKNESSER

ROUTER

RANDOM-ORBIT SANDER

wider than 6in (15cm). An 8in (20cm) machine is better, but usually at least twice the price of the more common 6in surfacers; wider machines are even pricier.

So, buy the widest surfacer you can afford and fit into your workshop. Make sure it is accurate, its cast-iron surfacing tables machined dead flat and precisely aligned and its cutterhead sufficiently powered (1½ HP, 230V motor). Longer tables are better than shorter, as they make it easier to true the edge or face of a long board.

Thicknesser

The most specialized tool in the workshop, a thicknesser's only task is to reduce boards to uniform thickness. It consists of a cutterhead and one or more powered rollers suspended over and parallel to a machined table. Depending on the make, either the table or the cutterhead is moved up or down to determine the depth of cut and the thickness of the board.

For many years thicknessers were too expensive for most home workshop woodworkers. Today, a number of portable 12in (30cm) planers as well as heftier 12in to 15in (30-38cm) models are modestly priced. If you can afford one, buy a heavier, stationary machine, and make sure it has enough power: you will often be planing a stack of boards one after the other, and it is frustrating to keep blowing fuses in the process. A 2 HP motor is the minimum. Equipped with a surfacer and thicknesser, you can determine the thickness and ensure that boards are dead flat.

Router

An electric hand-held router is versatile and is useful for cutting grooves, dadoes, mouldings, mortises, tenons, dovetails, even flattening and thicknessing boards. Fixed upside-down in a table, it becomes a small, low-cost spindle moulder. One with a ¼in (6mm) chuck and 1 HP motor is a good choice for beginners. More expensive and versatile, plunge routers can be lowered into the cut, an advantage for routing stopped grooves. High-speed steel bits are less expensive than tungsten carbide tipped bits, but dull much quicker.

Combination machines

The home workshop woodworker's machinery dilemma can be summarized succinctly: 'Can I find machinery of adequate capacity at affordable prices that will fit into limited space?' Universal machines offer an elegant solution. One make, for example, puts a 9in (23cm) tablesaw, 8in (20cm) surfacer and thicknesser, a spindle moulder, and a horizontal mortiser in the space occupied by an ordinary 10in (25cm) tablesaw. The machine is well-engineered and constructed, and much cheaper than the combined prices of comparable individual tools.

Bandsaw

Though not an essential machine, a bandsaw is the first machine you should consider after acquiring a tablesaw, surfacer and thicknesser. A bandsaw lets you cut the curves of a round tabletop or a cabriole leg. It is also a safer tool than a tablesaw for cutting tenon cheeks, ripping long boards, and resawing thick boards into thinner ones.

A bandsaw comprises a continuous thin, narrow saw blade running on two or three wheels. A 14in (35cm) model is adequate for home workshops. (The dimension indicates the distance between the blade and support column.) The three-wheel models have a reputation for being temperamental. A good general-purpose blade is ¼in (6mm) wide with 4 to 6 teeth per inch (tpi).

Drill press

Another optional machine, the drill press, offers the advantages of accuracy and stability over a brace and bit and hand drills (electric and manual). Repetitious hole boring, such as clearing waste from mortises, is easier and more accurate on a drill press. Look for a drill press with a ½in (13mm) capacity chuck, and stepped pulleys allowing variable speeds.

Random-orbit sander

A random-orbit sander is capable of removing wood quickly while offering control of precision sanding. Very much an optional purchase, it can save you considerable time preparing tabletops and other wide surfaces.

A BASIC TOOL KIT

Asterisk* indicates optional tool. Sizes are suggested; others can be substituted.

HAND TOOLS

Saws (measurements indicate blade length; ppi is tooth points per inch.)
Crosscut saw, 25in (63cm) 10 ppi.
Tenon saw, 14in (35cm) 15 ppi.
Coping saw, 6½in (17cm)
*Ripsaw, 26in (65cm) 6 ppi.
*Dovetail saw, 8in (20cm) 20 ppi.

Planes (plane measurements are approximate sole lengths)
Bench plane: one or more of try, 22in (56cm); jack, 14in (36cm); or smooth, 9in (23cm)
Block, 6½in (17cm)
Shoulder, 6in (15cm)
*Spokeshave, flat bottom, 10in (25cm) (includes handles)
*Scraper blade, 3in by 5in (72mm by 127mm)

Chisels
Bevel-edge chisels (width of cutting edges in inches)
1 (25mm), ¾ (19mm), ⅝ (16mm), ½ (12mm), ⅜ (9mm), *⁵⁄₁₆ (8mm), ¼ (6mm), *³⁄₁₆ (5mm), ⅛ (3mm)
Skew carving chisel, ¼in (6mm)
Paring chisel, ½in (13mm) (straight or crank-neck)
Mallet, 340g

Boring tools
Brace, 14in (36cm) with 5in (13cm) offset
Auger bits: ¼in to 1in (6-25mm) in ⅛in or ¹⁄₁₆in increments
Adjustable expansion auger bit
Hand drill, 12in (30cm) with ¼in (6mm) chuck
*Electric hand drill, ⅜in (9mm) chuck
Brad-point twist bits: ⅛in to ½in (3-13mm), ¹⁄₁₆in increments
High-speed steel twist bits: ¹⁄₁₆in to ½in (2-13mm) in ¹⁄₃₂in to ¹⁄₁₆in increments
*Flat or Forstner bits: sizes as needed

Measuring and layout tools
Steel framing square, 18in by 24in (45 by 61cm)
Tape measure, 10ft to 25ft (3m to 7·6m)
Combination square, 12in (30cm) blade, 4in (10cm) stock
Try square, 7in (18cm) blade, 4in (10cm) stock
Sliding bevel, 8in (20cm) blade, 5½in (14cm) stock
Marking knife (thin blade)
Bradawl
Steel rule, 12in (30cm)
Mortise gauge
*Marking gauge, pencil point
*Marking gauge, knife point

Clamps
Sash clamps (pipe or bar), various lengths
Quick-action clamps, 12in or 16in (30 or 40cm) bars, 2½in (64mm) jaws
*G-clamps, various sizes
*Spring clamps

POWER TOOLS

Tablesaw
10in (25cm), 1½ HP to 3 HP motor
Combination blade
*Dado head (grooving blades) set

Surfacer
6in (15cm) or wider tables, 1 HP to 2 HP motor

Thicknesser
12in (30cm) width, 2 HP motor

Router
1 HP, ¼in (6mm) collet. Bits as needed

*Random-orbit sander

*Universal machine
9in or 10in (23 or 25cm) tablesaw, 8in to 12in (20-30cm) surfacer/thicknesser, 1in (25mm) diameter spindle moulder, horizontal mortiser. (Replaces individual machines.)

*Bandsaw
14in (36cm), ½ HP motor

*Drill press
½in (13mm) chuck, variable speed

5

SHARPENING

Of all the skills covered in this book, sharpening may be the most important. Without sharp tools, woodworking becomes an ordeal, difficult and sometimes dangerous. Dull handsaws wander from the line, blunt chisels and plane blades tear and crush wood fibres – when they cut at all. Dull power tools burn the wood and are more prone to grab or kick back, sometimes throwing the wood or the tool back at the user. Whether hand or power, blunt tools require extra force, reducing control and inviting injury. You're more likely to draw blood muscling a dull chisel than slicing cleanly with a sharp one. For sharpening, tools fall into two classes: saws and edge tools.

SAWS

It is best to have saws sharpened professionally. Carbide-tipped power-saw blades require special equipment to sharpen; sharpening handsaws is an art, and takes time to master. Sharpening saws isn't an expensive proposition, and properly sharpened handsaws and power-saw blades often serve well for months before they need resharpening. Have two each of your most often used saws so one can be at hand if the other is at the sharpener's.

Purchased new, good quality hand and power saws will already be properly sharpened. Used tools usually are not, and it is a good idea to have them sharpened before use. Teeth of uniform size and set (see p.33) make a handsaw much easier to control, so ask your sharpener to grind off the old teeth on handsaws you buy used and cut new ones from scratch. If most of your backsawing is done on tenons and dovetails where the cuts are predominantly along the grain, have those saw teeth recut as rip teeth, rather than the crosscut teeth provided by the manufacturer. (Ripsaw teeth are also easier to touch up yourself when they become slightly dull.)

For most woodworkers, saw sharpening is an infrequent need. If you are a beginner, it makes sense to spend your time acquiring other skills first. If your town lacks a competent saw sharpener you have two options. Contact the manufacturer to see if they offer the service or can recommend someone, or learn to sharpen them yourself. With basic instruction and practice, saw sharpening can be mastered. A good instruction book is listed in 'Further Reading'. Buy a couple of old saws at a second-hand sale and start filing.

Edge tools

Unlike saws, chisels and plane irons are in almost constant need of sharpening, so you have to be able to do the job yourself. (Surfacer and thicknesser knives and router bits are best sent out, for the same reasons that saws are.) While sharpening these tools requires neither expensive equipment nor unusual talent, the task frustrates beginners. Often, the difficulty lies not in sharpening technique, but in knowing when a chisel or plane iron is truly sharp. Master craftsman work with truly sharp edge tools. Once you know what 'sharp' really is, it will not take much practice to achieve it on your own tools.

Theoretically, a sharp edge is an edge that is not there. Like the mathematician's straight line, this ideally sharp edge has length but no thickness. In the world of theory, such an edge would slice through the toughest wood with ease, unhindered and undulled, there being no surfaces to create friction or become blunt.

In the real world, the cutting edge of a chisel or plane iron is formed by the juncture of two surfaces, the back and the bevel. If those surfaces are rough, the cutting edge they form will be rough and irregular. Working wood with such an edge is like shaving with a worn razor blade. The smoother the surfaces are, the more the edge formed will resemble the ideal – all length and no thickness – and the easier it will slice through wood.

Sharpness is not all that is required of a cutting edge. If it were, we would use razor blades for plane irons. But we would need a lot of them, because razor blades, sharp as they are, would not last very long slicing through oak. A cutting edge must be durable as well as sharp. In addition to the type, quality and hardness of the steel in a blade, durability is affected by the amount of steel immediately behind the cutting edge. A larger angle between bevel and back puts more steel behind the edge. More steel gives more support and absorbs more of the impact with the wood. Given two identical and equally sharp plane irons, one with a smaller angle will slice through wood more easily than one with a larger angle. If the angle is too large, you'll end up scraping the wood fibres rather than shearing them.

Sharpening edge tools involves just two simple tasks. You must grind an angle between bevel and back that balances durability and quality of cut. Then you must make those surfaces as smooth as possible by polishing them with increasingly fine abrasives.

GRINDING

There are all sorts of machines and wheels for grinding edge tools. All your grinding can be done on an inexpensive

---

SHARPENING AND HONING EDGE TOOLS

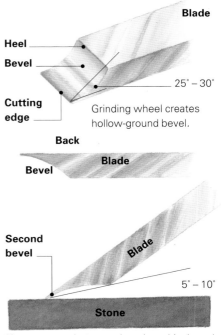

Hone a second, steeper bevel on chisels and plane irons.

Opposite: Sharp chisels and plane irons are essential for quality work.

Engage the wheel carefully when grinding, then move the blade horizontally, maintaining contact with as much of the wheel's edge as possible. Very little pressure is needed to cut against a wheel whose pores are not clogged.

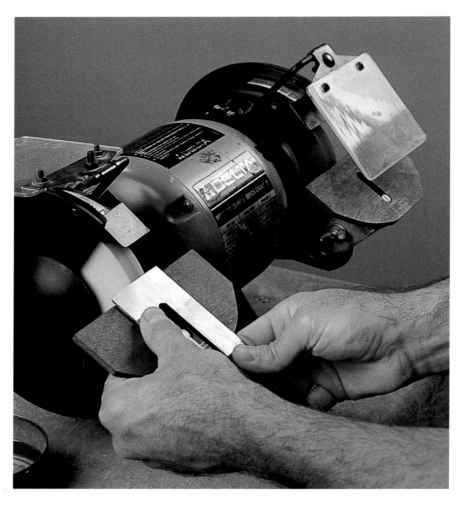

bench grinder, a ¼ HP motor with 152mm grinding wheels mounted each end. The hollow-ground bevel the machine produces is a little easier to hone (this is explained later), and the machines and wheels are inexpensive, compared to other sharpening set-ups. An 80-grit, grey aluminium-oxide wheel and a 100-grit white aluminium-oxide wheel can handle your needs.

Most grinding can be done on the 100-grit wheel, which is designed to cut faster and cooler than the grey wheels. Heat still builds up very quickly in the thin steel near the cutting edge. Burned steel loses its temper and becomes hard and brittle. It takes an edge, but the edge will not last. If it is badly burned, you have got to spend time at the wheel grinding away the burned part. Sometimes a burned edge indicates that your wheel has become clogged with metal particles. Use a dressing stick, a wheel-dresser or a diamond dresser to clear the pores and true the wheel.

For most work, the grinding angle of 25° to 30° provided on most new chisels and plane irons will work fine. If you work mostly soft woods such as pine, shade either side of 25°; for harder woods, grind bevels around 30°. You need not measure the angles, just adjust the tool rest one way or the other by eye when you regrind. If you are uncertain, check the angle against a protractor.

Different types of wood and work may require different angles on chisels, plane irons or specialized tools. When in doubt, experiment. Once you get the hang of it, grinding and honing a tool doesn't take more than four or five minutes. So try different angles for different tools and different jobs until you find what works best for you.

Some woodworkers can grind tools freehand, steadying the tool on an edge of the rest and establishing the angle by eye and feel. Most of us, however, need a steady platform set at the correct angle to guide the tool. The result is a bevel with a single, clean hollow-ground surface, not one formed by a mass of overlapping arcs, each at a slightly different angle. The rests on some grinders don't provide enough bearing surface. You can rig up new rests with pieces of angle iron and wood. Several manufacturers offer rest accessories that do the same thing.

You will use the grinder often, so put it in a handy location and at a height that avoids backache. You may find it comfortable to position the tool rests a little below the base of your sternum. If you grind and hone on your workbench, protect the worktop from oil and steel dust with plastic or a piece of canvas.

With the tool rest establishing the desired bevel angle, grinding is a straightforward task. Bring the bevel carefully up to engage the wheel and move the blade horizontally. Exert very little pressure against the wheel – it is better to make several light passes than one heavy one that risks burning the steel. You may find that you are most likely to remove too much steel or to burn the edge at the beginning or end of a pass, so try to be particularly sensitive to the feel of the tool as it engages and leaves the wheel.

The tool need not make contact across the full width of the wheel, but it's not a bad goal to try for. If you are working on one part of the cutting edge, skew the tool slightly and work near the outside of the wheel's edge. Frequent dips in a handy can of water minimize chances of burning.

When you buy a chisel or plane iron, whether it is new or used, you will

The chisel on the right is straight from the grinder, the one on the left has been honed to form a second bevel, much narrower and at a slightly greater angle than the ground bevel. Careful honing on stones and strop removes the deep grooves from the grinder, producing a polished second bevel and razor sharp edge.

probably need to do some grinding to get it in shape. First, check the cutting edge with a square to see if it is straight and at right angles to at least one of the adjacent edges of the blade. Then check the angle of the bevel against one of your other tools, a protractor or a template. If the cutting edge is slightly irregular or out of square, but the bevel is all right, set the rest to the existing bevel angle and carefully grind off the high spots.

If the cutting edge is considerably out of square or irregular, you may find it helpful to set the rest perpendicular to the wheel's edge and grind the edge straight, square and blunt. Then, setting the rest at the correct bevel angle, grind the bevel until it meets the back of the tool. The blunt edge dissipates heat readily, so you can remove a lot of steel before the edge thins enough to have to worry about burning it.

Burning is the main concern when altering an existing bevel. If the bevel angle is too steep, you can just set the tool rest and grind away. Since the steel is removed from the heel first, you needn't worry about burning until you approach the cutting edge on the last few passes. When increasing a shallow bevel, however, steel comes off the cutting edge first, and burning is a possibility on every pass. If the adjustment is slight, burning should not pose a problem – you will only need a few passes. If you are steepening the angle considerably, blunt the cutting edge as described previously, then grind the new bevel to meet it.

Once you have the tool in shape, subsequent grinding is necessary only when you have honed the edge so often that it becomes difficult or time-consuming to renew it on the stones. A few passes made with a light touch will usually remove all of the honed second bevel (which will be explained soon), and you are ready to hone again. Since this 'renewal' grinding can be done quickly, you might hone a blade only two or three times before you regrind.

HONING

For machine woodworking, a carefully ground edge is sometimes sufficient. The microscopic irregularites in the edge cause few problems when the tool or work is moving at great speed. But they become all too evident – torn wood, arduous work – when the tool is pushed along by hand.

Removing these minuscule ridges and valleys in the steel with abrasives is called honing. For centuries, woodworkers honed their tools on natural stones, and some regions and quarries became famous for stones with desirable grit and structure. Man-made stones, which make use of a variety of materials – reconstituted stone, ceramics, industrial diamonds – are more uniform and often cheaper, and have largely replaced quarried stone in all but the finest grits.

Sharpening stones are divided, in general, into two categories: those lubricated with oil and those lubricated with water. A lubricant floats particles of steel and crushed abrasive above the surface of the stone, keeping them from clogging the pores. This stone, steel and lubricant soup, called a slurry, also has abrasive qualities. Both types are messy. You need to wipe your tools and wash your hands after sharpening or you end up with smudged wood.

The honing techniques described here are for oil stones but will also work for water stones. There are a number of different types of stone to try, but all your honing can be done with just two. From the grinder, move to a man-made fine India stone, then to a natural soft Arkansas stone. Buy stones at least 50mm wide and 150-–200mm long. Larger stones are nice, but not necessary. (One side of the India stone is fine silicon carbide, but you may seldom use it.) Ordinary engine oil works just fine for lubrication. Thinner weights are better, but you can use whatever you happen to be running in the car at the time.

It is quicker and easier to hone a second bevel on your edge tools than honing the entire ground bevel. The slightly steeper angle of the second bevel also puts a little more steel behind the cutting edge.

The tool rest on the grinder is a handy jig for establishing the bevel angle, but many woodworkers prefer to hone free-hand. With a little practice, you can learn to maintain the angle you want by feel. A number of honing jigs are available, but free-hand honing is faster and it really does not matter if the second bevel differs by a degree or two each time you hone.

The back of a blade or chisel should be flat and polished, at least adjacent to the cutting edge. Repeated honings have extended the polished surfaces on this chisel. The duller areas are still fractionally lower than the surrounding bright surfaces.

You can hold chisels and plane irons with one hand and steady the stone with the other, or you may find it more effective to use a two-handed grip. Either one can get you started. With a little experience, you will modify them anyway or develop your own. The grip is far less important than what you do with it.

Start by dribbling a little oil on the fine India stone. Grip the tool and rest the bevel on the stone. Even after you have honed a tool once or twice it is easy to feel when the heel and cutting edge of a hollow-ground bevel are in contact with the stone. Then tilt the blade up just slightly, between 5° and 10°, to form the second bevel. Do not bother trying to measure the angle – your eye and sense of feel will get you close enough.

Now, imagining that your forearm, wrist, hand and the blade are a single entity, draw the blade down the length of the stone, pulling from your elbow and shoulder. When you are near the end of the stone, lift the tool (do not 'break' your wrist), move it back to the other end of the stone and do it again. If you have trouble maintaining the angle from stroke to stroke, try a continuous stroke, such as tracing a figure of eight on the stone. To avoid wearing the stone unevenly, try to move the strokes around to cover most of its surface. The figure of eight accomplishes much the same thing.

Remember: it doesn't matter how you hold the blade, or what sort of pattern you trace with it on the stone. The only thing that matters is maintaining the angle you have established, stroke after stroke. You want a flat second bevel, not a rounded one.

The back of the blade

Having spent a great deal of time attending to the bevel, beginners often forget that it takes two surfaces to form the cutting edge. The back of the blade (at least the part of it that is adjacent to the cutting edge) needs to be polished as smooth as the bevel. And it must be dead flat.

HONING

1–2 To hone free hand, you can hold the tool with one hand (left) or two (centre). You can sharpen on the pull stroke only, move the tool back and forth, or move it

in a figure eight. Most importantly, lock the blade, hands and wrists as a unit, so that the tool doesn't rock as you move it, creating a rounded bevel.

3 As you work on each stone, hone the back of the blade as well as the front. Be sure to keep the tool dead flat on the stone.

So, after giving the bevel ten or twelve strokes on the fine India stone, turn the blade over. Hold the back flat on the surface with one or both hands and move it back and forth on the stone ten to twelve times. Just make sure to keep it flat on the stone.

Next, wipe the slurry off and examine the back near the cutting edge. What you hope to see are tiny scratches left by the India stone along the entire surface adjacent to the cutting edge. Unfortunately, the back of a new plane iron or chisel may not be flat and what you are likely to see is a patchwork of scratched and unscratched areas along that surface. If so, you need to continue flattening the back on the stone. This can be a tedious, time-consuming process. If you need to remove much steel, hasten the process by using a coarser stone or a special 'lapping' plate or 'lapping' stone comprising a surface impregnated with tiny industrial diamonds. Fortunately, once you have established a flat surface along the length of the

cutting edge, subsequent honing of the back will extend it.

The process of grinding and honing forms a small wire-like burr of steel along the cutting edge. After two or three groups of strokes on the India stone (a group being a dozen or so strokes each on the second bevel and on the back), you should be able to feel a distinct burr. Pull your finger gently across the edge, not along it, to feel the burr. If you are touching up the edge on a tool that you have not had to regrind, start on the India stone and work on it until you have created a smaller burr, one that is more easily felt with a finger than seen.

Now move to the soft Arkansas stone and hone on it in exactly the same way as described for the India stone. Establish the angle of the second bevel, lock everything in place and stroke away. Turn the blade over and work on the back – make sure it is flat on the stone. Shifting from bevel to back bends the burr back and forth and it is soon worked off. Sometimes there is not much burr to start with. If so, turn the blade on its back and push the cutting edge gently against your thumbnail. The sharper the tool, the lower the angle at which the edge will catch on the nail.

Stropping

Finish the cutting edge on a leather strop, the same sort of thing a barber uses to tune up a cut-throat razor. Your strop can be a piece of belt leather, about 3mm thick and 50mm wide. The rough side of the leather should be abrasive enough to do the job, particularly after a little use, which impregnates it with slurry from the stones. You can also dress the leather with a fine abrasive, rubbing it on the leather from time to time.

When the burr is gone and the edge catches your nail at a fairly low angle, move to the strop. With the strop on a flat surface, hold the blade and stroke the bevel and back just as if the strop were a stone. (Pull the tool only, or you'll cut into the leather.) Because the strop is softer than the stone, there is a temptation to rock the tool up slightly when stropping the back. Don't – keep

it flat. Be patient and keep at it. It should not take too much stropping to produce an edge that will shave the hair off the back of your hand.

A word of encouragement

After one or two sessions on the stones, you may well feel like cursing. Things do not always happen in the ideal way outlined here. For example, you may sometimes find yourself working a tiny wire edge off on the strop, rather than on the stone. And you will not always end up with a razor edge. But then, you do not always need one. If you are rough-planing a stack of boards, a sharp edge, rather than a razor-sharp edge is sufficient. When you are ready to finish-plane the stack, then you want an edge that will trim the hair off your hand.

So, keep at it. Learn to produce a razor edge, and to understand wood, tools and techniques well enough to know when you need one. It may take you hours of grinding and honing. But once you get the hang of it (and you will), it will be simple.

STROPPING

Finish off the cutting edge by honing the bevel forward and back on a strop. Hold and move the blade as you would do if the strop were a stone.

4 Test for sharpness: with the blade on its back, push the cutting edge gently on your thumbnail. The edge catches the nail at a lower angle when sharper.

BASIC WOOD PREPARATION

Woodworking demands many skills, but none are more important than those needed to produce boards whose surfaces are flat, straight, and square, and whose dimensions are accurate. Indeed, the more sophisticated skills depend on these simple beginnings. If project parts are cupped, bowed, or twisted, or if they are even a fraction too long, too short, or out of square, joints will be difficult to lay out, cut, and fit, and assembly will be a struggle. Master the basic preparatory skills covered in this section, and your woodworking will be on solid footing.

Opposite: Skimming paper-thin shavings off the edge of a board with a sharp handplane is one of the many small pleasures of producing accurately dimensioned stock.

6

ROUGHING OUT

The process of dimensioning rough timber is much the same whether the final product is to be a basic bookcase or a bombay-fronted chest of drawers. It is satisfying to transform a pile of rough boards into a stack of project parts, each part with flat, parallel faces, its edges and ends trued perpendicular to those faces and to each other.

Most woodworkers dimension stock on machines, but hand methods are also valuable. A handsaw and bench plane allow you to tackle stock of any width, length or thickness, to cut long boards to length, and to clean up table-tops and carcass sides too wide for the machines. Understanding hand techniques will also help you to use your machines more skilfully.

To ensure accuracy, one face, edge, and end of each board is marked as a 'working' surface. Whenever you lay out a joint with a square or marking gauge, do so from the working surface. Though you will have to remark them later, you can select working surfaces when roughing parts to length and width.

DOWN TO SIZE

Working from your cutting list, begin by cutting parts to rough length and width. This makes them easier to handle and reduces waste during subsequent dimensioning. A badly bowed 300cm board may yield three relatively straight 90cm drawer fronts each of which will finish thicker than if the whole board had been flattened first. The same logic applies to width, as shown on p.50. Start by marking the parts out on the board, according to the figure and grain direction appropriate for each part.

Most timber is sold 'straight-line ripped' along one and often both edges, so it is easy to lay out lengths with a framing square. If you are using 'waney edged' timber, where the edges follow the irregular contour of the tree, you will need to place the framing square along an imagined straight edge. In either case, leave 5mm or so extra length to allow for final trimming.

Opposite: For many preparation tasks, the surfacer replaces hours of hand planing.

Sawing to length by hand

Long boards are unwieldy on the table-saw. Lacking a radial-arm saw, which is designed for this sort of work, a sharp 8- or 10-point handsaw and a pair of sawhorses does the job. In our machine age, the skill of cutting to a line with a handsaw is too often over-looked. Frequently, however, it is quicker and safer to pick up a handsaw than to turn to a machine.

Fundamentals of hand sawing are the same whether you are cross-cutting or ripping. Support the work at a comfortable height (about knee high) on one or two sawhorses. If you are right-handed, place the thumb of your left hand on the line to guide and steady the saw blade at the start of the cut. Your left hand should be sufficient to steady smaller boards; add a knee or clamp if necessary for larger work.

To saw straight and square, you must keep the saw blade at right angles to the surface of the board and aligned with the line of the cut. To do so, first imagine a plane rising along the line of the cut and perpendicular to the work. Think of your arm and the saw as a single, piston-like unit, aligned with that plane. Then, position your head over the saw so the imaginary plane cuts right between your eyes. When the blade is perpendicular to the work, you see only the top edge. Tilt the saw to the right, and your left eye picks up the left face of the blade; tilt it to the left and your right eye sees the right face. As you cut, focus your eyes on the pencil line and you'll be able to see both sides of the saw at once. Any movement of the saw from the perpendicular will still be betrayed by the appearance of just one face or the other in your field of vision. Beginners may want to place a square beside the saw blade as an aid to training the eyes.

Begin the cut with the middle of the saw blade against your thumb, the saw about 45° to the board's face (about 60° for a rip saw). Slowly drag the teeth backwards 25mm or so, then push forward about the same distance. As you repeat this movement and the teeth

---

CUTTING BY HAND

1 Align the saw blade, arm, and eyes along an imaginary plane rising at right angles from the saw cut. Place the thumb next to the line to start the cut.

2 Note the angle of the saw (it should be 45° for crosscutting, 60° for ripping). Make long, regular strokes, using as many of the saw teeth as possible.

RIPPING LONG BOARDS

1 At the beginning of the cut the left hand pushes the board on to the table and into the fence, the right supports most of its weight.

2 As the cut proceeds, shuffle your hands back and forth to keep the board moving. (The saw guard has been removed here for clarity.)

3 As the board end nears the saw blade, drop the left hand away as the right completes the cut. Turn off the saw before retrieving the waste or the board.

PLAN AHEAD

Cupped board

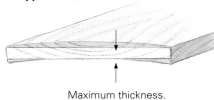

Maximum thickness.

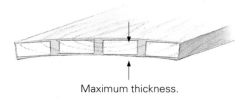

Maximum thickness.

To get the most out of the material, rip narrow parts from wide boards before flattening and thicknessing them.

catch, move your thumb away (your hand can stay put to steady the work) and lengthen the stroke until you are cutting with at least two-thirds of the blade's length. Saw rhythmically, do not rush; let the saw do the work. A sharp, properly set saw cuts with very little effort – if you have to push hard, your saw is dull. If the saw wanders from the line or tilts away from perpendicular, you can coax it back by applying corrective pressure through the hand on the saw handle over the course of several strokes.

When crosscutting, long or heavy waste needs support as the cut nears completion or there is a risk that the wood might splinter. Often you can hold the waste with your left hand; if it is too heavy, you will need to enlist an assistant, either a person or another sawhorse or support. Make sure the support does not lift the waste slightly and close the saw kerf, causing the saw to bind. Near the end of the cut, shorten the strokes and apply less pressure to avoid splintering.

CUTTING TO WIDTH

While the tablesaw isn't the best tool for crosscutting long boards, it is a good choice for ripping them to width. Set the rip fence about 5mm wider than the finished dimension to allow for subsequent planing and jointing. If the 'mill edge' is not sufficiently straight, handplane or run it over the surfacer before ripping.

If you are restricted to hand tools, a sharp 6 to 8 point hand ripsaw used as described above makes surprisingly short work of a pile of boards. Use a handsaw or bandsaw to establish a straight edge on waney-edged boards.

Ripping long boards

There are two requirements for ripping long boards on the tablesaw. First, the board must have one straight edge to bear against the rip fence. Second, you need some way of supporting the pieces as they emerge from the saw blade.

Most long boards can be safely fed into the saw by a single person, but you will need a helper to support the piece beyond the blade. Providing the assistant follows a simple rule – never pull the board, just support it at table height as the operator pushes it through – this is a safe, effective method. Outfeed rollers set at the height of the saw table enable you to work alone. Alternatively you can add fixed or free-standing extensions to the tabletop .

During the entire cut, keep your eyes focused on the point where the blade meets the wood – if you are watching the blade at all times, you are less likely to push your hands into it. (The saw guard has been removed in the photos for clarity. Do not remove yours.)

Initially, the weight of the board is more-or-less balanced between the operator and the front of the table. The left hand pushes the board down on to the table and sideways into the fence. The right (sometimes aided by the right hip) supports most of the board's off-table weight. Keep your feet about shoulder-width apart for stability.

During the cut, the hands shuffle back and forth to keep the board moving at a steady, controlled rate. (Stopping the board's movement can burn its edges and prematurely dull saw blades.) Pushed forward by the right hand, the board slides by the left hand, which stays near the front edge of the table exerting pressure to keep the board flush against the rip fence. When the front edge of the saw table stops the forward motion of the right hand, the left hand must push forward while the right is quickly replaced farther back on the board. Never allow your left hand to move beyond the front edge of the blade. Doing so pushes the offcut into the blade, causing burning or, possibly, kickback. It also puts your hand near the blade for no good reason.

The cut proceeds like this until your right hand reaches the end of the board. With the outfeed weight supported by a helper, rollers, or a table, you are free to concentrate on finishing the cut safely. Thumb hooked over the board's end, the right hand pushes across the table. As it passes the left hand not far from the table's front edge, the left drops from the board, its job done. Now the right must also exert

sideways pressure to keep fence and board in contact. Passing between the blade and the fence, the right hand disengages only when the board has cleared the blade's back edge. If you are working alone, turn the saw off and retrieve the boards from the other side – do not pull them back over the spinning blade.

Ripping short or narrow boards

Short boards – between about 20–30cm and 90–100cm long – account for most of the ripping in many workshops. Drawer fronts, door rails, stiles, and panels: most furniture parts fall in this range. These are easier to handle than long pieces and require less shuffling of hands to rip. At the end of a cut, if the board can be easily lifted with one hand, slide it to the end of the fence, let its leading end drop and slide it to the right, away from the blade and over the rip fence, then back on the tabletop to the right of the fence.

Ripping very short pieces can be dangerous. Once severed, they can too easily bind between the blade and fence and come shooting back at you. If possible, lay out several short pieces of the same width end to end, rip the longer board, then cut the pieces to length. You can rip short pieces safely on the bandsaw or by hand.

Narrow boards, long or short, are impossible to push safely with your hand between the blade and the fence. A saw blade is like a spider's web – even the slightest contact ensnares the victim. Use push sticks to finish off cuts where the distance between blade and fence is less than about 75mm. Push sticks can be made in all shapes and sizes, from a notched piece of scrap wood to elaborate shaped affairs.

Use a push stick near the end of the cut. Just before you drop your left hand away from guiding the board, apply the stick to the end of the board with your right, closer to the fence than the blade. The stick must do double duty, pushing at the same time into the fence and through the cut; it may take a while to get the knack of this.

RIPPING SHORT BOARDS

1 **When ripping short boards or narrow boards, the right hand pushes the work past the more-or-less stationary left hand keeping the board flush with the fence.**

2 **When the end of the board is approximately 20cm from the front of the blade, replace both hands with a push stick to finish the cut.**

7

FLATTENING AND THICKNESSING

The first task after roughing out is to establish a straight, flat working face. You do not have to woodwork very long to discover that few of the boards you buy are flat. Timber planed both sides (PBS) is flatter than roughsawn stock, but seldom flat enough for quality work.

If a board is not flat, it will be cupped across the grain, bowed with the grain, or twisted along its length. Frequently, it is all three at once. Cupping and bowing are easy to see. Just sight along the end or edge, or check against a straight-edge. (The sole of your plane, held on edge, makes a handy straight-edge.) Twists are not so apparent. Even if both ends are flat and both edges straight, a board can still be twisted. The simplest way to check for twist is to place the piece on a flat surface (your benchtop or tablesaw) and push gently on diagonal corners. If the board rocks, it is twisted. Mark the diagonal pair of high corners so you can plane them off.

If the board is larger than the available flat surfaces, a pair of 'winding sticks' will indicate twist. (A twisted board is said to be 'in winding' or 'wound' hence 'winding' sticks.) They are simply two long, narrow pieces of wood of exactly the same width. Place a stick across the grain at each end of the board, then kneel and sight along their upper edges. Align the edges at one end of the sticks, then move your eye down their length. If the edges diverge, the board is twisted. The mis-alignment is often very slight, so you will need to do some careful squinting. (Winding sticks are easier to use if the top edges are two contrasting colours.)

HAND TECHNIQUES

Hand techniques provide valuable insight into the problems of flattening and thicknessing. You will not need many tools – your bench plane, work-bench, a straightedge, and marking gauge. The longer the plane, the more it will bridge across high spots on a board, rather than riding up and down them. If you use one plane for all your needs, its throat is likely to be set for finer work and thick shavings may clog. Craftsmen used to use wooden planes with wide throats and blades slightly rounded across their width to remove wood quickly.

Make sure that the top of your work-bench is flat. It is difficult to plane a board flat, particularly a thin one, when it is supported by an undulating surface. Planing a benchtop is an ideal way to practice flattening a surface – it is thick enough so you can keep at it until you get it right.

Plane pointers

As hand tools go, bench planes are fairly complicated. New tools from quality manufacturers are usually set up properly, and will perform well, but it is helpful to know your way around the tool.

The most common adjustment is to change the size of the throat by altering the position of the frog (see p.54); wider for coarser shavings, narrower for finer. Do not be afraid to experiment to find the best settings for different woods, or a single setting that performs well for a range of tasks.

Modern bench planes almost always have a cap iron (also called a 'chip-breaker'). Set close to the cutting edge, the cap iron curls shavings upwards, breaking the fibres so they do not act as little levers prying wood up ahead of the cut. The cap iron should never protrude beneath the sole of the plane. The thinner the shavings, the closer the cap iron should be to the cutting edge. For the relatively thick shavings taken when flattening boards, set it back from the cutting edge between 1mm and 2mm, depending on how hard the wood is. (A plane with a heavy cutting iron and wider throat can take thicker shavings and will need greater clearance.)

The lever cap hooks over a screw set into the frog; pushing down on the lever fixes the cutting iron and cap iron tight to the frog. Adjust the screw so the cap is as tight as possible, but not a struggle to remove for sharpening.

After sharpening, set the cap iron, slip the blade iron onto the frog and snap the lever cap in place. Turn the plane over and sight the blade coming through the sole as you move the adjustment screw located beneath the frog. Move the lateral adjustment lever to bring the cutting edge parallel with the sole. Set the iron so it is just barely visible beneath the sole, then lower it during the first few strokes to take a comfortable shaving that is thick enough to make the job go as quickly as possible, yet thin enough to make it as easy as possible.

How to push a plane

Hand-planing a stack of boards (even a short stack) is hard work. But it need not be back-breaking work and is easier

Opposite: Flat parts of uniform thickness provide the basis for accurate joinery.

Right: You can check for twist by sighting along a pair of winding sticks. Divergence of the sticks' upper edges indicates the board is twisted.

ANATOMY OF A PLANE

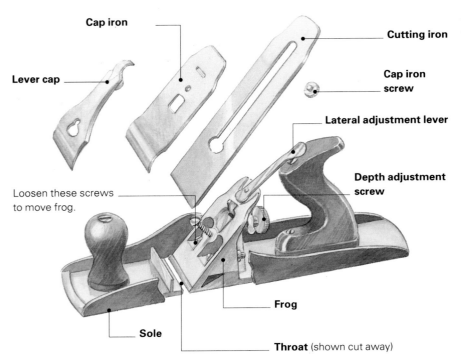

Cap iron

Lever cap

Cutting iron

Cap iron screw

Lateral adjustment lever

Depth adjustment screw

Loosen these screws to move frog.

Frog

Sole

Throat (shown cut away)

HOW TO PLANE

1–2 When you plane, use your entire body not just your arms. Shift your weight as the stroke progresses to bring your back and legs into play. At the start of the stroke, bear down on the front end of the plane. As the front end comes off the board, shift pressure to the back of the plane.

when you get into a rhythm. Lean a little into the direction of the cut and with one foot in front of the other for stability, rock on your heels and toes as your weight shifts from the beginning to the end of the stroke. Lift the plane, then repeat the stroke movement over and over. Hands and wrists hold and guide the plane; legs, back and arms provide the force.

At the beginning of each stroke, overcome the tendency to let the unsupported rear end of the sole drop by applying increased pressure with your leading hand on the front of the plane. Likewise, don't let the front of the plane drop at the end of the stroke. As you work your way down a long board, move your body too, rather than just extending your arms farther and farther. Finally, be sure to take the time to sharpen the plane iron when it begins to lose its edge, not after it is long gone. It is amazing how much less work it is to plane with a sharp tool than a dull one.

Flattening by hand

Correcting cupped, bowed, or twisted boards is simply a matter of planing off all of the high spots. Unfortunately, most boards are cupped *and* bowed *and* twisted, so you will most often need to feel your way along, checking your progress frequently with a straightedge, flat surface, or winding sticks, and adjusting your tactics accordingly. Be careful when planing cupped or bowed boards that you do not plane a twist into them by removing more wood on one edge, or end, than the other. Remember to plane both of the diagonally opposed high corners of a twisted board.

Because surface finish is less important than removing wood quickly, flattening boards is one of the few instances when it is desirable to plane across the direction of the grain. Vary the angle between about 30° and 90°, whatever it takes to reduce high spots effectively. It is usually easier to plane the concave face of a board first; it can be difficult to keep the plane from following a convex curvature.

When the board is flat, plane with the grain to take a few thinner shavings off the entire surface. Like a cat whose fur is stroked the wrong way, wood resents being planed against the grain, resisting the tool and leaving a rough, torn surface. The quickest way to determine the direction of the grain is by planing – if you are going against the grain, you will usually feel and see it. A less nerve-wracking method is to examine the annual rings as they appear on the edge of the board, planing with rising grain rather than into it. Planing with the grain now removes much roughness, but isn't the final surface, which will be worked much later in the project.

Flattening boards can be frustrating work at first. You will plane away and then wonder why the thing still rocks. But as you gain experience, you willl develop a sense of just where to plane, and the boards, rather than your spirits, will get flattened quickly.

Thicknessing by hand

Planing a board to thickness is a much simpler task than flattening its first face, though it may be more strenuous work if there is a lot of wood to remove. All you do is scribe the desired thickness on the edges and ends of the board with a marking gauge and plane down to the line. Use a pin gauge rather than a pencil gauge.

As before, plane diagonally, taking thick shavings to remove wood quickly. It is important to check with the straightedge or winding sticks to make sure you are not introducing bow, cup or wind. If you are working up a lot of boards, flatten and thickness each one in turn, then sharpen the plane and take a few very fine shavings off all the faces to finish the job.

MACHINE TECHNIQUES

A surfacer and thicknesser are direct mechanical descendants of the handplane. They also flatten and thickness boards by cutting off the high spots, only here the board moves past the cutting edge, which is travelling at very high speed.

Flattening on the surfacer

A surfacer comprises independently adjustable infeed and outfeed tables either side of a cutterhead. Moving the

FLATTENING THE WORKING FACE

Cupped: convex face

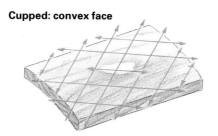

Cupped: concave face

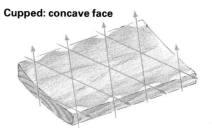

Twisted

┌ High spot

└ High spot

Final strokes

Flatten a working face by removing wood from high spots. First establish flat surfaces (lighter areas), then extend them with diagonal strokes. Finish with a few strokes along the grain. Plane with the rising grain (indicated by annual rings on the edge of the board) for the smoothest surface.

FLATTENING BY HAND

1-2 To remove wood quickly, plane diagonally. Work in from the edges to minimize tear out. Develop rhythm with the plane to reduce fatigue. Work up and down the board, frequently checking your progress with a straightedge or winding sticks. When the surface is flat, make strokes with the grain to remove tears .

FLATTENING ON THE JOINTER

1-2 Begin the cut by pressing the board down on the infeed table and against the fence with your left hand, moving it into the cutterhead with your right. As the cut **proceeds, transfer downward pressure to the outfeed table as soon as possible. Push the board's end over the cutterhead with a push stick to protect your fingers.**

MAKING THE SMOOTHEST CUT

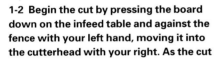

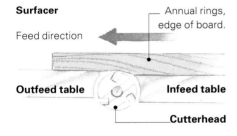

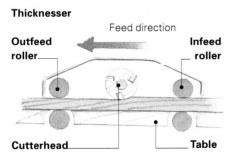

Surface and thickness plane with rising grain as indicated by the annual rings on the board's edges.

infeed table up or down sets the depth of cut. Except for some types of speciality planing, the outfeed table is always set even with the highest point in the arc of the cutterhead. If the table is higher, the board will taper end to end; lower, and the trailing end of the board will be gouged as it drops off the infeed table onto the cutterhead. If you keep surfacer knives sharp and the machine accurately adjusted, work on it will be much easier and safer. (Consult the owner's manual for information on making adjustments to the machine.)

Set the machine's fence to fit the width of the face you are flattening. (You can position narrow boards over the sharpest part of the cutterhead.) Boards slide easily on tables polished with a thin coat of paste wax – the less force required to push the board across the cutterhead, the better.

When flattening boards on the surfacer, keep your fingers on or above the top face of the board at all times, don't let them hang down over edges or ends. Use a push stick or push pad to further

remove your hands from possible danger. Keep your eyes on the cutterhead throughout the cut and you will be less likely to run your fingers into it.

The convex face of a cupped or bowed board will rock on the tables, so flatten the concave face first whenever possible. For twisted boards, flatten the face that rocks least. Check the grain on the edge of the board, and plane with rising grain to avoid tear out. If grain direction changes several times along the length, take light cuts (1mm or so) first to see which direction of feed produces least tear out. Though your surfacer may accommodate heavier cuts, you should seldom take off more than about 1.5mm to minimize tearout and maximize control. Harder woods or highly figured ones require thinner cuts.

Start the cut with your left hand pressing the board firmly onto the infeed table and against the fence, your right hand pushing the board into the cutterhead. As the board passes the cutterhead, downward pressure shifts to the outfeed table for the rest of the cut. Firm contact with the outfeed table ensures that the remaining wood will be pulled over the cutterhead in the same plane as the newly flattened surface. When enough board has passed the cutterhead, you can often move both hands over the outfeed table. If you need more horizontal force, push the board through with a push stick in your right hand, making sure most downward pressure continues to be applied by your left hand over the outfeed table.

Use only enough downward pressure to maintain firm contact with the tables. Too much pressure can deflect the board – after planing, it will spring back to its original shape. If a board is badly bowed along its length, you can lower it onto the machine so it straddles the cutterhead. Plane off the trailing end, reverse the board and repeat until the board is straight enough to make an end-to-end pass.

Flattening twisted boards without wasting a lot of wood is tricky. To see the problem, balance the board on two diagonally opposed high corners, so that the other corners are an equal height above the tabletop. Then push

USING A PUSH PAD AND PUSH STICK

A commercially made push pad (left hand) and a homemade push stick (right hand) make planing narrow boards on the surfacer safer.

one floating corner down on the table, and note how the gap between the remaining floating corner and the table-top increases. The amount the gap widens equals the extra thickness you'd need to remove if you flattened that face with three corners contacting the surfacer tables.

The trick, then, is to balance a twisted face on the two high corners as you push it over the cutterhead. One or two balanced passes should create enough of a flat surface on the two corners to support the face for the remainder of the procedure. Do not rock the board during the initial passes or you will just create a new twist. The same balancing act is necessary if you must flatten the convex face of a board. Balance the face so all four floating corners are about equidistant above the infeed table, push the piece carefully over the cutterhead to establish a single flat plane, then extend it with subsequent passes.

Because planer knives dull quickly if left in contact with stationary wood, it is important to keep the board moving. Hard or heavily figured wood should be fed more slowly to minimize tear out. Long boards require the same sort of positioning and hand shuffling described earlier for the tablesaw. Use a roller 'assistant' if necessary to support long boards coming off the outfeed table.

Narrow boards (less than 75mm wide) can be worked much more safely using a combination of a push pad and push stick. Push pads are rubber-bottomed plastic handles that grip the board by friction. Very short (less than 200mm) and/or narrow pieces (less than 50mm) are best worked by hand or laid out end-to-end or side-by-side; flatten and thickness the longer board, then cut the pieces to length or width.

Thicknessing on the planer

Thicknessers consist of a cutterhead suspended above and parallel to a flat table, called the bed. A powered infeed roller above the bed pushes the board onto the bed and feeds it into the cutterhead. An outfeed roller, often but not always powered, keeps the board pressed on the bed as it emerges from the cutter. Some machines also have rollers that protrude slightly above the surface of the bed to ease the wood's passage. In some machines, depth of cut is adjusted by moving the bed; in others the cutterhead moves. The thicknesser, like any machine, works best when it is sharp and properly adjusted. Misalignment of the bed rollers is one of the most common problems. High rollers can produce a 'snipe' or gouge on the first and last few centimetres of the cut.

The thicknesser is perhaps the only home-workshop woodworking machine that requires almost no skill to use successfully. Orient the boards so the machine cuts with rising grain, lay the already flattened working face down on the bed, slide it in to engage the feed roller, and the machine does the rest. Of course, you will need to support longer boards into and out of the machine.

The depth of cut depends on your machine's capabilities and the wood's qualities. Unless your thicknesser has a big motor, you will be lucky to manage

THICKNESSING ON A PLANER

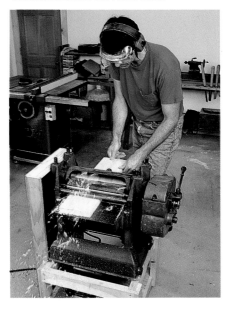

Running a thicknesser is simple. Place the previously flattened face down on the bed, and engage the board with the infeed roller.

2mm cuts on any but narrow boards or soft woods. Harder woods and those with highly figured grain (which is prone to tear out) require finer cuts and, if your machine has them, slower feed speeds.

You can save time and aggravation by thicknessing all the boards for a project at the same time. This also ensures that parts meant to be the same thickness will be so. Organize the boards from thickest to thinnest; figure out the best direction of feed for each, and stack them with the lead end toward the thicknesser. Stack them with the same orientation as they exit, so they'll be ready for the next pass without re-sorting. Change the depth of cut only when you reach boards in the stack that are too thin for the current setting.

Thin boards often get chewed up in a thicknesser. (The thickness at which this happens varies according to the wood and the machine.) Feeding a thin piece through on top of a piece of 20mm cabinet-grade plywood of the same length and 25mm or so wider cuts down on chatter and damage.

8

TRUING EDGES

Once the faces are flat and the board at the desired thickness, you need to true a working edge. Sometimes you can true an edge after flattening the first face; this is easy to do when working on the surfacer. If you are preparing a number of boards by hand, you will find the rhythm and concentration of truing all the edges at once increases your accuracy. On the surfacer, ganging this work allows you to make sure the fence adjustments are exact and to place the fence so you are working over the sharpest part of the cutterhead. (Truing edges with a hand plane is also called 'shooting' or 'jointing'; the latter term is also used on the surfacer.)

SHOOTING EDGES BY HAND

Once again, use your longest plane for working edges because it contacts more of the edge than a shorter plane. Whatever size plane you use, a razor-sharp plane iron is essential.

Opposite: Straight, flat edges help ensure parts will be straight later on.

Edges, like faces, can be bowed or twisted along their length. (Concave edges are called bowed, convex edges are 'crowned.') Because they are so narrow, edges are seldom cupped across their width – unless the plane iron has a convex cutting edge. As for flattening a face, the idea is to remove the high spots.

Having already ripped the parts to rough width, truing a working edge on most project parts is relatively straightforward. These edges are usually reasonably straight and square to start with, and a few passes with the plane will clean off saw marks and correct minor problems. Check for squareness of edge and face by sliding a square along the length of the edge. Use a long straight edge to check for bowing or crowning along the length of the edge. The sole of a jointer plane works well for boards as long as 150cm; just slide the sole along the edge and evaluate in segments of 60cm or so.

Hold boards in the face vice on the workbench. An adjustable support is handy for working on long boards. (Fasten a pipe clamp to the front leg and rest long boards on it.) Held in a vice, long narrow boards can be distorted as the weight of the plane bends the unsupported ends. If possible, plane them on the bench top against a stop or between dogs.

The key to handplaning an edge is to keep the sole of the plane perpendicular to the faces of the board. When the edge is square to start with, this is simple. Rest the sole on the edge and lock your hands and wrists in that position. (This locking is a mental as much as a physical action.) When the edge is out of square, positioning the plane at a right angle to the face is more difficult. Using a square to do so is far too awkward and time consuming. With practice, you can develop a 'feel' for squareness. You may find that keeping the fingers of your left hand in touch with the face of the board helps you to keep the plane square.

As for face planing, the force for the stroke comes from the upper arms,

---

TWISTED EDGE

Opposing gaps at opposite ends of the board indicate a twisted edge. (Reference the square from the working face at both ends.)

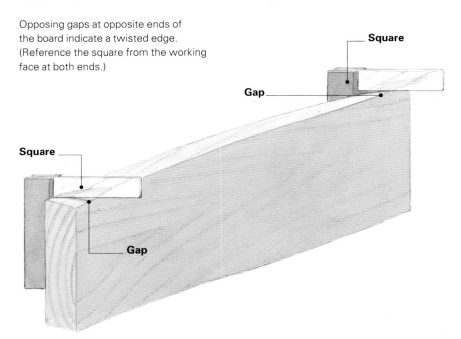

CHECKING THE EDGE

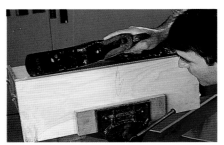

Slide a square along the edge to see if it is perpendicular to the working face. The sole of a long jointer plane can reveal bow or crown along an edge.

POSITIONING THE PLANE

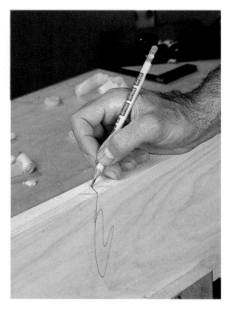

1–2 Position the plane's sole at a right angle to the board's working face, locking your wrists and forearms in place to maintain the angle. Use the fingertips of your left hand to help keep the plane square to the board's face. Mark the working edge and face for reference during subsequent procedures.

shoulders, torso and legs. Depending on your height and reach, you can plane boards of 100–130cm in length in one motion, shifting your weight from back leg to front leg, and extending your arms to finish the stroke. Longer boards require a choreographed shuffle down their length: arms, torso and legs shifting along as smoothly as possible while you keep the plane moving and square to the board's face. Mark the working edge with a 'V' that meets the mark indicating the working face.

To adjust an edge that is out of square to the face, take one or more shavings off the high side of the edge along the full length until the shaving extends across the full width. Keep the sole of the plane square to the face of the board. Don't try to correct square-ness by angling the cutting edge to the plane's sole – you'll drive yourself around the bend trying to figure out the compensating angle for every edge.

For heavily bowed or crowned edges, you will need to establish flats by planing the ends of the bow or the

TRUING AN EDGE BY HAND

1–3 These photos show how to true the edge of a short board in a single motion. Position the plane's sole at a right angle to the board's working face. Start the stroke by pressing down on the edge with the leading hand. Shift your weight as the stroke progresses, powering the plane with your upper arms, upper body and legs, while maintaining the angle of the sole with your hands. Press down on the back of the plane and ease off on the front at the end of the stroke.

9

MAKING WIDE BOARDS

Depleted stands of old-growth timber and modern industrial sawmilling practices have made wide boards hard to come by. Today, if you want a solid-oak tabletop 90cm wide, you will have to make it of several narrower boards glued edge to edge.

There is nothing second-rate about a glued-up tabletop or carcass side. Several boards can often be combined to produce patterns of grain or colour more interesting than those of a single, wide plank. By picking and choosing from a dealer's pile you can usually piece together a handsome panel. Even better, if you can buy boards cut from the same tree, or resaw thick planks, you can make symmetrical or repeating patterns, as you would with veneers.

LAYING OUT A WIDE PANEL
Select and arrange the boards before starting on the edges. As you arrange the boards, keep an eye on grain direction as well as appearance. If you can lay out the boards so that all rising grain rises in the same direction, the planing and scraping you do after you glue-up will be easier. But if the surface pattern you prefer requires alternating grain direction, it is not difficult to change planing direction on the glued-up panel.

Likewise, pay attention to the orientation of the growth rings on the ends of the boards in a panel. If a board cups, it will cup away from the heart side – the side closest to the centre of the tree. Alternating the orientation of the rings will produce a panel that will stay flatter. For tabletops and cabinet sides fixed firmly across their width and for panels confined in frames, you can let the grain patterns on the boards' faces determine the arrangement.

MATING THE EDGES
When you have selected the boards, cut them roughly to length and, if necessary, rip them to produce roughly parallel edges. Flatten a face on each board and plane them to thickness. Then lay out the milled boards, refine the arrangement if you wish, and mark

Opposite: Solid-wood tabletops and case work involve gluing up wide parts.

two sides of a large triangle across their faces. The marks will help you maintain the order through all subsequent steps.

Plane the mating edges. (Boards with two mating edges should be ripped to a uniform width first.) You can do this entirely by hand or machine, or combine techniques, taking advantage of the machine's speed and the superior surface produced by the hand plane. First, work the edges in pairs on the surfacer. Joint the first edge with the triangle-marked face against the fence and joint the second edge with the unmarked face against the fence. Alternating the faces in this manner will produce a flat surface, even if the fence is not set at exactly 90° (see p.64).

If your surfacer is accurately adjusted and the knives are sharp, gluing the edges straight from the machine will produce an acceptably strong joint. If you examine a machined edge, however, you will notice tiny undulations on its surface. Planing these off with a very sharp, finely set handplane will produce an extremely strong joint with an invisible glue line.

When you have taken a fine shaving off each edge of a mating pair, stack the boards in a vice to check the joint. Ideally, the top board should rest firmly on the bottom, the edges should meet along their entire length, with no gaps visible when viewed from either the front or back faces. A straightedge should rest on the faces of the stacked boards in a single plane, as shown on p.65.

On those happy occasions when the edges mate perfectly, all that remains is to glue-up. Before doing so, 'spring' the joint slightly, planing a slight concave bow into each edge so the joint fits tight at the ends and gaps slightly in the middle. (The gap might be 0.5mm in 90cm). Pulling the gap together at assembly makes the ends of the joint less likely to open up when the humidity changes. Apply very little pressure on the plane at the beginning and end of the stroke, but a little more in the middle. You can also start the cut 5cm or so from one end and stop the same

---

LAYING OUT A WIDE PANEL

For flatness and ease of planing

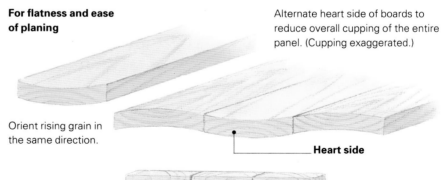

Orient rising grain in the same direction.

Alternate heart side of boards to reduce overall cupping of the entire panel. (Cupping exaggerated.)

Heart side

For appearance

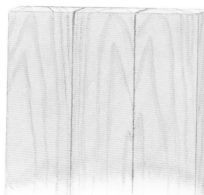

Match straight grain to straight grain.

Match figured grain to figured grain.

PLANING MATING EDGES

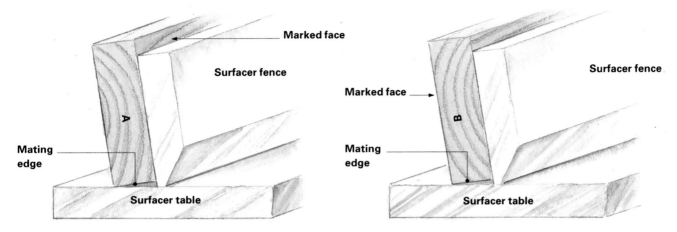

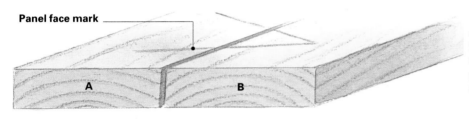

Alternating faces of adjacent boards against the surfacer fence will ensure complementary mating edges and a flat panel, even if the fence is not square to the surfacer tables. (Angles exaggerated.)

distance from the other end. After a stroke on each edge, re-stack the boards and check the joint again before moving on to the next pair.

Sometimes, the edges of stacked boards don't match up. They may be bowed, twisted or out of square. To check for bow and twist, push down on one end of the top board and look closely at the joint from the other end. If the surfaces touch only at one corner, at least one of the two edges is twisted. If the joint gaps all the way across the end, one of the edges is bowed. Finally, check with a straightedge to see if the stacked faces are in a single plane; if not, one or both edges is out of square.

GLUING UP

With all the edges jointed, planed and mated, you are ready to glue-up, as shown on p.66. Clear your workbench and spread newspaper or a sheet of plastic to protect it from dripping glue.

Clamp the panel dry (without glue) to position the clamps. Given well

cut joints, you can glue panels up to 100cm and sometimes 150cm long with just three sash clamps. The panel rests on two clamps, one 15cm or so in from each end. The third clamp, placed in the centre, rests on top of the boards. If the joint doesn't pull together satisfactorily, use additional clamps. But do not rely on additional clamps or excessive pressure to pull tight a poorly mated joint – take the time to return to the bench and get it right.

Longer panels require more clamps. If possible, add pairs of clamps so the total is always an odd number. This allows you to alternate clamps above and below the work and still have clamps at each end to support the boards. Alternating clamps top and bottom counters the tendency for the boards to bow away from the clamp bar. Rotating the clamp so its screw aligns with the centre of the edge of boards thinner than 20mm can help keep them flat.

When you are satisfied that everything is ready, stand the boards on edge

and run a bead of glue down all mating surfaces, spreading it to cover before pushing the edges together. You do not need any fancy gear to spread glue – a thin strip of wood, a cheap, bristly brush, or a small paint roller all work well. The point is to spread the glue evenly and quickly.

Lay the boards down on the clamps and rub the mating edges together, aligning the triangular marks on the faces. When all boards are in place, tighten the centre clamp and work out. Crank each clamp down just enough to engage the edges, then check to see that the faces are aligned before moving to the next clamp. Sometimes you are able to align the faces with your fingers, but white and yellow glues 'grab' very quickly. Sharp blows of a hammer on a hardwood block placed near the joint usually persuade the surfaces into alignment. (The banging can loosen clamps, so make sure you keep checking them.)

Check that the faces of the boards are flush with the surface of the bars or

Here, a three-board panel is stacked edge-to-edge to check the joints. If the faces bow or cup against the straightedge, one or more edges are not square.

pipes – this helps ensure that the panel will remain flat. The edges frequently creep up the jaws, so knock them down on to the pipe again with hammer and block. (Don't try to drive the top clamps down onto the boards – loosen the jaws and reposition them.)

As you tighten each clamp, give the previous ones a little turn to keep them engaged. Finally, when all clamps are drawn up, and the surfaces are aligned, tighten all the screws to a more-or-less consistent pressure. Remember, it shouldn't take white-knuckle pressure to pull the joints together enough to make a virtually invisible seam.

If you plan to leave the panel on the bench while the glue cures, sight across the clamps as you would across winding sticks and insert shims if necessary to bring them into line. If the panel isn't resting flat it may retain the twist when the clamps are removed. If you stand a glued panel up against a wall, lean it so the clamps are in line, keeping the panel flat.

When the glue has cured, remove the clamps and clean off the faces with a handplane, using the techniques described previously for flattening a face. Unless the joints are badly misaligned, you shouldn't have to remove so much wood that the board's thickness will be significantly affected. Plane or joint a working edge for the assembled panel, then cut it to final width and length.

A GLUE-UP CHECK LIST

Of all the tasks a woodworker faces, few are more anxiety ridden than gluing up a complex project. Weeks of careful preparation – joint cutting, surface preparation, carving – are all on the line as you race to apply glue, assemble and pull everything together before the glue sets. For the beginner gluing up even a simple tabletop or panel can be a daunting prospect.

It is possible, however, to reduce the level of anxiety, channelling it into a useful rush of adrenalin rather than panic or paralysis. Of primary importance, of course, are well cut, snug-fitting joints. Whether it's a three-board coffee-table top or an elaborate sideboard, glue and clamps are not magic curatives for ill-fitting joinery.

That said, preparing carefully and planning ahead can make a big difference in how your projects go together. You may find these few general principles helpful.

Clean up the work area. Gluing up in the midst of a mess is asking for disaster. Glue, like time and taxes, waits for no one – if you have to stop halfway through a glue-up to clear something out of the way, you're likely to end up with half a project.

Glue-up on a flat surface. Almost everything you glue-up needs to end up flat and/or square. It is depressing, to say the least, to discover that the tabletop or carcass for which you carefully flattened the stock and cut the joints is twisted or out of square because the surface on which the clamps rested during glue-up was twisted. The top of a

Mark the panel with a triangle as an aid to alignment when working on subsequent operations.

GLUING UP

1 After a thorough dry-run test, run a bead of glue down each edge, then spread it evenly over the surface.

2 Working out from the centre of the panel, tighten the clamps while aligning the faces.

3 A sharp hammer blow on a block of hardwood (to protect the panel surface) brings mating faces into alignment.

tablesaw is ideal in small workshops where space is at a premium. If you have sufficient room, a special assembly table is a welcome luxury. Commercially made clamp cradles, used two to a clamp, are expensive but handy.

Organize your work before you spread any glue. More glue-up fiascos are caused by lack of planning than anything else. Always walk through a no-glue trial first, even if you're just gluing two boards together edge-to-edge. You need to decide where to place the clamps to ensure that the joints close, and to make sure everything is ready – glue, glue spreader, wet rag for drips or gluey fingers, hammer and block to persuade the two surfaces to level up. And you need to work out where to put all this so it is handy, but not in the way. More complicated assemblies require more forethought. What goes together first? How do I clamp across here if I've already got a clamp across there? The time you spend deciding exactly what you are going to do will be repaid a thousandfold.

CHOOSING A GLUE

For many of us, woodworking is a welcome oasis in an increasingly busy and complicated world. Many of the tools we use and the constructions we employ have remained virtually unchanged for hundreds, sometimes thousands, of years.

Not so woodworking glues. While it is possible to rely on animal-hide glues that would have been familiar to ancient Egyptian craftsmen, the majority of wood-workers opt for one or more of the impressive array of adhesives produced by modern science. In general, these glues are superior to hide glues in strength, ease of application and durability. (However, technical superiority does not necessarily make modern glues 'better' for woodworking – an awful lot of superb furniture remains stuck soundly together by hide glues.)

Technological advances create more choices, but make choice more difficult. For most household furniture and fittings, a white polyvinyl actetate (PVA) glue forms a bond stronger than the natural bond between wood fibres. At workshop temperatures (18°C or so) it sets up slowly enough to give you time to assemble and clamp most complex constructions. (This period of workability is often called 'open assembly time'.) It cures sufficiently in an hour or so to allow you to remove the clamps – a real advantage for a clamp-poor workshop. (This period is called 'closed assembly time'.) Squeeze-out can be cleaned up with a damp cloth; the cured glue is clear and does not discolour the wood.

A large number of woodworkers use modified PVA glues. Yellow in colour, they are often referred to as 'yellow' glues. In many ways they out-perform white PVAs: greater rigidity, improved heat resistance, better 'grabbing' ability, greater tolerance of unfavourable conditions, and less clogging of sandpaper. Some woodworkers find these advantages are outweighed by the reduced open assembly time of many modified PVA glues, which makes gluing-up too much of a race.

Close to a universal glue as white PVA is, it has several drawbacks. Because of its low water resistance, it is not appropriate for outside use or for indoor projects that come in regular contact with water (chopping boards, kitchen worktops) or high humidity. And sometimes white glue sets too fast to allow you to assemble a complicated project.

In these situations, you can use a urea-formaldehyde glue such as Cascamite. In addition to good water resistance, these glues have a long open assembly time, so they are ideal for really complicated assemblies. They cure rock hard, so are easy to sand and do not have the tendency to 'creep' in certain circumstances like the softer PVA glues. The only reason you may not want to use them all the time is that they are less convenient (you have to mix up just what you need each time) and the closed assembly time is long – work needs to remain in clamps 12 hours or more. Several manufacturers now offer pre-mixed, water-resistant glues that provide working qualities and assembly times similar to PVA glues.

Only rarely are the above glues not up to the task. If you need a waterproof joint, rather than a water-resistant one, use a resorcinol glue, which is effective but expensive. Oily woods such as teak and rosewood can be difficult to glue. White and yellow glues and urea-formaldehyde glues can be adequate if you wipe the mating surfaces prior to gluing with a solvent. Epoxies are probably more dependable, but also a greater nuisance to use and they can produce a thick glue line. Given what is at stake (expensive wood, lots of time in a project), it is prudent to phone a glue manufacturer for advice on gluing the particular wood, or to conduct your own experiments to find the best glue.

It is worth reiterating that glue is only as good as the joint to which it is applied. Cleanly cut, snug-fitting joints are likely to last. The smoother the surfaces to be joined, the better the glue will work. This is particularly important to remember for edge joints that, unlike dovetails or mortise-and-tenons, have no interlocking mechanical strength.

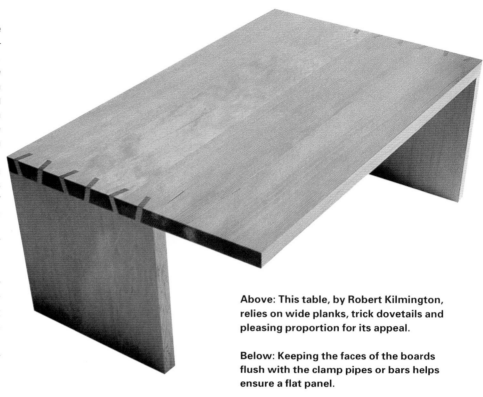

Above: This table, by Robert Kilmington, relies on wide planks, trick dovetails and pleasing proportion for its appeal.

Below: Keeping the faces of the boards flush with the clamp pipes or bars helps ensure a flat panel.

The best edge joint is one whose mating surfaces come straight from a razor-sharp hand plane. Roughing up the surfaces of any joint to form little 'pockets' for the glue will just weaken the joint.

A note on dowels and splines
For years, popular magazines told woodworkers to use dowels or splines to align and strengthen edge joints. (Splines are loose tongues that fit into grooves cut in mating edges.) If you work with modern glues, however, splined or dowelled joints are not stronger in any meaningful way.

Subjected to enough stress, the wood will fail before the glue joint.

Likewise, if the boards you are gluing are flat and the edges planed true, alignment is an easy task. You may have to apply a little persuasion here and there with a block and mallet, but that takes less time than you would spend dowelling or splining. Aligning edge joints with dowels or splines can make sense where tolerances for slippage are very small, such as when edge-gluing two veneered panels to form a flat surface or when assembling a large surface of a great many pieces.

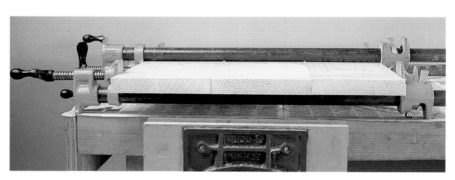

10

FINAL DIMENSIONS

This is the final stage of preparation before you embark on cutting joints. Having established a working face and working edge, all that remains is to trim parts to desired width, establish a working end, then cut to length.

RIPPING TO WIDTH

Unless you are a committed hand-tool woodworker, the tablesaw is the best tool for accurate ripping to width. The techniques for ripping narrower parts (rails and stiles for frame-and-panel construction, for example) are exactly the same as described in chapter 6, 'Roughing Out'. Wider, glued-up panels (or man-made boards such as plywood) are handled a little differently. Regardless of width, the fence is usually set to cut about 1mm wider than the final dimension to allow for a pass over the surfacer and a fine shaving with the bench plane. If you wait to joint or plane

Opposite: Exact dimensioning requires razor-sharp tools and concentration.

the newly sawn edge until after you have cut joints, the contrast of its rougher surface with the planed working edge will make it easier to distinguish between the two and ensure that you are always marking out from the working edge.

CUTTING TO LENGTH

Usually you can treat the creating of straight, square ends and precise cutting to length as part of the joinery or assembly processes. It makes more sense to lay out the finished length of a piece at the same time you are laying out the location of mortises, tenons, dovetails, or other joints. (Boards that will be glued up to form tabletops or panels are best trimmed after assembly, to allow correction of slight misalignment during gluing.)

The basic process, which is covered here, involves establishing a working end, straight and square to the working face and working edge, then measuring from that end and cutting the part to the required length. Depending on

your tool preferences and the accuracy the part requires (having dead square ends or exact length is more important for some parts than for others), you may use a handsaw, tablesaw, handplane, or surfacer. For precise work, the tablesaw and handplane usually produce good results.

Squaring an end on the tablesaw

The task of squaring an end is so conveniently accomplished on the tablesaw that many woodworkers don't bother to check rough-sawn ends for squareness, but automatically trim an end on the tablesaw.

Most tablesaws use a mitre fence for crosscutting. Mitre fence consist of a cast metal head (the fence), attached to a thin steel bar that is about 10mm thick, 20mm wide and 30 to 45cm long. The bar slides in a slot machined in the saw table, 10cm or so from and parallel to the saw blade. The fence pivots on the bar and can be locked at any angle to it and, therefore, to the blade.

An accurately set up machine can produce square ends straight from the saw. Several gadgets are sold to aid adjustment of the blade and mitre fence, but a try square and a little patience work reasonably well, as shown on p.70. To check accuracy, cut a piece of scrap using the fence and check the angle with the try square. Screw a piece of hardwood or plywood to the mitre fence to increase bearing surface; make sure this auxilliary fence is dead straight and flat. Positioning the fence so the blade cuts through it helps to reduce tear-out on the back edge of the work piece as the blade exits the cut.

The trick, if there is one, to accurate crosscutting is holding the workpiece securely against the mitre fence while you move the fence and work steadily through the blade. (As for ripping, you will not succeed unless the edge bearing on the fence is straight to begin with.) Sliding the board into place, the right hand grasps the fence, its fingers simultaneously pushing the work down on the table and pulling it into the fence. The position of the left hand varies somewhat depending on the width of the workpiece. In general, it bears on

RIPPING TO WIDTH

1–2 When ripping a wide panel, keep the working edge flush to the rip fence with your left hand, push the panel ahead with your right. When the end of the

board reaches the front of the table, shift your left hand to the board's end, well away from the line of the cut, and push the board through.

SAW SET UP

A precision square sets the blade square to the table (top) and the mitre fence square to the blade (above). The auxiliary fence increases bearing surface.

SQUARING AN END ON THE TABLESAW

For precision crosscutting, position your hands in line with the mitre bar (top). For narrower work, balance the hands either side of the bar (above).

CROSS CUTTING WIDE PIECES

1 One strategy for crosscutting wide pieces such as table tops and carcass sides is to reverse the mitre fence to start the cut.

2 When the fence reaches the edge of the table, turn off the saw and place the fence in its 'ordinary' position to complete the cut.

the leading edge of the workpiece, exerting even pressure down and back against the fence. Both hands are centred, as much as possible, on or either side of the line of the mitre bar, making the movement of arms, hands, mitre fence and workpiece in a straight line as easy as possible.

Carefully align the cutting mark on the workpiece with the saw blade before cutting. During the cut, think of your hands, the workpiece, and mitre fence as a single unit. Keep your eyes on the saw blade. If there is a little side-to-side play in the fit of the mitre-fence bar and table slot, you can exert subtle pressure with your hands to keep the blade on a pencilled or scribed line. Never move the workpiece sideways along the fence during a cut. This brings the already cut wood into contact with the blade, putting stress on the blade (and the operator), leading to burned wood, a burned blade, or both. If the cut is off line, pull the work back from the blade and reposition it.

When the cut is complete, a little sideways pressure from your fingers will slide the workpiece away from the blade far enough to allow you to pull it and the mitre fence back or to slide the workpiece sideways and out of the way. Turn the saw off before removing small offcuts near the blade. Do not knock them away with a stick: shoved into the blade, they can become high-speed projectiles.

Most crosscutting involves pieces of manageable size – up to, say, 120cm long and 30cm or less wide. Long, heavy boards are difficult to hold down on the table while you are paying attention to the cut at the same time – rest the end on a support. Unless you have an experienced helper, it is probably best not to have someone hold the other end. Their slightest movement can skew the workpiece to the blade, causing it to bind or even kick back.

The distance between the front of the table and the saw blade (usually about 30cm) limits the width of pieces that can be crosscut as described above. If the width of the piece exceeds this space by several centimetres, you can easily pull the mitre fence out in front of the table, with the bar engaged in the slot,

SQUARING AN END WITH A TENON SAW

1 To establish a working end, scribe against a square with a sharp pencil or a knife. Make sure the square is referencing on the working edge.

2 Hold the work firmly against the bench hook. Align the saw blade, hand, arm and sight line. Begin the cut at a slight angle, then lower the saw as the cut progresses.

3 Make the cut right to the centre of the scribe line, where the knife has severed the fibres. Bisecting a line in such a way will require very little clean-up.

and make the cut. It is possible to cut wide pieces where the mitre-fence bar is barely engaged in the slot. But the farther you extend the fence from the table, the more difficult it becomes to control the cut.

Another method is to turn the fence around and push the workpiece against it, so the fence is supported by the tabletop at the beginning of the cut. Cut until the mitre fence reaches the rear edge of the saw, shut off the saw, move the mitre fence to the 'ordinary' position, then cut through the other half. Obviously, both edges of the workpiece must be straight and parallel to each other for this to work. The distance from the blade to the back edge of the table is the limiting factor here; on most saw you can cut about 30 to 35cm before you run out of table.

Squaring an end with a tenon saw

Though most woodworkers will use a tablesaw (or radial-arm saw) for precise crosscutting, it is useful to know how to do so with a handsaw. For hand-tool

aficionados, of course, it is the preferred method. Many of the parts you will be cutting to length will be narrow – rails and stiles for frame and panel construction, table legs, drawer runners and sides. Measuring under about 15cm wide, these pieces can be accurately cut with a tenon saw (the larger backsaw) while holding the work against a bench hook. Wider boards can be cut using a crosscut saw and the same techniques described before for rough crosscutting; a finer saw (12 point) and greater care help. For greatest accuracy, you can trim the ends with a handplane after sawing, as described later.

A tablesaw can trim millimetres off the end of a board, but this is difficult to do with a handsaw. If you are planning a hand-tool project, rough cut pieces a couple of centimetres longer than the finished dimension to provide enough length to make cutting easy.

Holding an accurate square against the working edge, mark across the end with a sharp pencil or, for very precise work, a knife. Some woodworkers

CUTTING TO A LINE

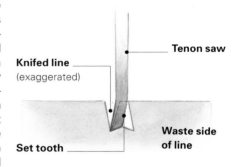

Cut to the centre of a knifed line for greatest accuracy.

extend this line down one edge as an aid to keeping the cut square to the face; others carry it all around the piece. Press the work firmly against the bench hook with your left hand (or right hand, if you are left-handed); support long pieces with scrap the same thickness as the hook.

The technique for this type of sawing is similar to that described for

SQUARING AN END WITH A HANDPLANE

1 When planing end grain of narrow boards, the fingers of the left hand steady the plane, pull it through the cut, and keep it from going too far or too fast.

2 A shooting board places the work and the plane at right angles. Adjust the pressure applied to tool and work with your hands for greatest accuracy.

JOINTING WIDE BOARDS

You can joint the ends of wide boards as you would an edge; it can sometimes be difficult to hold long parts (length is vertical here) flush against the fence.

handsaws in chapter 6, 'Roughing Out'. Use your left thumb or forefinger to position the blade on the mark, align your hands and forearm with the saw blade as best you can, and position your head so that you can see both sides of the blade simultaneously. Start the cut gently, with the saw at a shallow angle to the work. As the cut proceeds, lower the saw until it is horizontal, lengthening your strokes to make use of most of the teeth. You can leave your left forefinger in place as a guide for most of the cut. With practice, you should be able to bisect a thin knifed scribe line. Cuts right to the 'centre' of the line require very little clean-up.

Squaring an end with a handplane

Parts whose working ends must be dead square usually require some trimming with a handplane, no matter how carefully you have set up your tablesaw or wielded the tenon saw. For wider boards or glued-up panels, where machine or handsawing is difficult, the working surface is frequently

established on a roughsawn end with a handplane alone.

The technique is very similar to that described in chapter 8 'Truing Edges'. Most important is to develop a sensitive touch that allows you to keep the sole of the plane at right angles to the face of the work. Some woodworkers plane the ends of parts as narrow as 50mm with a try plane, making use of the tool's weight and balance to maintain its orientation to the work. Others prefer an block plane for narrow work. To prevent splintering at the end of the cut, stop the plane before it reaches the far edge, then plane in from that edge.

A shooting board provides a somewhat easier, though not skill-free, method of squaring ends of boards up to about 30cm in width. You will still need to develop a 'touch' for the process, as subtle changes in the pressure on the plane or the workpiece affect the cut.

Wider boards can be handplaned or run across the surfacer. (For safety, don't joint end grain of boards less than about 30cm wide.) The main difference between handplaning edges and ends is that you produce shavings with the former and dust with the latter. Use an accurate framing square to check for squareness with the working edge; a smaller square will do for checking squareness with the working face. End and edge jointing techniques on the surfacer are likewise similar. To prevent splintering on the surfacer, cut in about 25mm from one edge, then reverse the panel and take the full cut.

CUTTING TO FINAL LENGTH

The same techniques described above for tablesaw, tenon saw, and plane can be used to cut parts to exact length. Measure from the working end, square a line across the face and off you go.

Pieces that are wide but not too long – carcass sides, drawer bottoms and so on – can be crosscut to length against the rip fence. Place the working end against the fence and feed it slowly through the saw as described above for ripping a wide part. Take care to keep the end firmly in contact with the rip fence throughout the entire cut.

CUTTING TO LENGTH

1 Wide parts can be crosscut to length against the rip fence providing the length of the uncut piece is not more than approximately twice its width.

2 Clamp stop blocks on an auxiliary mitre fence to cut several parts to identical lengths. Remember to push the squared working end against the stop.

3 For short identical pieces, set a thick stop block on the rip fence in front of the saw blade. Set the desired length between the block and the blade.

Don't do this with parts less than 30cm wide, and parts whose length exceeds the width by too much. While a carcass side 45cm wide and 75cm long can be safely trimmed to length against a rip fence, a shelf the same length but only 30cm wide doesn't have enough bearing surface in relation to its length – the chances of its binding between blade and fence are uncomfortably large.

Cutting to identical lengths

Almost every project calls for at least one pair of identical parts and usually a lot more – drawer fronts, door rails and stiles, table and chair legs for example. Accurate marking out is essential. Instead of measuring each part with a ruler, measure one part, then use it to lay out its mates. If the parts must be exactly the same length, stack one on top of the other after you have cut and planed the second ends. Align the ends with your fingers – you will be surprised at the sensitivity of your fingers in detecting even the smallest differences in length.

Parts that are not too long or too wide can be easily cut to identical lengths on a tablesaw. (A radial-arm saw is ideal for this work and can handle much longer stock.) The mitre fences on some saws come equipped with a set of adjustable rods designed for just this purpose. One rod fits into the fence, secured by a thumbscrew, and one or more additional rods (depending on the length of the pieces to be cut) attach to it, the last one having a hooked end, which engages the end of the workpiece. Lacking rods, you can accomplish the same thing by clamping a block to a long wooden auxiliary fence. If you enjoy gadgets, there are a number of more elaborate commercially made stop systems and ones you can make yourself incorporating grooves, sliding blocks, thumbscrews and more.

All these set-ups could not be easier to use. Just set the rod or block, push the pieces against it and cut as described previously. It is important to remember, however, to establish a working end on all the pieces and push that end against the stop. (Some systems have flip-down stops, which allow you to flip the stop up to cut the working end, then flip it down to cut to length.)

Stop blocks like these are useful as long as the finished pieces are longer than 15 to 20cm. Shorter than that and there isn't enough room for your hand to hold the piece against the mitre-gauge and clear the saw blade safely as you make the cut. An alternative is to clamp a stop block to the rip fence, so that the distance between the face of the block and the blade equals the desired length. Use a thick block and attach it about 15cm in front of the saw blade. Push the work up to the block, then advance the gauge to make the cut. Because the space between the blade and the fence is greater than the length of the severed piece, the chances of the severed parts binding and kicking back are considerably reduced.

FRAME CONSTRUCTION

Of all the ways of sticking pieces of wood together for some useful purpose, few are as versatile, or permit as much variation, as the frame. The chair you sit on, the table you eat at, even the house you live in are all likely to be or to contain framed constructions. Add a wooden (or fabric, plaster or glass) panel between the framed members, and you have doors and windows or wall and ceiling coverings. Virtually any kind of furniture – tables, chairs, chests, desks, dressers – can be made with the frame and frame-and-panel construction presented in this section.

Opposite: A frame and panel construction can be starkly simple or elaborately embellished. A narrow maple framework supports panels of waterproof paper in this screen by Alison White.

11

MORTISE-AND-TENON BASICS

For centuries, virtually every wooden frame, from massive post-and-beam buildings to doors of display cases, was held together by mortise-and-tenon joints. Cultures as different as those of Europe and Japan developed remarkably similar systems of joinery based on the mortise-and-tenon, a heritage they share with numerous other cultures around the world. Despite the fact that new materials, fasteners, and glues have lessened our dependence on the joint, it is still indispensable to anyone making quality woodwork.

It is not hard to understand why woodworkers in so many far-flung places would all arrive at the same method of sticking a frame together. A well made mortise-and-tenon joint has great strength: it is as strong in compression as the wood itself and pinned, wedged or glued together, it is virtually impossible to pull apart. Although they

Opposite: With practice, cutting a tenon is as fast with a handsaw as by machine.

are simple things, mortise-and-tenon joints can take complex forms. Some of the Japanese timber-framing joints are wondrous affairs, worth making just for the challenge, if nothing else. But beneath the complexity lies the same basic idea. Learn to lay out and cut the simple version shown on these pages, and you will know much of what you need to make many of the others.

There are numerous ways to cut mortises and tenons, from chisels and handsaws to high-speed horizontal boring machines and double-end tenoners. In between come alternatives involving bandsaws, tablesaws, routers, spindle moulders, drill presses and a world of ingenious (and sometimes wacky) jigs and fixtures. Here, we will show how to cut mortises by clearing most of the waste with an auger bit (powered by hand or drill press) then finishing the job with paring chisels. A tenon saw and shoulder plane are sufficient to cut and trim basic tenons; we will also show how to use a bandsaw and a tablesaw to cut tenons.

MORTISE-AND-TENON ANATOMY

Despite its simplicity, a mortise-and-tenon joint can be a maddening thing to discuss because some of the terms used to describe the parts are far from standard. The drawing on this page shows the names we use here. Most people agree on the terms 'cheek' and 'shoulder'. Confusion often arises concerning the other terms. Note that in this case the width, length and thickness of the tenon correspond to the length, depth and width, respectively, of the mortise.

The proportions and placement of mortises and tenons vary according to the type of piece being built and the positions of the joints on it, as you will see in the projects in this section. As a general rule, tenons are about one third the thickness of the piece on which they are cut, with shoulders of equal width (centring the tenon). Most tenons also have 'short' shoulders, which reinforce the joint's resistance to stress from racking, and hide any bruises created when chiselling the ends of the mortise. The length and width of the mortise are, of course, sized to correspond to the tenon.

The depth of the mortise, and therefore the length of the tenon, is determined by the width of the mortised piece. The deeper the mortise, the greater the strength of the joint, due to increased gluing surfaces. The blind, or stopped, mortise-and-tenon we make here is not quite as strong as the through-wedged tenon you will meet in the next chapter, but it is used more often and is a bit easier to cut, making it a better sample joint.

For convenience, in this chapter we call the tenoned piece the rail, and the mortised piece the stile, terms commonly used to denote the horizontal (rail) and vertical (stile) parts of an open frame or frame-and-panel construction.

LAYING OUT THE JOINT

If you want to make the sample joint shown here, prepare two pieces 75mm wide, 380mm long, and 25mm thick. (Dimensions can vary according to scrap you have on hand; you will do best with stock at least 20mm thick.) Make sure that the faces of the stock

ANATOMY OF A MORTISE -AND -TENON JOINT

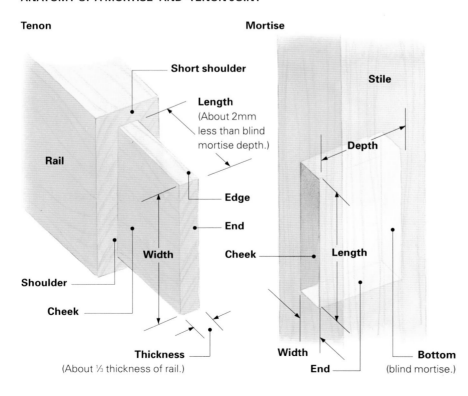

Tenon

Mortise

Short shoulder

Length
(About 2mm less than blind mortise depth.)

Rail

Edge

End

Width

Cheek

Shoulder

Cheek

Thickness
(About ⅓ thickness of rail.)

Stile

Depth

Length

Width

End

Bottom
(blind mortise.)

are flat and the edges are square to them; the ends need not be perfectly square. Mark a working face and edge on each piece and remember to measure and mark only from them. (If you want to try the machine techniques too, prepare an additional two or three pieces to use for setting up machines.)

To lay out, you will need a pencil, thin-bladed marking knife, mortise gauge, and an accurate square. A single-pin gauge will work just fine, but will require resetting for each cheek; use two single-pin gauges if you have them.

Although we cut only one sample joint here, many projects require two or more identical or nearly identical joints – a cabinet door, for instance, has four, one at each corner. Whether you are making two identical joints or a dozen, you can save time and avoid errors by organizing your work. Scribe the shoulder lines of all the tenons with a sharp knife, then scribe all the cheeks with the mortise gauge. And remember, always hold the square or gauge fence against the 'working' face and edge.

Tenon layout

To mark the tenon shoulders measure in from the end of the rail a distance about 2mm less than the depth of the mortise, and make a tick with a pencil. (The difference in length provides room at the bottom of the mortise for excess glue that the tenon pushes ahead of it at assembly.) Remember that the length of the tenon is dependent upon the depth of the mortise. Because the waste is cleared from the mortise with an auger bit, the mortise must not be so deep that the lead point of the bit penetrates the opposite edge of the stile. To determine mortise depth quickly, mark it on the stile directly from the bit.

A pencil mark is too thick to provide the accuracy needed when sawing the tenon shoulders, so scribe the actual shoulder lines (at the position of the pencil tick) with the knife. Extend the knifed lines across both faces and edges, making sure that the stock of the square bears only against the working face and edge.

Now lay out the tenon cheeks. Set the double points of the mortise gauge to the thickness of the tenon. Keeping in mind the one-third proportion, size the tenon slightly thicker than the diameter of a standard auger bit. Here, for example, with rail and stile 25mm thick, set the gauge to scribe a tenon slightly less than 10mm thick. Using the same setting to lay out the mortise will allow you to clear waste with an 8mm bit and leave a shaving or so on each cheek to pare off with a chisel.

With the pins set, position the mortise-gauge fence to centre the tenon on the edge of the rail. Then, with the fence against the working face, start at the knifed shoulder line on one edge and scribe up the edge, across the end and down the other edge to the other shoulder line. Now set the rail aside – you will lay out the width of the tenon later.

A single-pin gauge also works for scribing cheeks. If you use one, don't be tempted to scribe from both faces even though the tenons and mortises are centred on the pieces. Because of

LAYING OUT THE TENON

1 Mark the depth of a blind mortise so that the waste-clearing bit's point will not penetrate the edge. Mark the mortise depth at the position of the bit's cutters.

2 Scribe the tenon's shoulder lines with a sharp knife and square held against the working edge. Extend the lines around both edges and faces of the rail.

3 To scribe the cheeks, begin at the shoulder line on one edge and scribe along the edge, across the end, and down the other edge to the shoulder line.

variations in the thickness of the pieces, chances are you will end up with different sized mortises and tenons and some irritating trimming to do. Instead, scribe both cheeks from the working face, resetting the gauge for the second. (Or use two gauges.)

Mortise layout

First, position the mortise on the edge of the stile. While the mortise on this sample could go anywhere along the edge, mortises for real projects are placed so that the edges of the rail or other tenoned member fall where you want them. So, square a pencil line across the working edge of the stile, about 25mm from an end, and assume that is where you want to position the outer edge of the rail.

Butt the rail against the stile, aligning its top edge with the pencil mark. The width of the mortise will be the width of the rail less the short shoulders on each edge. Make a short pencil mark across the juncture of the stile and rail about 6mm in from each edge of the

rail. (The exact distance is not critical for this joint, so you can guess these measurements.) Squaring the line across the edge of the stile with a pencil positions the mortise. Squaring lines across the end of the rail fixes the width of the tenon.

Now scribe the mortise cheeks. Use the same gauge setting as for the tenon and run the fence against the stile's working face. (For projects where the face of the rail is offset from that of the stile, you will need to reset the fence, but not the double pins.) As an aid to positioning the waste-clearing auger bit, scribe a centre line down the mortise with a single-pin gauge.

CUTTING THE MORTISE

It is easier to fit a tenon to a mortise than the other way around, so cut mortises first. (See photos on p.80.) For a blind mortise, you will need to stop the bit that clears the waste at the proper depth. On a drill press, just adjust the machine's depth stop. When boring with a brace and bit, wrap a piece of

tape around the bit and watch for it to reach the wood. If you want a stop that prevents you from boring too far, try fixing a block of wood to the bit or buy a commercially made stop. It is important to maintain the bit parallel to the faces of the stile. If you need to, use a square to check your progress. Bore the first holes near each end of the mortise, then work on the waste between. Whether you are working with a drill press or by hand, the holes will be easier to bore if you leave a little wood between them – these "bridges" are no trouble to remove with a chisel.

Now, remove the remaining waste with chisels. Deepen the scribe marks slightly with a wide, very sharp chisel. Then, break out some of the "bridge" wood with a narrow chisel. To pare the cheeks, you can guide the wide chisel with your left hand and power it with your right, striving to create flat surfaces, parallel to the faces of the piece. With a chisel equal to or slightly narrower than the width of the mortise, pare the ends. If the end grain offers

---

LAYING OUT THE MORTISE

1 Position the rail where it will join the stile, then mark the width of the mortise on to the stile directly from the rail, about 6mm in from each rail edge.

2 Square the lines across the edge of the stile to establish the position of the ends of the mortise. Pencil lines are accurate enough for these marks.

3 Finally, scribe cheek lines with the previously set mortise gauge. Add a centre line, as shown here, to aid positioning the waste-clearing bit.

CUTTING THE MORTISE

1–3 Clear waste from the mortise with a bit slightly smaller than the final width (left). Bore holes in each end, then clear waste from the middle. Use a square if necessary to keep the bit parallel to the faces of the stile. After removing some of the 'bridge' waste, pare the mortise cheeks with a wide, sharp chisel (centre). The final paring cuts should remove the last traces of the auger bit from the cheeks. A narrow chisel cleans waste from the mortise ends (right).

HAND-CUTTING THE TENON

1-3 Start each cheek by making angled cuts from the edges (left). Then, using the angled saw kerfs as a guide, cut to the tenon shoulder. Cut right on the knife line to make the shoulders (centre). Start the cut at an angle, then lower the saw until the kerf extends across the entire rail. After marking the width of the tenon with a pencil gauge, cut along the grain, then cut exactly on the knife lines on each edge to create the short shoulders (right).

more resistance, a little persuasion with a mallet may help. During this process, you will need to move between the various chisels as necessary to deepen the mortise. Rest the cutting edge of the chisel in the deepened scribe line for the final paring, which should clear the last traces of the auger-bit holes from each of the cheeks. Clear waste from the bottom of the mortise with a narrow chisel worked bevel down.

HAND-CUTTING THE TENON

Probably the most difficult part of making these joints by hand is cutting the cheeks and shoulders of the tenons with a tenon saw. Simple as it looks, cutting to a straight line with a saw is not easy, but requires patient practice – regular workouts with scrap wood repay the effort handsomely.

A sharp, properly set saw is essential; don't even attempt it with a dull saw. Most tenon saws have crosscut teeth, and if sharp will work satisfactorily cutting tenons. But, as mentioned in the sharpening chapter, tenon cheeks are cut with the grain, and are most easily cut with a saw sharpened as a ripsaw. A rip-sharpened saw will also produce clean shoulders even though those cuts are across the grain because the surface fibres have already been severed with a knife.

Make the cheek cuts first. Cut each cheek in three stages. The first two cuts are at an angle, one from each edge. Starting at the corner, when complete, the angled cut extends from the shoulder line on the edge of the rail to about the mid-point of the scribed cheek line on the end of the rail. Try to split the scribe marks in half with the saw cut, as shown on p.71. For the third cut, the saw is parallel to the shoulder line and is guided by the kerfs of the first two cuts. Despite the little 'jig' formed by the angled saw kerfs, you will still need to exert pressure here and there to keep the saw on track.

Cut the shoulders on the knifed lines with a tenon saw, holding the rail with a bench hook. Start the cut on the near or far edge (whichever you prefer) and lower the saw slowly as you go until you're cutting across the full width of

the rail. The fibres break cleanly at the knifed line, providing a good indicator for manipulating the saw as you lower it along the line. Raking light that throws a shadow in the knife line will help you see what's going on. Strive for even strokes and use as much of the blade as possible, keeping it perpendicular to the face of the rail.

With the cheek waste removed, lay out and cut the tenon to width. When you marked the mortise, you also pencilled lines across the end of the tenon to indicate its width. (If you forgot to mark the width earlier, just hold the tenon to the mortise and tick off the width with a pencil.) Now extend those lines down one cheek of the tenon with a pencil-point marking gauge. Hold the rail in the vice while cutting along these lines. To make fitting and assembly easier, cut the line away, so the tenon will be just slightly narrower than its mortise; 1mm is plenty. (It is the cheek-to-cheek fit that must be snug.) Free the waste with cuts across the edges on the knife lines to create the short shoulders.

MACHINE-CUTTING TENONS

Of all the machine methods for cutting tenons, the safest and most straightforward is to cut the cheeks on a bandsaw and the shoulders on a tablesaw. Unless you have a special jig, the technique of cutting tenon cheeks on a tablesaw is too dangerous. Holding the workpiece vertically against the rip fence provides too many possibilities for kickback and injury, particularly when working with narrow parts or when cutting long tenons.

The bandsaw is suited for making cheek cuts. It is easy to control a piece fed horizontally on the bandsaw, and the thin bandsaw blade creates less resistance than a tablesaw blade and offers less opportunity for injury. A wide, sharp blade in a well tuned bandsaw is ideal, though success can be had with a 6mm- or a 13mm-blade. Dull blades of any width can wander or make a mess of things.

The technique, as shown on p.82, is simple. Set the rip fence to cut the first cheek, working face against the fence. Then reset the fence for the

second cheek. (Again, because of variation in the thickness of rails and stiles, resist the temptation to turn the piece over and cut both cheeks against the same fence setting.) By making trial cuts in a piece of scrap milled to the same thickness as the rail, you can fine-tune the fence settings. If your saw is well set up, and the mortise accurately cut, you can bandsaw the cheeks so the tenon fits snugly in the mortise straight from the saw. Otherwise, make it slightly oversize – it is much easier to take wood off later than put it on.

To cut the shoulders on the tablesaw, set the mitre fence very accurately at 90° to a sharp blade. Then wind the blade down so it just projects into the bandsaw kerf at the top of its arc. Hold the material against the gauge and make the cut. (See chapter 10 for tips on accurate crosscutting on the tablesaw.) With practice, you can cut right to the line, just as you would with a handsaw. Because you are cutting on both faces, you cannot place the working edge against the mitre fence for both cuts. Prepare the stock carefully so both edges are parallel and the shoulders should come out square. It can be difficult to hold a long piece in place while cutting a shoulder. An accurately set up radial-arm saw works better, because the blade moves over the stationary work.

With the waste gone from the cheeks, mark the width of the tenon as described previously, then return to the bandsaw and cut the edges of the tenon. Remember that making the tenon slightly narrower than the mortise makes the joint easier to fit. Cut the short shoulders against the mitre fence on the tablesaw.

Machines are, of course, well suited for cutting several identical parts. Once the fences and gauges are set, it is easy to make the same cut over and over. Because of this, you may not need to lay out cheek lines and scribe shoulders on all identical parts. It is a good idea to lay them out anyway, to give an easy way to check the cuts as you go along. The machines most of us use (not to mention their operators) are not infallible.

MACHINE-CUTTING TENONS

1 First bandsaw the cheek farthest from the fence, then one closest to it. Reset the fence for each cut so the working face is always bearing against the fence.

2 Cut the shoulders on the tablesaw using an accurately set mitre fence and a sharp blade. The blade is hidden from view, so steady hands are essential.

3 After bandsawing the tenon to the desired width, remove the waste by cutting the short shoulders on the tablesaw.

TENONING WITH A DADO HEAD

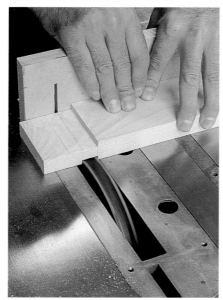

To cut tenons with a dado head on the tablesaw, set the height of the blades to the cheek scribe, and cut away the waste to the shoulder scribe.

If you do not possess a bandsaw, you can cut tenons with a dado head on the tablesaw. A full set of dado blades cuts a groove about 20mm wide, so the job goes quickly, too. The main drawback of this method is the necessity of working from both faces of the rail, rather than just the working face. Unless the tenon is exactly centred, it will be necessary to fiddle with the height of the dado blades for each cheek, or the tenon will end up either too thick or too thin. Likewise, if you are tenoning several rails, any variation in the rails' thickness will affect the tenons. It certainly helps to have several pieces of scrap the same thickness as the rail to use in setting up the saw for each cheek cut.

FINAL FITTING

If all of your saw and chisel work has been exact, the joint should now slip snugly together without forcing, the cheeks of mortise and tenon making contact along their entire surfaces, the shoulders seating on the edges of the stile showing no gaps under even the closest scrutiny. You may often come close to this ideal state of affairs, but will seldom escape having to trim a little something somewhere. And when you are learning, you spend a long time fiddling. Although this can be frustrating, keep at it – as you gain experience the job becomes easier.

If the tenon will not fit in all the way, check the mortise first to see if the cheeks are parallel to each other and to the working face of the stile. You will just have to sight this: look for the little scalloped vestiges of the auger bit on the cheeks and pare these away with a wide chisel.

Next, turn to the tenon, which is easier to trim. A shoulder plane is indispensable for this job. A rectangular steel block, small enough to fit comfortably in the palm of the hand, the shoulder plane's blade extends across the width of the 25mm-wide sole and its edges are flush with the plane body's machined faces. You can use it to trim tenon cheeks and shoulders. For

FINAL FITTING

1–2 A shoulder plane works well for trimming tenon cheeks as well as for squaring up shoulders. Take fine shavings and check the fit of the joint

frequently to avoid removing too much material. On the shoulders, work in from both edges to avoid splintering the edges of the rail.

3 It may take you a dozen tries to get the techniques right, but making a neat, snug-fitting mortise-and-tenon joint can be very satisfying.

large tenons, you can use a block plane for the top part of the tenon.

When you are setting up the shoulder plane, it is important that the blade is flush with the sides of the plane, particularly for work on the shoulders. If the blade protrudes, it will dig into the cheek. If it is recessed, it will not get right into the juncture of cheek and shoulder, and the plane will move farther from the cheek with each pass.

Grinding the blade flush with both sides of the plane allows you to cut on the push or the pull stroke. At the end of a cut along the shoulder, for example, you can turn the plane around and plane into the wood, rather than planing off the edge and risk chipping the wood.

When trimming tenon cheeks, make sure that the working faces of the rail and stile stay aligned in the same plane. To check, assemble the joint and hold a straightedge across adjoining faces. If the straightedge reveals misalignment, you'll need to remove wood from only

one cheek, perhaps near the end, perhaps near the shoulder. Proceed cautiously. Begin cutting away wood before you know where the problem lies, and you may quickly find yourself with a joint that is loose-fitting as well as misaligned. Remember that the trouble may as easily be found with the mortise cheeks as the tenon cheeks. When you think you have isolated the problem, take only a few shavings before checking the assembled joint again.

Once you get the hang of cutting mortise-and-tenon joints, you will not need to fool too much with the cheeks. But because even a tiny gap in the shoulders is noticeable, you will regularly spend time fitting them. Fortunately, it is easy to do with a shoulder plane. If the knifed lines are still evident, plane down to them. Otherwise, check with a square to see if the shoulders are 90° to the working edge and, with the square against the working face, check to see if both shoulders are at the same level.

Plane to correct any faults, then push the joint home. Mark any remaining high

spots with a pencil, disassemble the joint and plane them off. As you proceed, check matching parts, such as trestle uprights, or pairs of rails and stiles in a door frame, to make sure that the distance between shoulders is the same.

Fitting is a process of trial and paring. Try the tenon in the mortise, then trim off material that is preventing the joint from closing tightly or aligning properly. It is not always easy to see where the problem lies, so proceed with caution, taking a shaving or two then trying tenon to mortise again.

Tenons that are too thin are more troublesome – it is always far simpler to remove material than to add it. You can glue veneers to tenons to fatten them up, but the process is tedious and not terribly successful. Unfortunately, most of the time the best solution to an anaemic tenon is to make a new rail. Nobody likes to start again, but you must admit that if you are in the pickle to begin with, you could benefit from the extra practice.

Right
CLIVE HOWDLE
The narrow back slats of this oak chair flex when leaned against, comfort the sitter and lighten the design both visually and physically.

Above
SAMUEL CHAN
With the addition of two planks, a mortise-and-tenoned bench becomes a side chair.

Right
STEMMER & SHARP
Turned rungs connect ash legs in this folding clothes stand, an amusing piece of minimalist design. Dark details are stained a deep blue colour.

Below
RUPERT WILLIAMSON
Undulating sycamore rails
and solid yew legs support
the yew-veneered top of
this small apron-rail table.
The rails are housed in
dados cut in the legs and
are mitred at the corner.

Right
ROBERT WILLIAMS
Through-wedged mortise-
and-tenon joints join the
solid front and laminated
back legs to the side rails
of this ash side chair. Blind
tenons joint the front and
rear rails to the legs.

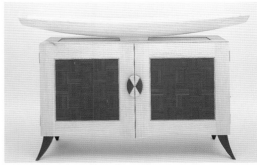

Above
ROSANNE SOMERSON
The traditional frame-
and-panel construction
of this oak and purple-
heart cabinet contrast
with the sculptural form
hovering over it.

12

A SIMPLE TRESTLE TABLE

Simply engineered and easy to make, trestle tables have a long history. Every school-child's vision of a medieval castle includes a Great Hall with a large plank tabletop on hefty trestles. Today you can find refined descendants of these behemoths serving as desks in the offices of large corporations – perhaps as a plate-glass top hovering over 'saw horse' trestles. Most contemporary trestle tables, however, are humbler creations for the kitchens and dining rooms of ordinary folk.

The table we will make in this chapter (see p.88) is loosely based on several Shaker tables admirable for their simplicity and pleasing proportions. Lacking legs at each corner, tables like this are ideal for houses where there is a frequent need to squeeze in an unexpected guest at a meal. Our version has a top of Ponderosa pine on a poplar underframe which can be painted. The combination

Opposite: Clive Howdle's simple trestle table would suit a workshop or office.

of a natural-wood top and a painted base was common in Shaker pieces and can be striking. An oil-finished cherry top on a deep-green trestle looks better and better as the cherry ages to a rich russet colour. If you prefer a smaller table, it's easy to reduce the size. A smaller version (top 50 by 95cm, 48cm high), could serve as a coffee table or a children's table.

MAKING THE TABLETOP
The basic techniques for making a wide tabletop like this are covered in chapter 9, so only a few comments are needed here. If you make the tabletop first, while the glue cures you can begin on the trestle. If the top ends up a different size than planned (longer, shorter, narrower, depending on what you get out of the material), you can adjust the size of the trestle accordingly.

The top is a full 25mm thick, so that it can span the unsupported distance between the two trestles without sagging. This thickness also looks better – even were it strong enough, a thinner

top would appear skimpy and out of proportion. To ensure that the top will finish at least 25mm thick after flattening and thicknessing, start with rough timber 32mm thick.

The unbroken expanse of a tabletop can be a showcase for handsome wood, and woodworkers often stockpile attractive boards for that particular purpose. If you do not have a special stash, you can usually produce a good-looking tabletop by spending a little time arranging the available boards. The more material you have to choose from the better your chances of finding good matches. If you cannot pick through the timberyard piles, increase your choices by ordering at least 50 per cent more than the minimum amount of timber the top requires.

Working with long and/or wide boards for a large tabletop can be more demanding than working with smaller pieces. A 20cm surfacer with long tables is particularly handy for flattening and edge-jointing long boards. A narrower surfacer forces you to rip boards

MAKING THE TABLETOP

1 Mate the edges on the surfacer and handplane, then glue-up the top. The quick action clamps pull the boards flush with the sash clamps to keep the top flat.

2 Provide a level support so no twist occurs. When the glue has cured, plane both faces of the top to clean off excess glue and eliminate slight misalignments.

3 Sometimes you have to improvise in the workshop. After planing the edges of the tabletop straight and parallel, you need to plane ends square to the edges.

TRESTLE TABLE

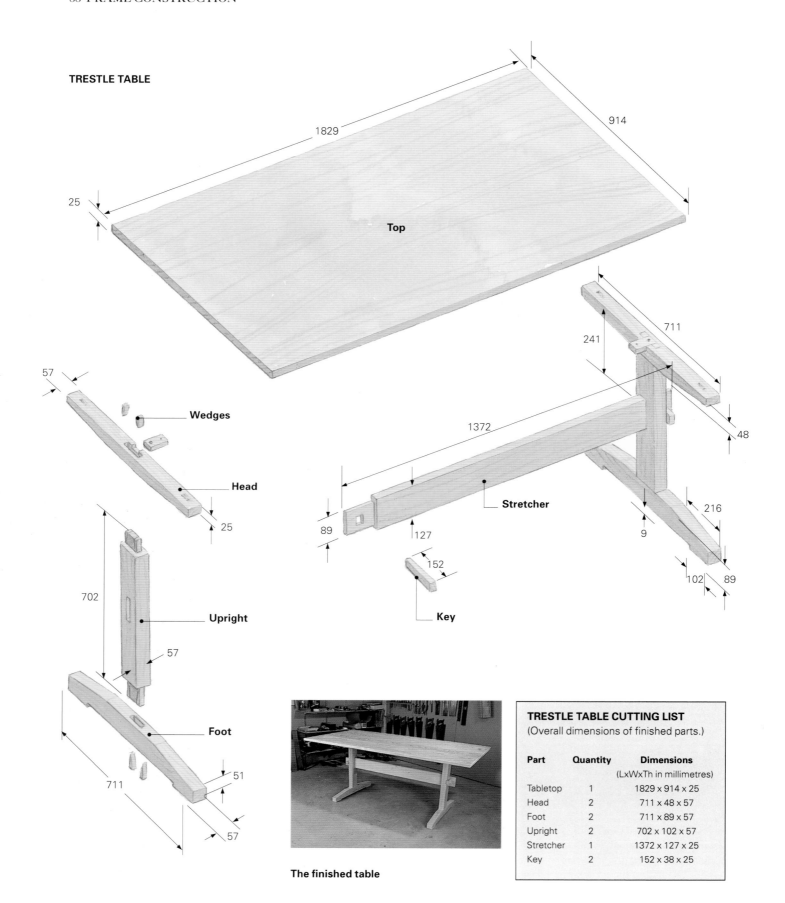

1829

914

25

Top

57

Wedges

Head

25

241

711

48

1372

Stretcher

89

127

9

216

102   89

702

Upright

57

152

Key

Foot

51

711

57

The finished table

TRESTLE TABLE CUTTING LIST
(Overall dimensions of finished parts.)

Part	Quantity	Dimensions
		(LxWxTh in millimetres)
Tabletop	1	1829 x 914 x 25
Head	2	711 x 48 x 57
Foot	2	711 x 89 x 57
Upright	2	702 x 102 x 57
Stretcher	1	1372 x 127 x 25
Key	2	152 x 38 x 25

THROUGH-WEDGED MORTISE-AND-TENON JOINTS

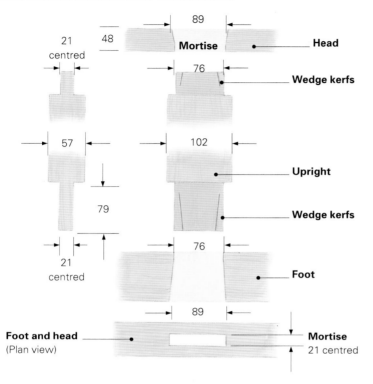

89 — Mortise — Head

21 centred

48

76 — Wedge kerfs

57

102 — Upright

79

76 — Wedge kerfs

21 centred

76 — Foot

89

Foot and head
(Plan view) — Mortise
21 centred

RESAWING

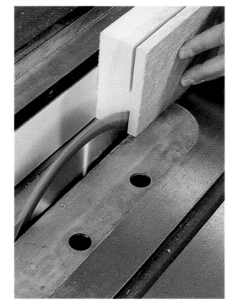

If a board is much thicker than you need, you can resaw it on the tablesaw in two cuts, each a little more than half-way through the board.

LAYOUT

Mark identical parts together to ensure accuracy. Here the mortise on the second foot is being marked from the first.

---

into narrow widths; reglued, they often do not look as good as a top assembled of a few wide boards. And it is more difficult to flatten and straighten the bowed faces and edges of long boards on a surfacer with short infeed and outfeed tables. If your surfacer is small, you might want to sharpen up your handplane to prepare a large top like this.

BUILDING THE TRESTLE

This underframe employs two types of through-tenon. The trestle legs are assembled with through-wedged tenons which are arguably the strongest mortise-and-tenon joint. Through-tenons with loose keys join the legs to the stretcher; this 'knockdown' joint makes removal or storage of the table easy.

Poplar was used for this trestle because it is strong, relatively easy to work and paints well. It is also one of the few woods that can be obtained in thicknesses greater than 50mm to accommodate the legs (head, upright, and foot), which finish at 57mm thick. If you cannot get the wood you want in sufficient thickness, you can glue two thinner boards face to face for each part. Cut 32mm or 38mm stock at least 6mm over final rough length and width to allow for slippage when gluing. Flatten two faces (you need not thickness the boards), spread glue evenly on them with a brush or roller, and clamp them together with quick-action or G-clamps. Lightweight clamps may not exert enough pressure to squeeze out excess glue, leaving a noticeable glue line. Clean off the cured glue, and proceed to flatten, thickness and so on as you would for roughsawn boards.

Layout

Mill all the parts to size, making sure that the faces of the stock are flat and the edges are square to them. Instead of creating a mountain of shavings planing the 75mm rough poplar down to 57mm, flatten a working face, then resaw the parts to about 60mm thick before finishing the job on the thickness planer. You can resaw with a bandsaw or a tablesaw. The 13 to 16mm-thick poplar offcuts come in handy for other projects. In addition,

CUTTING THE THROUGH-MORTISE

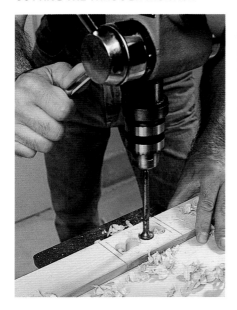

1–2 A drill press provides accuracy and speed for clearing mortise waste. For through-mortises, bore in from both edges to prevent breakout. Pare the

through-mortise cheeks with a wide, sharp chisel, working in from both edges. Take a couple of shavings to make them slightly concave to ease assembly.

KEYED MORTISE-AND-TENON JOINT

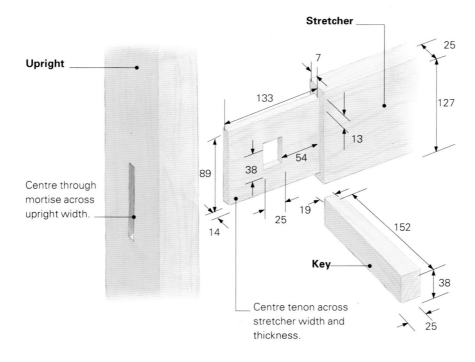

Upright

Centre through mortise across upright width.

Stretcher

Centre tenon across stretcher width and thickness.

Key

mill one or two pieces of scrap to the same thickness and width as the uprights which can be used later when setting machines to cut the tenons.

Lay out the mortises and tenons as described in chapter 11 'Mortise-and-tenon Basics'. Because these are through joints you will need to mark the mortises on both edges of the head and foot. As the drawing on p.89 shows, the mortises taper. Driving the wedges home at assembly spreads the tenon, making the joint impossible to pull apart. Remember to reference the square and marking gauge on the working face only when laying out the mortises on both edges. Speed and accuracy are enhanced by marking identical parts, such as the two head pieces or foot pieces, together, rather than measuring each separately.

The leg tenons are standard proportions, slightly less than one third the thickness for each shoulder, slightly more than a third for the tenon. As the thickness of the stretcher is much less than the width of the trestle upright into which it fits, the stretcher tenon can be proportionally thicker. The joint is not necessarily stronger, but the more substantial exposed tenon looks better. You will need to reset the marking gauge fence (but not the double pin setting) to scribe the cheeks of the stretcher tenon after scribing the mating mortise on the upright.

Cutting the joints

Clear waste from the through-mortises by boring from each edge. If you do this by hand, bore holes just over half-way through from one edge, then turn the piece over and bore in from the other edge. This ensures clean, aligned openings, even if the bit wanders slightly off course once or twice.

A carefully adjusted drill press is ideal for clearing waste from through mortises. Because bits sometimes wander even on a drill press, to ensure accuracy use a bit that is slightly less than the mortise width and bore the holes half-way from each face. Work from both faces when paring down to the scribe lines with a sharp chisel. Use the chisel as a straightedge to detect any bulges in the cheeks. The ends of the foot and head mortises taper; you need extend the taper to within only 10mm or so of the inside edge.

You can cut the tenons just as described in the previous chapter. If you work on the bandsaw and table-saw, fine-tune the fence and stop settings on scrap first, then be sure to make identical cuts on both leg or stretcher tenons before changing the settings. Because the stretcher tenon is exposed beyond the mortise, cut the tenon slightly oversize (both in thick-ness and in width), so you can clean off the saw marks and still have a snug fit.

Fitting

Through mortise-and-tenons should fit snugly, cheek-to-cheek, just like their blind cousins. The keyed joint is some-what trickier to fit because it must assemble and disassemble easily. The faces and edges of the exposed part of the tenon must be presentably smooth and there should be little visible gap between the mortise opening and the tenon. Begin fitting by marking around

FITTING

1 If all you need is a little gentle persuasion with a rubber hammer, the joint is a good fit. Trim the cheeks with a shoulder plane and chisel if necessary.

2 A keyed through-tenon must not be so tight that assembly and disassembly are difficult, but gaps should be uniform and as small as possible.

SHAPING THE HEAD AND FOOT

1 Clamp the bottom edges of the feet together and use a 20mm bit to form the tight radii at the ends of the relief.

2 Bandsaw the remainder of the relief against a rip fence to ensure a straight line; clean up if necessary with chisels.

3 After boring holes to define each end of the screw slots in the head piece, chisel out the remainder of the waste.

the tenon about 60mm from the shoulder – just a little more than the thickness of the upright. The tenon above this line extends beyond the mortise, and need not fit precisely to the mortise. Trim this portion with a sharp block plane to be slightly smaller than the mortise for easy assembly.

Work the lower portion of the stretcher tenon carefully with a shoulder plane, checking it frequently to the mortise. Remember that these surfaces will not show – they need not be smooth, just snug-fitting. When the cheeks fit well, trim the shoulders as needed to eliminate gaps.

Shaping the head and foot
Before assembling the legs, you need to taper the head and foot and relieve the underside of the foot. Without this relief, the full length of the foot would make contact with the floor and be much more likely to rock on uneven surfaces.

Use a 20mm drill bit to create the tight radius at each end of the relief, as shown on p.91. Clamp the two feet together, bottom edge to bottom edge. Position the centre point of the bit at the juncture of the surfaces and bore a hole half-way through the thickness. Turn the clamped pieces over and bore from the other side. Clear remaining

waste on the bandsaw or a router. As this surface is not visible on the finished table, you can leave it straight from the saw. If the sawcut is uneven, clean it up with a block plane. Bandsaw (or handsaw) the tapers, then clean them up with a sharp bench plane.

The tabletop is attached to each leg by three screws: one in the centre and two near each end of the head as shown on pp.94 and 95. The outside screws pass through slots to allow the top to expand and contract without splitting as the humidity changes. To keep them from digging into the wood and sticking in place, the screw-heads

Two trestles, crossing at right angles, support the oval, ash-veneered top of this handsome table. The top members of the trestles are turned on the lathe from black walnut; metal cross braces replace rails on the narrow trestle.

bear on washers. Make the slots by boring holes at each end, then pare the oblong recess and the slots with a chisel. Bore the larger recessing holes first, then the smaller-diameter slots. (You will add the support for the centre screw after assembling the legs.)

Assembly

Assemble the legs without glue to check the final fit and to position the clamps. Before gluing, cut kerfs for the wedges in the tenons of the trestle uprights. The kerfs angle from about 20mm in from the tenon edges at the end to a point about 6mm from the edge and 13mm from the shoulder. The thinner material near the shoulder forms a sort of hinge and makes it easier to drive the wedges and spread the tenon into the tapered mortise. Also, by cutting diagonally across the grain, the chances of a wedge opening a split in the tenon are lessened (it's a slim chance anyway). The joint would be serviceable without glue, but glue it anyway as extra insurance against gap-

ping at the shoulders, which is also why you draw the shoulders tightly together with clamps before driving the wedges. (See chapter 22, 'Surface Preparation' for a discussion of cleaning up squeezed-out glue.) Cut the wedges of poplar on the bandsaw or by hand; their taper should be similar to that of the mortise; they should be about 13mm longer than the saw kerf in the tenon. (The band-sawn offcuts from tapering the head make good wedges here.)

When the glue has cured (several hours or overnight depending on the glue and temperature), remove the clamps and plane the top faces flush with a sharp handplane. Because these joints are wedged, this could be done almost immediately, but you may prefer to let the glue set to ensure tight shoulders. Cut off the protruding wedges on the top edge of the head and bottom of the foot and plane these surfaces flat. The head, in particular, must have a flat bearing surface for the tabletop.

Chamfers are a nice touch on simple pieces like this table. A chamfer is a

ASSEMBLY

1 Before gluing, cut angled kerfs in the tenons of the trestle uprights for the wedges. Don't extend the cut too close to the edge of the tenon.

2 During assembly, pull the leg joints together with clamps, then drive wedges into the kerfed tenons. Gluing the wedges makes the joint even stror ger.

3 Using a sharp handplane, clean off the faces of the legs. Cut off the protruding wedges and plane so that they are flush.

CENTRE SCREW BLOCK

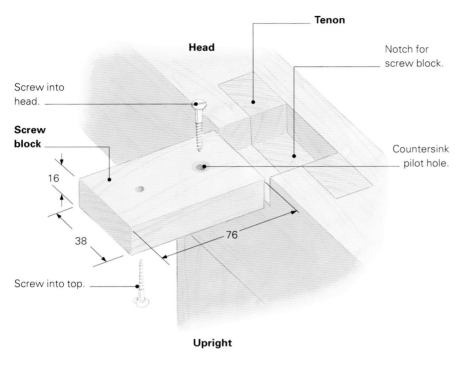

Tenon

Head

Screw into head.

Notch for screw block.

Screw block

16

38

76

Countersink pilot hole.

Screw into top.

Upright

CHAMFERING

A 45° router bit makes quick work of chamfering. The pilot runs against the work; a ball-bearing pilot will not burn the wood.

narrow surface created at the juncture of two wider faces, usually at a 45° angle. They create more opportunities for the play of light and shadow and they eliminate sharp corners, which can be easily damaged. The simplest method of chamfering is with a router and a 45° chamfer bit with a ball-bearing pilot. The pilot guides the bit, whose depth determines the size of the chamfer.

Chamfering with a handplane and, for curved surfaces, a spokeshave, is more time consuming, but it offers greater flexibility. If you want to chamfer by hand do so before gluing up. Dry assemble the legs and plane the faces flush. Mark where the chamfers begin and end, then disassemble the pieces and cut the chamfers, taking care not to cut beyond the marks.

Set the centre screw block flush with the top edge of the head. Use a marking gauge to scribe lines on the edge and inside face of the head to establish the length and depth of the recess. Holding the support even with the scribe line on

the top edge, knife along its sides to establish the recess width. A router clears most of the waste quickly, to full depth and to within 3mm or so of the length and width scribes. (Make the cuts in two or more shallow depth settings for greater control.) Finish the recess with a sharp chisel. Bore two screw clearance holes, as shown in the drawing on the left. (The top does not need to move in the centre.) Glue and screw the support to the recess.

Keying the stretcher tenon

The stretcher is pulled tight to each leg by driving a slightly tapered wooden key through a mortise cut in the stretcher tenon. The drawing on p.90 gives the dimensions, and you can layout and cut the key mortise as you have done the others. Note that the key mortise extends inside the leg mortise to ensure there is room to draw the joint tight. Insert the tenon and mark it along the face of the leg, then withdraw the tenon and establish the end of the mortise about 3mm closer to the shoulder.

Cut the key overlong so you have room to fine-tune its fit with the mortise. For a neater job, you can taper the outer end of the mortise to match the wedge. The key shown in the photos was made of pine, like the top, to provide additional contrast with the painted trestle. When key and mortise fit snugly, drawing the shoulders tight with a sharp rap of a mallet, mark and trim the ends of the key so it protrudes by about an equal amount either side of the tenon. If you like, chamfer the key and the exposed arrises on the tenon with a spokeshave and block plane. Begin the chamfer on the tenon beyond the face of the leg, or there will be a risk of unsightly gaps at the corners of the mortise.

Attaching the top

Place the top bottom-face-up on either saw horses or the workbench. (Covering the supports with a clean blanket will help prevent damage to the top.) Position the assembled trestle on the top and measure in from the edges and ends to centre it. Mark through the screw holes, slide the trestle out of the

SLOT SCREWS, HEAD TO TOP

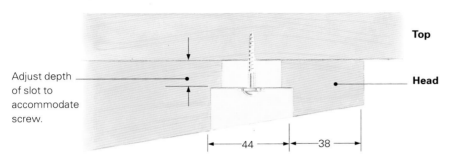

Top

Head

Adjust depth of slot to accommodate screw.

◄——44——►◄——38——►

Head (viewed from bottom face.)

Roundhead screw

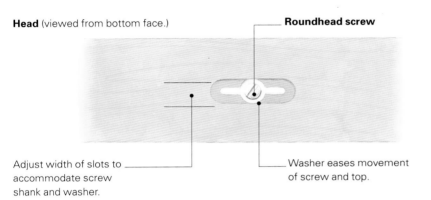

Adjust width of slots to accommodate screw shank and washer.

Washer eases movement of screw and top.

way and bore pilot holes – be careful not to bore through the top! Then screw the trestle to the top.

Traditional craftsmen often finish-planed the top face of a tabletop at this point, with the top fixed firmly to the base. If the top surface is in good shape, you can just finish sand it. (See chapter 22, 'Surface Preparation', for more on this.) You may like to chamfer the edges and ends of the top, too, and could do so now with a router or handplane.

A number of variations on this design are possible using the same basic joints. To provide more visual 'weight' beneath the table, you might double the uprights at each end, separating them by 30cm or more. Run two stretchers from end to end, or alternatively add a rail between pairs of legs and fix a single stretcher to the rail. You might also make a single broad, but thinner upright at each end; perhaps 455mm wide and 38mm thick. The upright might have either a curved outline or an internal cutout.

FITTING THE SCREW BLOCK

Notch the head of each leg for a screw block, then glue and screw the block in place. Screw up through the block into the tabletop.

ATTACHING THE TOP

Position the assembled trestle on the underside of the tabletop and centre it by measuring in from the edges and ends. Screw it in to place.

FINAL PLANING

The top is easier to plane when on the base. Screwing a top to its base can distort the surface. Flattened after fixing, it is likely to stay that way.

TRESTLE TABLES

Below
STEMMER AND SHARP
A wooden optical illusion, this whimsical console table is made of maple.

Right
ROBERT WILLIAMS
Interlocking triangles held together by a threaded brass rod comprise the knock-down pedestal base of this iroko garden table.

Left
ACHILLE CASTIGLIONI
Moving from the workshop to the office, these up-market beech saw horses support a plastic laminate work top. Pegged vertical risers in the centre of each A-frame end allow adjustment of the tabletop height.

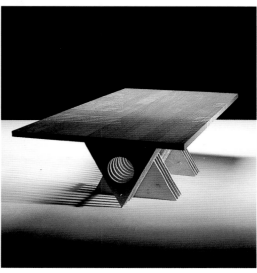

Above
MATHEW HILTON
Mathew Hilton has relied on sound joinery to keep the legs of his minimalist trestle table from splaying out without employing lower stretchers.

Top left
SHAKER CABINET MAKERS
Based on a Shaker design, this classic trestle table demonstrates the beauty of understated design. The top is cherry and the legs are hard maple.

Top right
NICHOLAS PRYKE
The sandblasted sycamore base provides sculptural support for the oak top, which maker Nicholas Pryke has bleached to echo the understructure.

13

APRON-RAIL TABLE

Say 'table' to almost anyone, and it is an apron-rail table that will be called to mind: four legs joined by narrow rails supporting a plank top. Dining tables, coffee tables, side tables, writing tables, work tables – the list goes on and on, with each type expressed in a panoramic range of styles.

The construction underlying this mind-numbing variety is remarkably uniform and reassuringly simple. Mortise-and-tenon joints fix rails to legs; screws attach tops to rails. The little table we will make in this chapter is kissing cousin to both the sturdy 'country' pine table found in so many kitchens and the elegant Sheraton hall table gracing a musuem gallery. The same basic construction can be used to make a stool or bench; extend two of the legs upward and you have a good start on a traditional side chair.

Apron-rail tables present one engineering challenge – stability. Made with heavy legs and rails of generous width, the kitchen table mentioned above will stand rock steady even when assaulted by a half dozen diners sawing away on the meat course. But toss a book on a refined hall table and its long thin legs and narrow anaemic rails may tremble under the impact. The taller the table, the thinner the legs, and the narrower the rails, the more susceptible it will be to this sort of induced vibration. Delicate tables can, of course, be made to support considerable weight – if the weight bears straight down. But apply force at an angle and narrow-rail-to-thin-leg joints may fail.

There are several methods of countering induced vibration or angled 'racking' forces. Wider apron rails resist racking by triangulation. Imagine diagonal braces contained within the width of the rail – the wider the rail the more effective the bracing. But wide rails may ruin the proportions of the piece or, for desks or dining tables, get in the way of knees. The little table shown on p.100 offers one solution to this dilemma: the rails are narrow in the centre, wider where they meet the legs. Where you

need not allow for knees or feet beneath the table, you can counter vibration and racking by placing additional rails lower down the legs.

MAKING THE TABLE

Almost all the techniques needed to make this table have been covered in previous chapters so the process is outlined here, with comments on a few new wrinkles as they arise.

Preparing the material does not take long, with just four legs, four rails and one tabletop to dimension and square up. Beginners sometimes have difficulty dimensioning table legs – it is maddening to end up with a rhombus instead of a square section. If you have both a surfacer and thicknesser, the procedure shown is dependable. Surfacing the second face is the critical step – make you keep the first face pressed firmly against the fence throughout the cut. If the fence is at right angles to the infeed and outfeed tables, the two adjacent faces will be square. Cut the legs about 13mm too long to provide 'horns'

that protect the thin end of the mortise until after assembly.

When you mark the joints, note that the rail faces are offset from the faces of the legs, so you will need to reset the mortise gauge during layout. The offset adds a little interest to the frame, producing an attractive shadow line in raking light. It also makes clean-up after assembly easier – you don't have to plane the faces flush.

To provide the maximum amount of gluing surface for tenons, mortises meet inside the legs and tenons are mitred. (See photos on p.101.) Mitre tenons with a tenon saw, or on the tablesaw. Cut them slightly shorter than the depth of the mortise; if mitres meet, they could prevent the tenon shoulders from seating. Take care when cutting and fitting mortises and tenons – tight-fitting joints are essential in tables this size and larger, where joints can be subjected to repeated racking stresses.

Tapering the legs and cutting a slight curve on the bottom edges of the rails

Opposite: Decorative pegs help fix rail to legs in Mathew Burt's table.

SQUARING LEGS

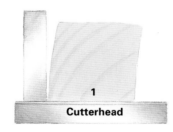

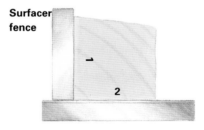

Surfacer: keep flattened, first face flush against surfacer fence to flatten second face – make several passes if necessary.

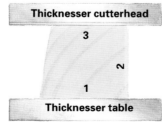

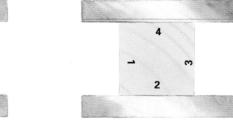

Thicknesser: complete squaring and dimensioning leg with two passes through the thicknesser.

APRON-RAIL TABLE

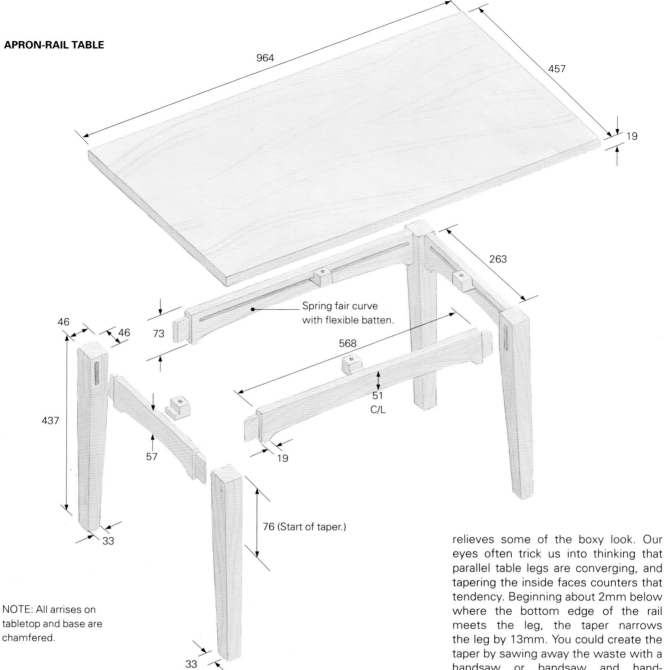

964

457

19

263

Spring fair curve
with flexible batten.

73

568

51
C/L

46

46

437

57

19

33

76 (Start of taper.)

33

NOTE: All arrises on
tabletop and base are
chamfered.

The finished table

CUTTING LIST
(Overall dimensions of finished parts.)

Part	Quantity	Dimensions
		(L x W x Th in millimetres)
Tabletop	1	964 x 457 x 19
Legs	4	437 x 46 x 46
Side rails	2	641 x 73 x 19
End rails	2	337 x 73 x 19
Buttons	4	35 x 25 x 19

relieves some of the boxy look. Our eyes often trick us into thinking that parallel table legs are converging, and tapering the inside faces counters that tendency. Beginning about 2mm below where the bottom edge of the rail meets the leg, the taper narrows the leg by 13mm. You could create the taper by sawing away the waste with a handsaw or bandsaw and hand-planing the final surface. Planing the taper is quicker, as shown on the opposite page.

Measure in 13mm from the two inside faces and draw pencil lines across the end grain on the bottom of the leg to establish the extent of the taper. With the surfacer switched off, find the top of the cutterhead arc, measure from that point along the fence the length of the taper (here it is 360mm) and fix a stop block. Pushing one face firmly against the surfacer fence, rest the end of the leg against the stop, then slowly lower the leg onto the spinning cutterhead and push it through the machine. Because the leg is supported on the outfeed table at the beginning, this produces a taper equal to the depth of cut. Repeat this operation as many times as necessary to reach the layout lines on the bottom of the leg. (It's usually best not to set the depth of cut deeper than about 2mm.) Because you are tapering adjacent faces, plan your planing so that you always have a square (not tapered) face running against the fence.

The curve on the bottom edge of the rail reduces its visual weight while allowing maximum width at the joint. It is easiest to lay out by springing a thin piece of wood or hardboard. After you have sawn off the waste with a bandsaw (a coping saw will do the job if necessary), clean up the edge with a sharp spokeshave. The concave curve is gentle enough for a flat-bottomed spokeshave; you

CUTTING THE JOINT

On the leg, set the depth of the waste-clearing bit so its cutting edges extend to the outside layout line of the adjacent mortise.

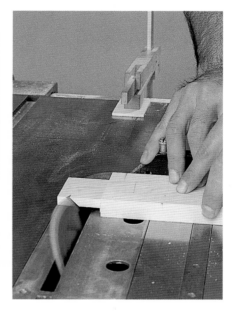

To ensure tenons of a consistent length, set a thin stop block (shown here clamped to the back of the table) that butts against the tenon shoulder.

APRON RAIL JOINTS

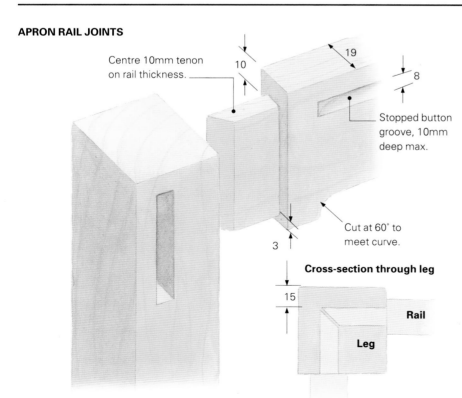

Centre 10mm tenon on rail thickness.

10

19

8

Stopped button groove, 10mm deep max.

3

Cut at 60° to meet curve.

Cross-section through leg

15

Rail

Leg

JOINTING THE LEG TAPER

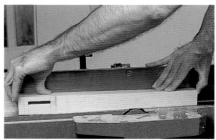

Set a stop block on the surfacer fence and lower the leg onto the spinning cutterhead. The depth of cut increases to full depth at the end.

CURVING THE RAILS

Spring a thin batten (hardboard here) to mark the curve on the rails; nails position the batten at the ends. Clean up bandsaw marks with a spokeshave.

MAKING THE BUTTONS

1 Several cuts on the tablesaw produce top-fixing buttons on a wide piece of scrap wood. First, make a tongue on both ends of the board, as shown here.

2 Working against an auxiliary fence to support the small pieces, cut off individual buttons. Bore holes for the screws to complete the buttons.

CUTTING A STOPPED GROOVE

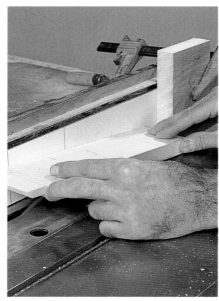

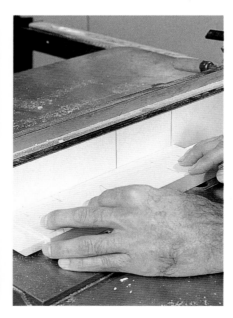

1–2 Fix a stop block so the cut will start behind the lead tenon. Mark on the fence where to end the cut. Holding the edge and trailing end of the rail firmly against rip fence, stop block, and saw table, carefully lower the lead end onto the spinning blade. Lift the rear end when the mark is reached.

need to be attentive to the grain direction to avoid tearing the grain. It may take you a while to get the hang of spokeshaving, particularly to overcome the tool's tendency to 'chatter' and produce a somewhat corrugated surface. Make sure the tool is razor sharp. Reducing the depth of cut and striving for good firm contact between the tool's sole and the work often help. The spokeshave will not fit into the last inch of the curve at each end, so finish there with a sharp chisel.

The tabletop is fixed to the base by small wooden 'buttons'. A button's tongue is free to slide in and out of a groove in the rail, thereby allowing the top to expand and contract with changes in humidity. The grooves need to be deep enough to allow as much movement as possible, but not so deep that they weaken the rail.

On relatively thin rails like these they can be up to half the rail's thickness. If you want a deep slot on a thin rail, cut individual mortises for the button tongues, rather than a continuous

TOP-FIXING BUTTONS

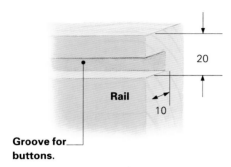

Groove for buttons.

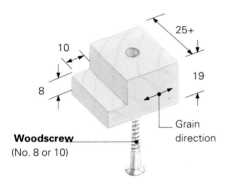

10

25+

10

8

19

Woodscrew (No. 8 or 10)

Grain direction

groove. The simplest and safest way to cut the grooves on the tablesaw is to cut them the full length of the rail, extending through the tenons. This reduces somewhat the amount of gluing surface and sometimes can affect the fit of the tenon. Some people prefer to stop the groove just short of the tenons.

A common, but somewhat nerve-wracking method for cutting stopped grooves is shown opposite. It involves lowering a rail onto a spinning tablesaw blade at the lead end, then raising the piece off the cut short of the tenon at the trailing end. This can be dangerous, and is not recommended for grooves deeper than about 9·5mm or for narrow or short rails. Small workpieces and deep grooves put fingers too close to danger and can bind between saw blade and fence, resulting in kickbacks. A plunge router is probably the safest tool for cutting stopped grooves; the time it takes to set up a jig for small pieces is well worth the peace of mind gained. If you lack both a router and the nerve to

lower pieces of wood onto a spinning blade, cut individual mortises by hand.

ASSEMBLY

Clean up the show faces of the legs and rails before assembly. It is harder to sand into the corners created by the offset rails of the base. Likewise, if you want to chamfer or round arrises, do so now. Some people go so far as to put a coat of finish on the rails and inside faces of the legs at this point (masking off the area around the mortises).

Assemble the base in two stages. Glue the ends together first; when the glue has cured, trim the 'horns' (the excess on the top end of the legs) by hand or on the tablesaw. Then tie the ends together with the long rails. Two tips are useful during this simple process. First, apply a healthy coating of glue inside the mortise, but only the barest film on the tenons. This will minimize glue squeeze out, which can be a nuisance to clean off the offset joints, while not weakening the joint. Second, position clamps and apply pressure carefully. Small imbalances in clamping pressure can throw open-ended frames like these out of square or into wind.

This is a good project to show off the grain of a single-board top. Otherwise glue-up several narrow boards as described in chapter 9. You can make the buttons that fix the top out of wide scrap wood. The buttons should be just slightly thinner than the distance from the bottom of the groove to the top edge of the rail so the screw draws the rail tight. Make the tongues by rebating the ends with two saw cuts, cut off a row of button blanks, then slice off individual buttons. Finish by boring the clearance holes for the screws.

A tabletop this size usually needs only one button each end. Some makers glue these into the grooves so any shrinkage or expansion will occur equally either side of the button; this is perhaps more useful on a top where the perimeter is flush with the legs or rails than on an oversailing top like this one. If the top is very flat, a single button in the middle of each long rail will suffice. If not, add another each side. Remember, these have to slide in and out of the grooves.

ASSEMBLING THE BASE

1–2 Assembling the base is straightforward. Pay attention to squareness by measuring diagonals, and to winding distortion by sighting over the rails.

FIXING THE TOP

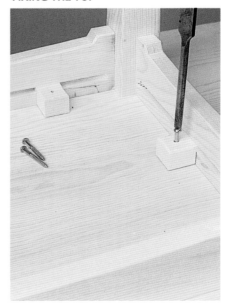

Position the base and the buttons on the top and screw the buttons in place. Make sure the screws are shorter than the combined thickness of button and top.

Above
ROBERT WILLIAMS
Triangulation of the
 thin members that
make up the legs and
rails produces light-
ness and rigidity in
this mahogany table.

Right
MATHEW BURT
This olive ash dining table
expands to twice its width.
The doubled legs house
single rails under the
tabletop and connect at
turned pads at the floor.

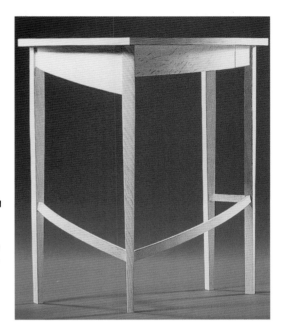

Left
STEMMER AND SHARP
Assembled with traditional mortise-and-tenons and simple lap joints, this unusual three-legged table is a hybrid between apron-rail and trestle design.

Below
ANDREW LAWTON
Heavy chamfers and through tenons with wedges of contrasting wood are eye-pleasing touches in this sturdy English oak table.

Above
JOHN CALLEN DESIGN
Asymmetrical leg spacing, drooping rails and stretchers lend an unusual air to this otherwise traditional side table in bleached and limed oak.

14

FRAME AND PANEL DOOR

Frame and panel is one of the most common construction types. It is pervasive in architecture, found in the structure of walls and ceilings, doors, and windows as well as in decorative detailing such as wainscotting and coffering. Likewise for furniture. Any case piece – chests, desks, dressers – as well as their doors and drawers, can be assembled of frame-and-panel parts. All manner of furnishings such as mirrors and even picture frames are frame and panel construction.

The appeal of frame and panel is due in part to a structural advantage. Wood moves, swelling as the surrounding air grows moist, shrinking as it dries. By suspending wide panels in narrow frames, the effects of movement are controlled. The panels are left free to expand into grooves in the frame, while the total expansion of the framework is a tiny fraction of the panel's width.

Opposite: Samuel Chan's cherry sideboard features frame and panel construction.

The other attraction of this construction is visual. You could work at it for years and not exhaust the decorative possibilities. A frame and panel can be starkly simple – a rectilinear frame surrounding a flat panel – or elaborately embellished. Both the frame and the panel provide a wealth of opportunities for moulding and for creating dramatic three-dimensional effects by varying the profiles and heights of the surfaces.

The making of the frame-and-panel door in this chapter will introduce you to the basic construction. The frame is assembled traditionally, with mortise-and-tenon joints. The panel is held in grooves – once the frame is assembled, the panel cannot be removed. We will also show how to make a rebated frame, which is best when the panel is breakable (glass or a mirror), is easily damaged, or needs periodic removal for cleaning (fabric). Finally, when you need the strength of a mortise-and-tenon joined frame, but are in a hurry, we will show how to make the simple, but sturdy bridle joint.

PROPORTION AND TERMINOLOGY

The names of the parts of a frame and panel are identified on the drawing on p.108. Most often, the vertical members of the frame, or stiles, are mortised, the horizontal members, the rails, are tenoned. (With modern glues there is no compelling structural reason for this, and you can reverse the construction for visual effect.) As long as the rails, stiles and panels are sturdy enough for the task, there are no hard-and-fast rules regarding their proportions. Simple examples like this often look best when the top rail and stiles are the same width and the bottom rail is noticeably wider.

Here, as in most mortise-and-tenon joints, the mortise is about one-third the thickness of the stile. The groove for the panel should be equal to or less than the width of the mortise and aligned with it. This allows you to plough the groove along the entire length of the stile which is much easier than having to stop it short of the ends. The tenon is 'haunched' as shown

CUTTING A HAUNCHED MORTISE AND TENON

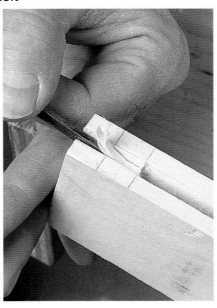

1 The mortise haunch is the same width as the mortise and slightly narrower than the groove. Cut the cheeks of the mortise haunch with a tenon saw.

2 Using chisels, pare the haunch down to the correct depth and clean up the cheeks of the mortise haunch to the scribed layout lines.

3. After cutting the tenon cheeks, mark the width of the tenon and position of the haunch from the mortise. Pencil mark at right indicates haunch.

FRAME AND PANEL DOOR

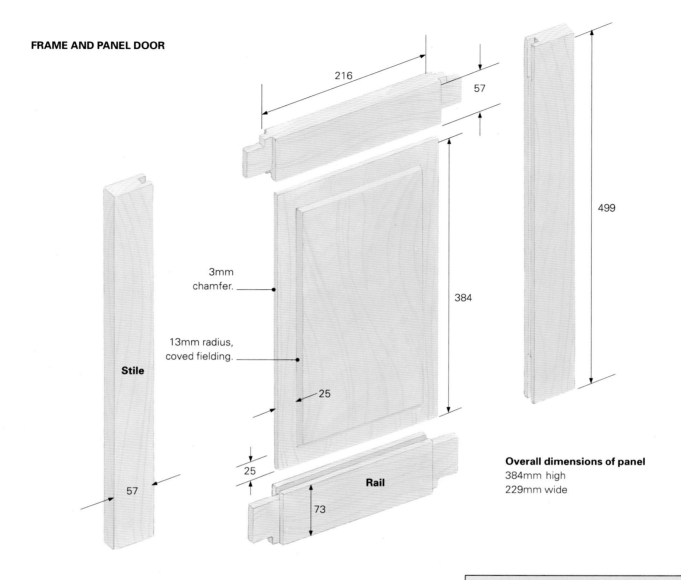

216

57

499

3mm chamfer.

384

13mm radius, coved fielding.

Stile

25

25

57

Rail

73

Overall dimensions of panel
384mm high
229mm wide

FRAME AND PANEL DOOR CUTTING LIST (Overall dimensions of finished parts.)		
Part	**Quantity**	**Dimensions**
		(L x W x Th in millimetres)
Stiles	2	499 x 57 x 19
Top rail	1	305 x 57 x 19
Bottom rail	1	305 x 73 x 19
Panel	1	384 x 229 x 13

FIELD PROFILES

Cove-fielded panel

10mm

Rail or stile

6mm (typical for cross-grain expansion of small panel.)

Traditional fielded profile
(proportions vary)

HAUNCHED MORTISE AND TENON

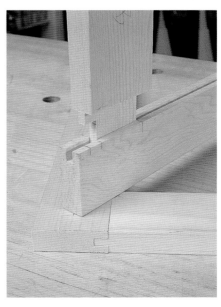

1 Cut the haunch to length with a tenon saw. The haunch should be long enough to fill the groove in the stile, but not keep the rail shoulders from seating.

2 It is easy to groove the rails and stiles on a tablesaw. The depth of the groove aligns with the bottom edge of the tenon and falls between the tenon's cheeks.

3 These completed joints show how the haunch fills the groove at the end of the stile. After assembly, cut the horn off the stile, as shown in the bottom joint.

---

above to fill the groove at the ends of the stile. Note that the other edge of the tenon aligns with the bottom of the groove in the rail. Grooves are commonly between 10 and 16mm deep, depending on the size of the panel and the type of wood – some woods expand and contract more than others.

MAKING THE FRAME

Take particular care to plane the surfaces of the frame parts flat and square. If the rails or stiles are twisted or warped, the assembled frame and panel will be too. Cut the stiles an inch or so longer than the finished dimensions to create 'horns', which provide insurance against damage to the thin end wall of the mortise during cutting and fitting. The 'horns' are easily cut off after assembly. You can glue-up and thickness solid-wood panels now, but don't cut them to finish size until the frame joints are cut and fitted.

Lay out the mortises and tenons as described in chapter 11. Make sure to place all the working faces on the same

HAUNCHED MORTISE AND TENON FOR FRAME AND PANEL DOOR

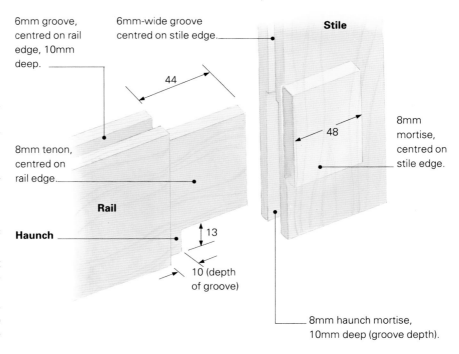

6mm groove, centred on rail edge, 10mm deep.

6mm-wide groove centred on stile edge.

Stile

44

8mm tenon, centred on rail edge.

48

8mm mortise, centred on stile edge.

Rail

Haunch

13

10 (depth of groove)

8mm haunch mortise, 10mm deep (groove depth).

FIELDING THE PANEL

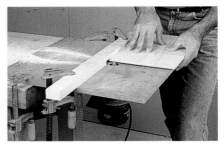
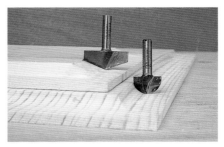

1–4 Create a tongue around the panel with a tablesawn rebate. The first cut, face down on the table, creates the rebate shoulder. The second cut, shown left, trims **the tongue to thickness – it should be a snug, but not tight, fit in the groove. You can shape a fielded panel on a router table (top right). You can make a** **temporary router-table by mounting a router base in a piece of plywood (centre). The base is held in a routed recess with wooden blocks.**

---

side of the frame; it's also useful to orient the working edges toward the inside of the frame. The squareness of the frame depends on making the distance between shoulder lines on the pairs of rails and pairs of stiles the same length – mark the second part from the first to help ensure this. Scribe the tenon cheeks with a mortise gauge; you will mark the haunches and the tenon width after you have cut the waste from the cheeks.

When laying out the mortises, remember that the stiles are overlong. The length of the mortises will be the width of the rails less the haunch and depth of the groove – it's easy to forget the latter when laying out.

It is often easier to cut and fit the mortises and tenons before making the groove. Some woodworkers cut the grooves first and use them to establish the mortise and tenon cheeks. For beginners, the advantages of grooving after cutting and fitting the joints usually outweigh the disadvantages. (When you are comfortable with your

skills, try the other method and choose the one you prefer.)

If you cut and fit first, make the mortise slightly wider than the groove, and you will save yourself the headache of trying to align the groove exactly with the mortise and tenon cheeks. After completing the full-depth mortise, you can cut the shallower mortise for the tenon haunch with a tenon saw, guided by the layout lines and the trimmed mortise cheeks, afterwards pare the waste away with a narrow chisel (see p.107).

After cutting the tenon cheeks, mark the width of the tenon and position of the haunch from the mortise. Square the lines along the tenon with a pencil-point marking gauge; measure to establish the length of the haunch. To make fitting and assembly easier, cut the tenon just slightly narrower than its mortise; 1mm is plenty. (It's the cheek-to-cheek fit that must be snug.) You can cut the haunch slightly long and trim it to fit its shallow mortise with no gaps. When you have fitted all the

joints individually, push the frame together dry, without glue. Measure across diagonals to check for squareness and examine each joint for gaps.

Most first-timers will find something out of line and need to trim a bit more to put it right. When the joints are tight and the frame square, check that the working faces of the rails and stiles are flush – all in the same plane. If they are not, shave them with a sharp hand-plane to correct the misalignment. (You can do this while the frame is dry-assembled.) The working faces must be flush to ensure alignment of the grooves you are about to cut.

The simplest way to cut grooves is on the tablesaw with a dado head or by making several passes over a single blade, as shown on p.109. Keep the working faces tight against the rip fence and the grooves will align at assembly. A table-mounted router fitted with a ball-bearing-guided slotting cutter also works well. Frame parts are usually too narrow to support the base of a hand-held router steadily.

THE PANEL

Plywood panels the same thickness as the groove are easy to fit. They slide right into place and need allow only for the possible expansion of the rails and stiles – cut them 2 to 3mm less than the distance between rails and stiles measured from the bottoms of the grooves.

Solid-wood panels are usually thicker than the grooves, so their edges and ends must be thinned to fit. They must also be sized to allow for movement with changes in humidity. To work best, the profile of a fielded panel (the raised part is called the field) should feature a flat tongue matched to the frame's groove – the tongue maintains a snug fit in the groove as it slides in and out with changes in humidity. Probably the simplest method is to rebate the edges and ends on the tablesaw.

The easiest solid-wood panel treatment is to leave the shoulders of the rebate square; the gap between the frame and the rebate shoulders provides interest through the play of light and shadow while permitting the panel to move. Or you could shape the shoulders of the rebate. All sorts of profiles are possible. The two shown are easy to make with a simple router set up. The cove is easier to sand smooth while retaining crisp arrises than is the more traditional 'sloped' profile. Remember that the flat side of a fielded panel can also be the front.

Large panels will expand and contract more than small, certain woods more than others. With some experience you will be able to estimate movement and pick a suitable panel width. This panel, for example, is 6mm narrower than the distance between the bottoms of the grooves in the stiles. The panel can expand 6mm before it bottoms out in the grooves, and it can contract almost 13mm before pulling out of the grooves. (If your workshop is humid, remember that the panel will shrink in a dry cen-trally heated atmosphere.) Wood movement along the grain is negligible, so cut the panel about 2 to 3mm shorter than the distance between groove bottoms in the rails.

ASSEMBLY

First dry-fit (without glue) the frame and panel. If you checked everything as you went along, all should go together nicely. If you want to chamfer or round the inner edges of the frame, do it now. It is also much easier to finish sand the faces of the panel and the inner edges of the frame before assembly than after. (Some people pre-finish these surfaces.) Apply glue sparingly to the parts of the joint near the panel – you don't want excess glue to fix the panel at the corners and restrict its ability to move.

After the glue has cured, trim the horns off the stiles with a tenon saw or on the tablesaw and plane the edges flush. A few very fine shavings off the faces of the frame should clean them up nicely. To ensure that shrinkage and expansion are divided equally between

---

ASSEMBLING A PANEL

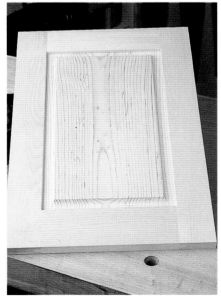

1–2 Dry-fit the panel before gluing up to make sure everything fits. Glue up on a flat surface to ensure that the panel will be flat. Protect the edges of the stiles

with scrap wood from damage by the clamp heads. You can wipe off glue with a damp rag as shown at centre, or slice it off with chisel or plane after it cures.

3 The play of light and shadow on the cove-fielded panel and the lightly chamfered inner arrises of the frame help this simple door please the eye.

both stiles (so the panel doesn't shrink out of the groove on one stile), you can fix the centre of the panel in place with small nails or dowels placed midway along the length of the rails.

REBATED FRAME WITH OFFSET SHOULDERS

Rebated frames come in handy for mirrors and other projects where a removable panel is necessary. While you could rebate a frame after assembly with an electric router and piloted rebating bit, the joint shown here is a more satisfying piece of craftsmanship. The offset shoulder fills the rebate that is cut along the full length of the stile, a more straightforward and neater solution than making a stopped rebate. And the joint is not much more difficult to cut than a standard mortise and tenon.

Precise layout is particularly important for joints with offset shoulders. Note that the rebate aligns with the outer cheeks of the mortise and tenon. Start by scribing the rebate on the inner edge and back face of each rail and stile with a single-pin marking gauge. Knife the front shoulder line across the edges and face of the rails. Then, aligning the pin for the outer cheek with the rebate, set the two-pin gauge and scribe the cheeks of the tenons and mortises. Measure carefully to position the tenon's offset shoulder on the rail's back face; it is offset from front shoulder by the width of the rebate.

Note that extending the rebate the entire length of the rail narrows the tenons by the width of the rebate. It is

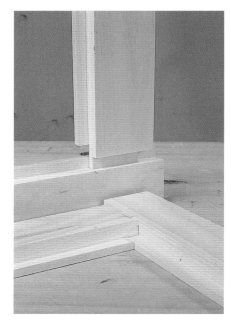

A rebated frame with offset shoulders (above) is ideal for use with mirrors and panels that may need to be removed or replaced. Nicholas Bentley has dressed up this simple mirror frame (right) with applied, carved, and painted ornaments.

easy to forget this and cut the mortises the full width of the rail. Measure to establish the correct mortise width, then pencil or knife lines across the edge of the stile to establish the ends of the mortise. Cutting the joint is little different than for a standard mortise and tenon. Cut the mortise and tenons first, then saw or rout the rebate and do final

fitting. Hold panels, mirrors, or glass in place with small strips of wood tacked or screwed to the rebate cheeks. Allow for movement of solid-wood panels.

THE BRIDLE JOINT

The mortise-and-tenon joint is strong, durable and versatile, but it can be time-consuming to produce. A bridle joint can save time. Sometimes called an open-mortise joint, the tenon slips into a slot open on three sides, rather than into a four-sided mortise. Sawing an open mortise is much quicker than clearing the waste from a standard mortise with auger bit and chisels, particularly if you have a bandsaw.

REBATED FRAME WITH OFFSET TENON SHOULDERS

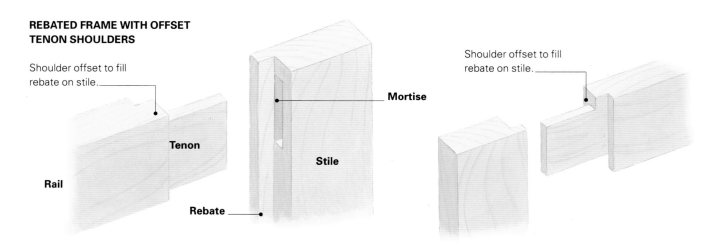

Shoulder offset to fill rebate on stile.

Tenon

Rail

Mortise

Stile

Rebate

Shoulder offset to fill rebate on stile.

Ease and speed come at a price. The bridle joint, with its open mortise, has no mechanical advantage against levering. Its strength depends heavily upon the glue bonding the cheeks of the tenon to those of the mortise. Fortunately, contemporary glues are up to the task, making the joint a viable option. In theory, you can substitute a bridle joint for any 'enclosed' mortise-and-tenon at the corner of a frame.

Lay out a bridle joint much like a standard mortise-and-tenon, but scribe the mortise cheeks on the end and both edges of the stile, as you do the tenon. Similarly, you saw the mortise cheeks just like those of the tenon, only on the other side of the scribe line. It is still a good idea to cut the mortises first, and trim tenons to fit.

A single hole bored on a drill press at the base of the mortise clears the

Left: A glued-up bridle-jointed frame can look a bit like a scaffold. Sash clamps pull the joints together in two directions; quick-action clamps and pressure-distributing blocks ensure good contact between mortise and tenon cheeks, and gap-free ends and edges.

Below: Easy and quick to cut, bridle joints also have a distinctive look due to the contrasting colours of end- and side-grain.

waste quickly. Bore the hole before making the cheek cuts (the saw kerfs can interfere with the bit's travel). Bore in from both edges to ensure accuracy. Pare down to the layout lines at the end of the mortise with a sharp chisel.

When the cheek cuts are complete, and the waste removed, trim cheeks and shoulders to ensure a snug fit. Open mortises are less rigid than closed ones, and a thick tenon can force the mortise cheeks apart. Aim for an easy but snug sliding fit, with the tenon and mortise cheeks in contact over their entire surfaces, particularly along the top and outside edge, which will be visible in the assembled joint.

Assembly

Although bridle joints are easier to cut than standard mortise-and-tenons, they are more trouble to assemble. While a standard joint requires a clamp in only one direction (to pull the tenon into the mortise), a corner bridle joint may require clamps in three directions

Brush glue evenly on the tenon and mortise cheeks and push the joint (or complete frame) together. Place sash clamps parallel to the rails to pull the tenon shoulders tight. Add sash clamps parallel to the stiles to pull the tenon against the end of the mortise. A G-clamp or quick-action clamp perpendicular to the cheeks draws them together to ensure the best glue bond and eliminate gaps along the visible outer edges. Cut wooden clamp pads the same size as the cheeks to distribute the pressure of the quick-action clamps. Sometimes the sash clamps can be removed after the cheek clamps are in place, but check that the shoulders don't open slightly when pressure is relieved.

BRIDLE JOINT

Saw to the inside of the scribed layout lines for the mortise and to the outside for the tenon.

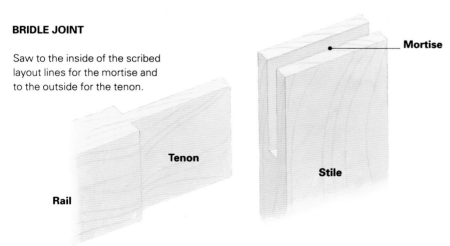

Mortise

Tenon

Stile

Rail

GALLERY
CABINETS

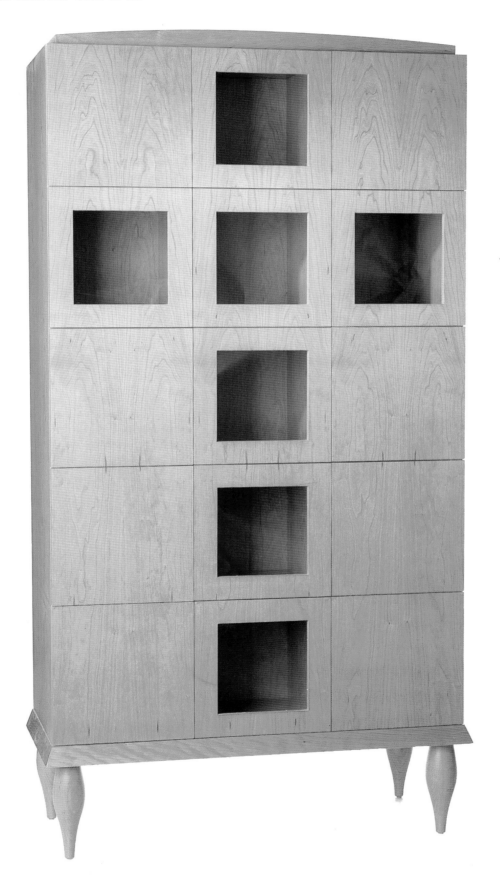

Left
ALISTAIR FLEMING
Veneered with American cherry, this storage cabinet has detachable doors, which can be rearranged so the glass forms different patterns.

Opposite, top
ROBERT WILLIAMS
Mimicking the structure of a tree, the top and bottom of each of the cases in this cabinet are 'end-grain' slabs, the grain running perpendicular to the top and bottom surfaces, like old-fashioned chopping boards. The case in the foreground swings shut to present a block of four 'columns.'

Opposite, below
JOHN COLEMAN
An elegant cabinet veneered in lacewood with lacquered drawers is perched atop a base of thin chromed steel.

Left
MIKE WALKER
Solid maple doors,
drawers, and top
are combined with a
veneered medium-
density fibreboard case
in a steel frame.

Below
ROBERT WILLIAMS
Stained trim contrasts
with sand-blasted
and limed panels,
all English oak, in
this dresser.

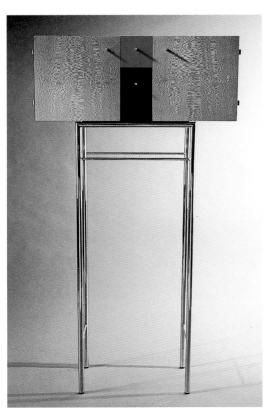

15

FRAME AND PANEL CHEST

Frame-and-panel construction has long been used for assembling case pieces – cupboards, wardrobes and desks of all sorts. Case sides, tops, bottoms, backs, as well as doors and drawer fronts can all be frame-and-panel construction.

While there is a wide variety of possibility in the treatment of the frames and in the materials for the panels (solid wood, man-made boards, glass, fabric, metal grillwork), most frame-and-panel case pieces take one of two forms. They can be assembled of flat, door-like frames similar to the one made in the last chapter. At each corner, the edge of one stile is joined to the face of another. Simple butt joints are often reinforced by nails or screws, though in many instances modern glues are strong enough on their own. A joint similar to the tongue-and-dado in chapter 16 is an excellent choice for assembling cases like these; it helps align the parts and provides some mechanical strength to reinforce the glue joint.

In perhaps the most common form of frame-and-panel construction, a single post or leg replaces the two joined stiles at each corner. Imagine adding bottom rails to the apron-rail table in chapter 13. Fill in between legs and rails with panels, and you're on the way to creating any of a variety of pieces.

The blanket chest made in this chapter (see p.118) is a simple variation on this second construction type. Supporting rails of side and end frames alike, the 'legs' of the chest are wide enough when viewed from the front or back to read as stiles of door-like frames. The design is based on one produced in the 1890s by a founder of the English Arts and Crafts Movement, Sydney Barnsley, whose chest may have been inspired by medieval pieces.

MAKING THE CHEST
The techniques used to make this chest are very similar to those required for last chapter's frame-and-panel door. This is a more complicated project, but it proceeds along the same lines. Here, operations covered in other chapters are summarized, and new tasks commented on at greater length.

Prepare stock to rough dimensions, making sure everything is flat and square. There are many parts in a piece like this, and it pays to be organized. Group the legs, rails, and stiles in assemblies (front, back, right end, left end, lid) as soon as you can and keep them together throughout the process.

Using numerous narrow vertical panels gives a very different look than if each frame contained a large single panel. In addition, by making the stiles on the lid the same width as the panels and carrying the chamfers across the rail-to-stile joints, the lid echoes the panel layout on the front and back sides. The narrow panels for this chest were resawn from 50mm thick stock and planed to 16mm thick.

Resawing (splitting a board in half through its thickness) creates pairs of panels with mirror-image grain patterns, which can be used to decorative advantage. (See p.120.) Keep the pairs marked as you dimension the panels.

Opposite: Oliver Morel's casket is made of Cuban mahogany, pear and walnut.

JOINTS
You will get plenty of mortise-and-tenon practice making the chest; there are more than twenty of these joints in all. Work carefully when laying out the mortises on each leg to ensure that those on the edge (for the front or back rails) align with those on the face (for the end rails). Lay out all mortises on one leg, then use this to position the mortises on the other three.

With the exception of the lid, none of the joints are flush on the exposed faces. The various surface levels give the piece more visual depth and interest than it would otherwise have, but they can make scribing with the mortise gauge tricky. The rails on the chest's front and back sides are flush with the inside face of the legs (making it easier to fit the chest bottom), so run the mortise-gauge fence on these faces to ensure accurate joints. A steady hand is required to scribe the mortises on the legs for the end rails, which are several centimetres from the edge that the gauge fence must run against.

CUTTING THE JOINTS

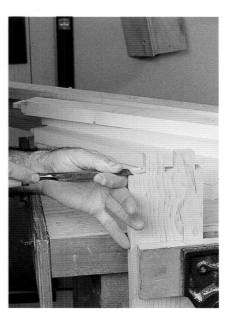

1 Cutting and fitting mortises and tenons accounts for the lion's share of the work on this chest. Here, the double mortises are being trimmed with a wide chisel.

2 After removing the waste with tenon saw and coping saw, trim down to the knifed shoulder lines on the double tenons with a sharp chisel.

FRAME-AND-PANEL CHEST

NOTE: Bottom left off for clarity.

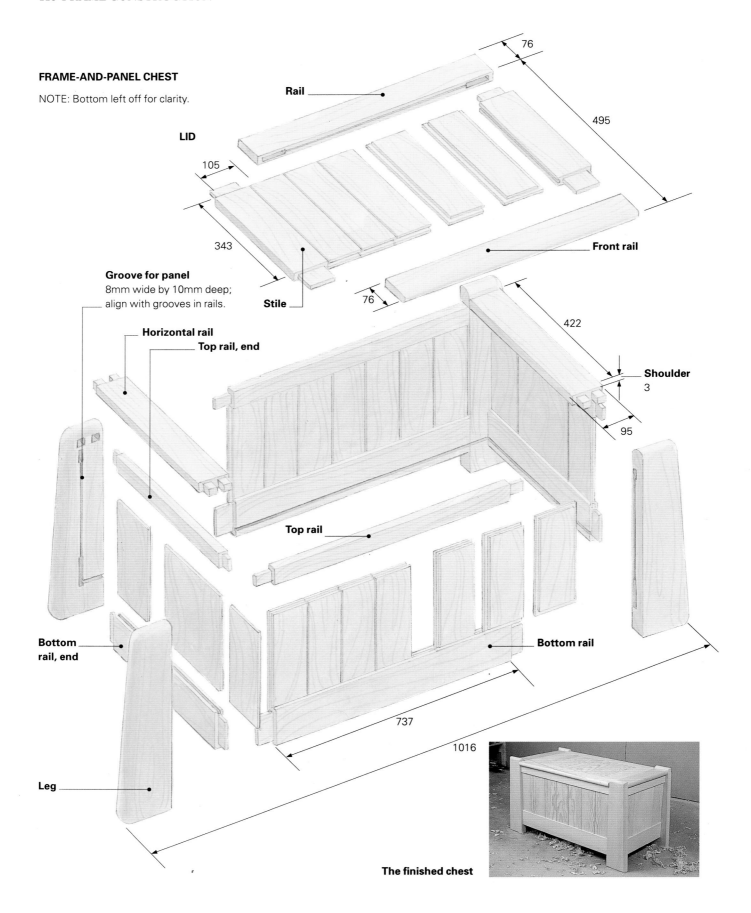

Rail

76

495

LID

105

343

Front rail

Groove for panel
8mm wide by 10mm deep;
align with grooves in rails.

Stile

76

Horizontal rail

Top rail, end

422

Shoulder
3

95

Top rail

Bottom rail, end

Bottom rail

737

1016

Leg

The finished chest

CUTTING LIST
(Overall dimensions of finished parts.)

Part	Quantity	Dimensions
		(L x W x Th in millimetres)
Chest case		
Legs	4	546 x 140 x 38
Top rail, front & back	2	838 x 51 x 25
Bottom rail, front & back	2	838 x 108 x 25
Top rail, ends	2	473 x 51 x 25
Bottom rail, ends	2	473 x108 x 25
Horizontal rail, ends	2	473 x 95 x 25
Chest bottom	1	870 x 441 x 19
Standard panels	14	289 x 114 x 16
End panels	4	289 x 124 x 16
Central end panels	2	289 x 219 x 16
Lid		
Stiles	2	445 x 105 x 25
Rails	2	737 x 76 x 25
Standard panels	4	359 x 114 x 16
End panel	1	359 x 124 x 16

JOINT DETAILS: CHEST

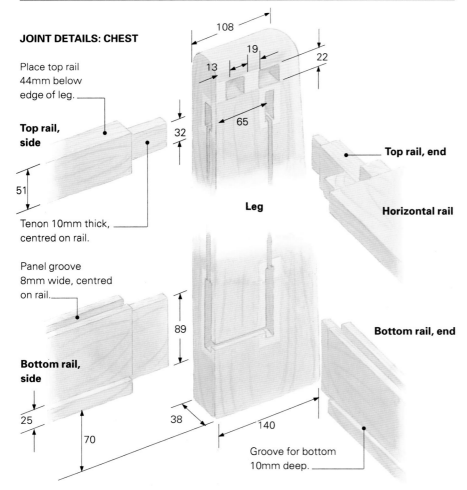

Place top rail 44mm below edge of leg.

Top rail, side

51

Tenon 10mm thick, centred on rail.

Panel groove 8mm wide, centred on rail.

Bottom rail, side

25

70

108

19

13

22

65

32

Leg

89

38

140

Groove for bottom 10mm deep.

Top rail, end

Horizontal rail

Bottom rail, end

Each end has two top rails, one with a vertical face, one with a horizontal face. Note that the horizontal rail-to-leg joint consists of two small mortises and tenons instead of one long joint. When mortises stretch across the grain, the mortise surfaces in contact with the tenons are largely end-grain, and glue does not bond end-grain-to-side-grain joints well. Making two small mortises and tenons doubles the side-grain-to-side-grain gluing surface, and makes a stronger joint. The bottom cheek of the double tenons is 'bare-faced' (no shoulder), the top has a narrow shoulder to hide bruising around the mortise.

PANELS
When the joints are cut and fitted, groove the rails and legs to take the panels. Cut grooves on the tablesaw with a dado head or several passes over a regular blade. The grooves run the length of the rails but must run between the mortises on the legs. You can cut stopped grooves on the tablesaw as described in chapter 13, or on a router table. Because the inside faces are flush on the front and back frames, use the same fence settings to groove those rails and legs. (First, dry-assemble the front and back frames and plane the inside faces flush to ensure that the grooves will align.) On the ends, groove the rails first, then dry-assemble the end frames, mark the position of the grooves on the legs and set the rip fence accordingly. Grooves in the bottom rails house the chest bottom; cut those now, too. The bottom requires short grooves in each leg too, but you'll cut those later.

Arrange the panel blanks to match or contrast grain patterns according to your taste. Then rebate the panels to create tongues that fit into the grooves and allow the panels to overlap, which keeps dust out of the chest. Cutting rebates is easy on the tablesaw (see p.110). But here the task requires considerable concentration to make sure that you cut the rebates on the correct faces. On all but the wider end panel, one rebate must be cut on the back face to form an overlap. Make liberal use of scrap pieces to work out the saw and fence settings and the

JOINT DETAILS: LID

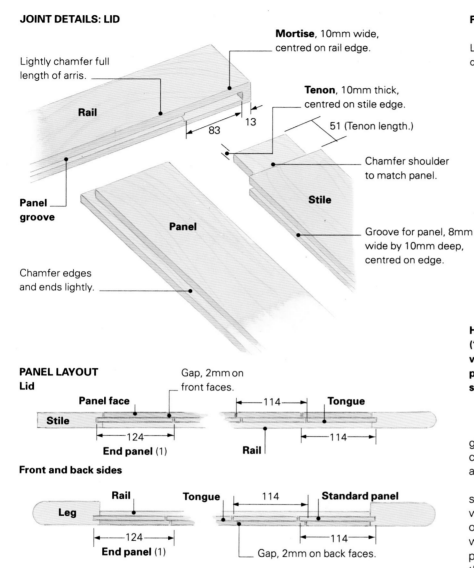

Lightly chamfer full length of arris.

Rail

Mortise, 10mm wide, centred on rail edge.

Tenon, 10mm thick, centred on stile edge.

83 13

51 (Tenon length.)

Chamfer shoulder to match panel.

Stile

Panel groove

Panel

Groove for panel, 8mm wide by 10mm deep, centred on edge.

Chamfer edges and ends lightly.

RESAWING

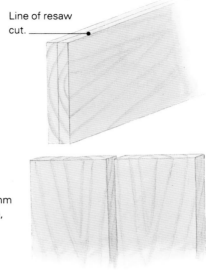

Line of resaw cut.

Halving a board through its thickness ('resawing') produces two thinner boards with two mirror-image faces. Opened like pages in a book, they create a symmetrical pattern.

PANEL LAYOUT
Lid

Gap, 2mm on front faces.

Panel face

Stile

124

End panel (1)

114

Tongue

114

Rail

Front and back sides

Rail **Tongue** 114 **Standard panel**

Leg

124

End panel (1)

114

Gap, 2mm on back faces.

NOTE: Chest ends have 1 wide centre panel, 1 standard panel, 1 end panel.

---

sequence of cuts. Organize the pieces carefully and work through them methodically; it doesn't hurt to have some spare panel blanks on hand in case you make a mistake. The tongues should be a snug, but not tight, fit in the grooves.

A gap of about 2mm between panels should accommodate expansion and contraction. Notice that the gaps are worked on the inside faces of the panels on the chest sides and ends, but on the outside faces for the lid. Cut the panels about 3mm shorter than the dis-

tance between the bottoms of the grooves. The width of the rebates is not critical on the panels for the sides and ends; just make them uniform. On the lid, cut the rebates on the ends of the panels so that the shoulders fit snugly between the rails. Cut those on the edges so the panels are uniform.

Assembly: stage one
It is much easier to assemble complicated projects in stages. Here, you will assemble the front and back sides, do some work to them after the

glue cures, then add the end rails and chest bottom in the second, and final, assembly stage.

Dry-assemble the sides to make sure the joints can all be drawn home with the panels in place. Now taper the outer edge of each leg. Saw away the waste by hand or on a bandsaw, then plane the edge flat and square. Round the top ends of the legs (see the discussion below), then glue-up the front and back frames, using the tapered waste pieces as clamping battens. You can glue-up the top now, too; chamfer all the exposed arrises on the rails, stiles, and panels; include those on the shoulders of the lid stiles (to make them appear to be panels).

The top end and outside edge of each leg are radiused, as is the front edge of the lid and outside edges of the horizontal end rails. Like the tapered legs, the radiused edges and careful chamfering of all arrises (also done now, before assembly) refine an otherwise simple design. Radiused edges are difficult to clamp, so round them

ASSEMBLY: STAGE ONE

Assemble the chest in stages. First, glue up the front and back sides. Waste pieces from tapering the leg make good clamping blocks.

ROUNDING THE LEGS

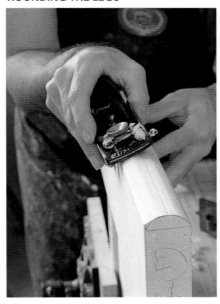

A sharp block plane rounds the end and edge of each leg. Create facets by taking shavings the full length, check progress against the layout lines frequently.

EXTENDING THE GROOVE

1-2 Insert the bottom end rail and knife the groove position on the leg. Knife along a straightedge to join these marks to the rail groove then chisel out the waste.

ASSEMBLY: STAGE TWO

1–2 Complicated pieces need to be repeatedly dry-assembled to make sure that joints fit properly. The final dry assembly, just before gluing up, should

simulate the conditions of a real assembly to determine the number and placement of clamps and bearers, and the best sequence of assembly.

3 Work quickly but methodically when gluing up. Note the heavy bearers, which were added to draw a stubborn bottom rail-to-leg joint tight.

Wide rails and stiles enclose a panel on Thomas Loeser's blanket chest. Painted plugs cover the screws that fix the front and back to the sides. Milk paint highlights heavy notches carved in the top and the sides.

after assembling the sides and lid. When you have rounded the edges of the legs, fit the horizontal end rails in place and cut them to width so their rounded edges will fall just behind the round on the legs.

You can round these surfaces with a router, but large bits can be expensive. It is not difficult to round them with a hand plane, as shown in the photo on p.121. Lay out the curves and scribe pencil lines to indicate where the round intersects with the edge and faces. (Make a template for the curve either by drawing a flattened arc freehand or by tracing around a cylindrical object.) Work down to the layout lines by planing facets of the curve all along the length of the edge (or across the width of the end). Finish the curve with a sanding block, taking care to keep crisp the juncture of the round with the leg faces.

After the glue cures on the assembled sides, extend the groove for the chest bottom across the legs (shown on p.121). The chest bottom can be solid wood, or plywood. Whatever the material, rebate the edges and ends to create tongues that fit snugly in the grooves. When fitting a solid-wood bottom, remember to allow for expansion and contraction across the width of the grain.

Assembly: stage two
Dry-assemble the chest by adding the end rails, panels and the chest bottom to the glued up front and back sides. This trial run is very important for complex assemblies. Once you spread glue, there is no time to find needed materials or make adjustments in the fit of things. So be very thorough now. Determine the fastest way to assemble the parts and where to place everything, including glue and clamps. Set the cramp heads to the proper spacing; cut and test clamp pads. An assistant can make a world of difference in a

complicated assembly, and it is often worth postponing assembly until one is available.

When you are ready for the real thing, double check your set up, then work quickly but methodically. Despite all your preparations, something unanticipated is likely to crop up. When gluing up this chest, for example, the bottom rail-to-leg joint on one end would not pull tight, leaving a slight, but irritating gap. Adding a pair of heavy bearers to the bottom clamps solved the problem, but the solution had to be identified and implemented very quickly. As you work, measure across diagonals to check that the assembly is square. If it is out of square, adjusting the position of the clamp heads can sometimes shorten a diagonal and correct the problem.

Hingeing the lid
There are a great many types of hinges on the market, but old-fashioned brass butt hinges are still an excellent choice. They are simple to install, unobtrusive yet handsome. Though expensive, extruded brass butts are worth the extra money. Die-formed and crisply machined, these hinges have a pleasing heft and don't rattle around like stamped or pressed butts, which are made by wrapping sheet brass around a pin. If extruded hinges are unavailable at your local hardware store, many speciality woodworking mail-order firms carry a selection.

Two hinges are plenty for a lid this size and for most chests and cabinet doors. Hinges come in a variety of combinations of length and width. Most catalogues specify by length and open width, in that order. The hinges used here are 76 by 44mm. The hinge barrel must protrude from the side of the chest to permit the lid to open fully. When the barrel is positioned correctly, the hinge leaf should be narrower than the thickness of the chest side by 3mm or more so the back of the hinge mortise will not break out.

Hinge installation is a fairly simple procedure. Begin by planing the lid to fit snugly between the chest's horizontal end rails. Set one marking gauge to the width of the hinge mortise, another (if you possess one) to its depth. Set both gauges just shy of the pin's centreline, as shown on the facing page. Deeper and the lid will not shut; shallower and the gap will be rather unsightly. Wider, the lid will not open completely; narrower and the protruding barrel will look unattractive .

Make light pencil marks indicating the hinge positions on the lid, then scribe the mortise width and depth between them. Align the edge of the hinge with the scribe mark for width, and knife lines against the ends of the leaf. The ends are seldom milled perfectly square to the edges; knifing the position ensures tight-fitting mortises. Put identifying marks on the leaf and the mortise to keep them paired.

With a sharp chisel, deepen the scribe marks, then score the waste as shown in the photo below. The mortise tapers front to back so that the back of the leaf is flush with the surface – angle the chisel accordingly. Scoring both across and with the grain makes the waste easier to remove. Stay about 2mm away from the scribe marks at this stage. Pare the scored waste away with a wide, sharp chisel. Start the final cuts by nestling the chisel's edge in the scribe mark for the depth. Trim to the knife and scribe lines, then check the fit with the appropriate hinge. Make the final cuts along the back edge carefully to avoid splitting off the remaining thin piece.

With the hinge in place, use an awl to mark the screw holes. Take some care positioning them. Fudge slightly toward the back, so the screw will pull the hinge tight to the back edge of the mortise. Bore the pilot holes, then screw the hinge down. (When fitting, attach three-hole hinges with only the centre screw – the hinge will need to

HINGE MORTISE LAYOUT

Gauge setting for hinge mortise width: position pin beyond face of rail so lid can open without binding.

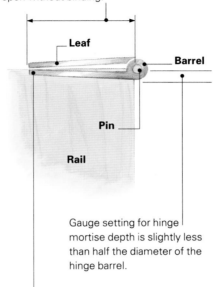

Gauge setting for hinge mortise depth is slightly less than half the diameter of the hinge barrel.

Taper depth of mortise so that back of hinge leaf is flush with edge of rail.

be on and off a couple times before fitting is completed.) In hard woods, use steel, rather than brass screws until the final installation; it's a terrible feeling to twist off a brass screw.

Position the lid, with hinges installed, on the chest and mark the hinge positions on the rail with the knife. Remove the hinges and use them to scribe the mortise ends, then cut and fit the mortises in the top rail as described above. When the hinges are installed, plane the edges of the lid stiles so the lid opens easily – a small gap each side will allow for expansion in humid weather.

Sometimes a little tinkering is necessary to get hinges to function just right. If the hinge barrels are set too deep, the lid may bind on the chest rail. To correct, shim the mortises with paper or veneer. You can also shim to adjust the width of the gap between rail and lid. When everything fits just right, polish the hinges and screw heads with steel wool. You can even line up the screw slots when you put them in.

FITTING THE HINGES

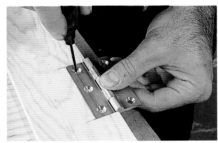

1–2 Scribe the width of the hinge mortise on the lid (top). Align the edge of the hinge leaf with the width scribe and knife against the ends of the leaf (bottom).

3–4 Score the mortise waste (top) and pare down to the depth scribe line (bottom). Carefully extend the mortise to its full length and width.

5–6 Mark positions of the screw holes with a bradawl (top). Knife the hinge positions on the chest's top rail (bottom) then cut those mortises in the same way.

PLANK
JOINERY

Many of the pieces of furniture in any house are little more than wide boards joined at right angles to each other. Join three boards to make a bench or table. Four boards produce a box for a bookcase or a kitchen cabinet. Slide several boxes into a larger box and you've got a chest of drawers. These simple forms are also ideal for displaying magnificent pieces of wood. The chapters in this section examine basic plank joinery, including woodworking's most intriguing and decorative joint, the dovetail.

**Opposite: Through mortise-and-tenon joints
fix the legs to the plank seat of Stephen
Hounslow's English ash bench.**

GALLERY
PLANK CONSTRUCTION FURNITURE

Left
PAT BOOTH
Made of solid cherry, the top and legs of this table fold flat for storage on specially designed woven stainless steel hinges. It can be used as a dining table, or by folding the top and swinging the legs back, as a narrow console table.

Below
HUGH SCRIVEN
Joinery is reduced to a minimum in these stools by bolting the solid cherry seat to two subtly curved laminated ply sides.

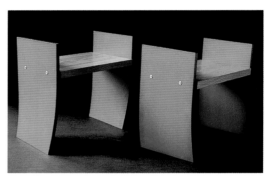

Right
JOHN CALLEN DESIGN
Today the 'planks' in plank construction are often man-made boards covered with striking veneers, as in the sycamore-veneered pedestals for this desk.

Left
STEPHEN HOUNSLOW
Dividing the oak legs
and wedging them
under tension to the
ash top produces a rigid
table unobstructed
beneath by stretchers.

Right
SAMUEL CHAN
Assembled of curved,
laminated slabs, Samuel
Chan's birch chair is a
clever marriage of
engineering and sculpture.
The curves all have the
same radius and can be
made on a single form.

16

REBATE, DADO, TONGUE-&-DADO JOINTS

The joints covered here can be quickly and accurately cut with a tablesaw and/or router. With them, you can join simple boxes together and install dividers, shelves, and even drawers in the boxes. While ideal for basic furniture, these joints are also used with more complex joints in the finest work.

A rebate is an L-shaped recess cut across the end or edge of a board. In plank construction, rebates are primarily used for corner joints, the end of one piece fitting into a rebate across the end of the other. The rebate's single shoulder provides its only advantages over its simpler cousin, the butt joint. Its sheer strength adds some resistance to racking forces (pressure diagonally across a carcass) and it helps position the pieces during assembly. As one of each pair of mating surfaces is end grain, the joint must have mechanical fasteners, such as nails or screws.

Opposite: These simple machine joints make quick construction easy.

In a dado joint, the end of one piece is housed in a shallow groove (the dado) cut across the face of another. (The joint is also called a housed joint.) The joint combines the sheer strength of a rebate with a surprising resistance to racking (if the joint fits snugly). The joint also eases assembly by positively locating all of the parts.

Like the rebate joint, the tongue-and-dado is primarily used to produce a 'flush' outside corner; where two carcass sides joint a top, for example. A little more trouble to cut than a rebate, it is a much superior joint, providing both strength and ease of assembly.

The procedures for making each of these joints are similar. As for all joinery, care in preparation will pay off; small errors of squareness at the corners and intermediate divisions of a carcass can add up to serious assembly headaches.

Mitre joints, where the mating ends are both cut at 45° angles and no end grain shows at the end of the assembled join, are also discussed at the end of the chapter.

MAKING A REBATE JOINT

There is little to master in making a corner rebate joint. For all but very long pieces, it is easy to cut the joint on a tablesaw. (A router with a ball-bearing-pilot rebating bit or a straight bit and fence will do the job for pieces too unwieldy for the tablesaw.)

You can set the rip fence for the shoulder cut by measurement or directly from the thickness of the mating piece. (For convenience here, we call the part being rebated the side, and the mating piece the top.) Make the shoulder slightly farther from the end than the thickness of the side so you will just have to plane a little end grain to clean up the joint after assembly. Keep the end tight against the rip fence during the cut. It's safer to use a mitre fence to push pieces narrower than about 125mm and pieces that are much longer than they are wide.

Cut the rebate cheek upright against the rip fence. The depth of the rebate (distance from the inner face of the side to the cheek) isn't critical. About two-

MAKING A REBATE JOINT

  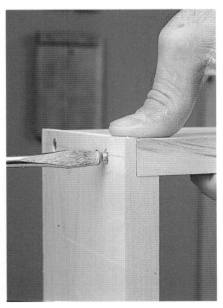

1 Keep the end of the board tight against the rip fence to cut the rebate's shoulder. Use a mitre fence (not visible in photo) to assist with narrow boards.

2 Reset the fence for the cheek cut. Note that the waste is to the outside of the blade, where it cannot bind between the blade and fence.

3 For quick assembly, hold the pieces in place by hand as you add screws. For tighter joints or more complex assemblies, clamp first, then screw.

ANATOMY OF A REBATE JOINT

Note: + indicates dimension should be just fractionally larger than the measurement referred to.

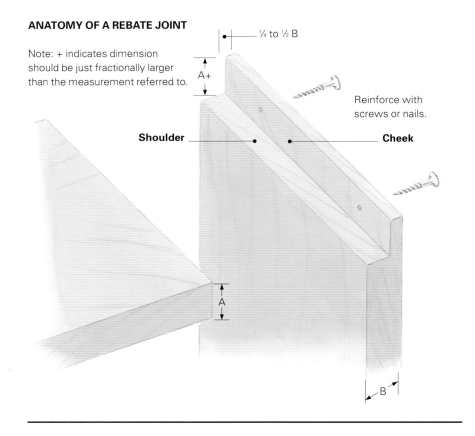

¼ to ½ B

A+

Reinforce with screws or nails.

Shoulder

Cheek

A

B

thirds the thickness of the side will work well in most situations. Screwing a tall auxilliary fence to the rip fence will make it easier to work with longer parts. If the part is too long and awkward to work vertically, you can make the shoulder cut, then clear the waste with several additional passes pushed through with a mitre fence.

Rebate joints can be assembled quickly with screws, which make a much stronger joint than nails. Angle the screws slightly so they pull the top into the corner of the rebate. To ensure a tight fit, draw the mating surfaces together with clamps, then screw. You will probably need to clamp horizontally and vertically to eliminate gaps.

MAKING A DADO JOINT

For centuries, woodworkers cut dados by hand, with tenon saw and chisel. The tablesaw and router have made this time-consuming hand work a matter of choice rather than necessity. The goal whether by hand or machine is a tight joint. Remember, however, that

the tighter the joint, the harder it will be to glue-up, particularly on wide boards. You should have to apply some pressure to assemble the joint dry, but you should not have to hammer it home. Check your machine set-up on scrap pieces before cutting the real thing. (For convenience in the discussions below, we call the dadoed piece the side, and the mating piece the shelf.)

For many applications it is quick and effective to cut the dado to take the full thickness of the shelf. Even boards run through the same planer settings have slight differences in the thickness, so you can ensure a tight joint by cutting the dado fractionally narrower than the shelf thickness and planing a few shavings off the shelf faces to fit the parts. Sometimes it is best to create a tongue on the end of a shelf by cutting one or two narrow shoulders, and cut the dado and tongue to match. This is useful for veneered man-made boards, which have little material to remove on the faces during fitting to a full-thickness dado.

Dadoing on the tablesaw

You can cut dados on the tablesaw by making multiple passes over a single blade, or a single pass over a multiple-cutter dado head set to match the thickness of the sides. Depending on the width and length of the board, you can groove by pushing the side through the cut with a mitre fence, by pushing its end along the rip fence, or by combining the two. The depth of the dado should not be more than half the thickness of the side.

Scribe with a sharp knife the position of the dado on the edges of the side (and across the faces if you wish). Aligning the edge marks accurately to the saw blade or dado head is the most important part of making the cuts; check rip fence or mitre-fence stop settings with a piece of scrap. During the cut, push the face of the board down firmly on the saw table so the dado will be uniformly deep.

Glue-up is straightforward. Use wide battens to distribute the clamping pressure across the faces of the sides. For wide sides, you can crown the battens slightly, placing the convex edge against the side so that clamping pressure will create pressure in the centre of the side. Despite the end-grain gluing surface, the mechanical advantage of a tight fit coupled with the modern glues produces a strong joint without screw or nail reinforcement.

Routing dados

Long or wide pieces that can be difficult to manoeuvre across a tablesaw are easy to dado with a router. Just fix the piece firmly to the workbench and move the lightweight tool across it, guided by a straightedge. A simple wooden straightedge is easy to make; take care to make the stock (which bears against the edge) exactly perpendicular to the fence. Because the thickness of the workpieces almost never matches the size of a standard router bit, it is best to rout dados by taking two passes with a smaller bit.

Again, the trickiest part of routing a dado is positioning the fence so the bit cuts exactly on the scribe lines. You can do this easily if you always use the same router bit with a particular

CUTTING A DADO JOINT ON THE TABLESAW

1–3 To dado with a single blade, make both shoulder cuts first. Then clear the waste between shoulders with repeated passes over the blade (left). A single pass **over a dado head cuts a full-width dado (top). Clamp a dado joint with a wide batten to pull the joint tight across the full width of the side (bottom).**

straightedge. For example, if you rout a lot of dados that are 20 to 25mm wide, make a straightedge for use with a 13mm router bit. Hold the router base firmly against the fence and rout across the stock with the bit. Aligning the appropriate shoulder of this groove with the knife mark of the dado shoulder you are cutting will correctly position the fence.

When dadoing a wide board, it is prudent to check the alignment of the fence at both ends. You can do this with blocks cut to the distances between the fence and the groove shoulders in the stock. Clamp the fence in position at both ends before routing. Most router collets (which hold the bit) are not centred exactly on the router base, so mark on the base the point of contact with the fence and always run that part of the base against the fence.

If you only have a few dados to cut and do not want to fuss with aligning a straightedge, you can rout out most of the waste between scribe lines, then trim to the lines with a wide, sharp chisel.

ROUTING DADOS

Two passes complete this dado routed against a straightedge. Note how the groove in the straightedge stock aligns with the dado shoulder being cut.

ANATOMY OF A DADO JOINT

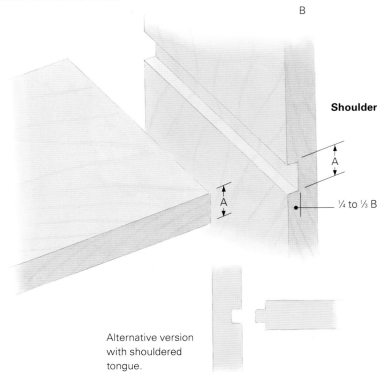

B

Shoulder

A

A

¼ to ⅓ B

Alternative version
with shouldered
tongue.

THE TONGUE-AND-DADO JOINT

This joint combines the techniques of dado and rebate: a dado across the end of one board (the side) mates with a tongue formed by rebating the end of the other board (the top). The thickness and length of tongue are not critical; one third the thickness of the mating pieces works well. For 19mm stock, therefore, the tongue would be 6 by 6mm. You can scribe the position of the dado with a mortise gauge. Set it so the side protrudes slightly beyond the surface of the assembled joint, to make clean-up easier.

You can cut the dado on the tablesaw or router as described before. In many instances it will be a great deal easier to guide the router by attaching a fence to its base rather than fixing a straightedge across the board. You can clamp a piece of wood to the base or use commercially made fences sold for most routers. Cut the dado just slightly deeper than the length of the tongue so the shoulder will be sure to seat.

A shallow rebate forms the small tongue. When making the shoulder cut on the tablesaw against a rip fence, it is safer to attach an auxiliary fence positioned to only make contact with the tongue. That way, the thin waste piece will not bind against the fence and possibly kick back. Turn the piece upright and run it against the fence for the cheek cut. Because the tongue is cut to fit the dado, have an ample supply of offcuts at hand for fine-tuning the fence setting.

No matter how carefully you set up the machines, you may need to take a few shavings with a shoulder plane to fit the tongue to the dado. (You could also take shavings off the face of the board with a bench plane.) The joint should be snug, but be careful when fitting not to snap off the narrow and somewhat weak strip of wood above the groove. The joint assembles much like other dados; because it is usually used at the corner, you can stretch more clamps across the top to draw it tight. A thin batten will protect the surface of the wood; several clamps spaced across the width of the side will be needed to draw the joint home.

ANATOMY OF A TONGUE-AND-DADO JOINT

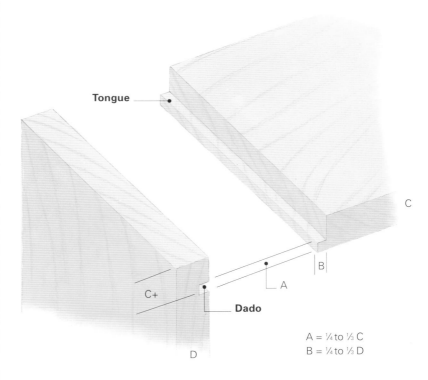

$A = \frac{1}{4}$ to $\frac{1}{3}$ C
$B = \frac{1}{4}$ to $\frac{1}{3}$ D

MAKING A TONGUE-AND-GROOVE JOINT

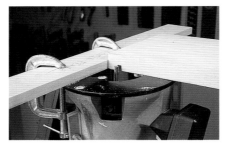

1–4 Rout the dado against a fence fixed to the router base (top left). On the tablesaw, cut a rebate to form the tongue; shoulder cut shown against an auxiliary fence (bottom left). If necessary, trim the tongue to a snug fit with a shoulder plane (top right). Draw the joint tight with clamps (bottom right).

MITRE JOINTS

Unlike the joints just discussed, mitres used as corner joints in plank construction can be difficult to cut, fit, and assemble. And, as the width of the boards increases, mitres become in every way more difficult. If the boards are not dead flat, they are difficult at any width. Were it not for the undeniable appeal of their clean look, few people would bother with them. The technique shown here should not cause beginners much trouble for boards up to around 150mm in width, which will cover many small cabinets, boxes, as well as plinths and cornices used on larger case pieces.

An accurately set up saw is essential. You can check the angle of the saw blade by mitring two pieces of scrap and seeing if they combine to form a 90° angle. (Any error in the saw angle is doubled, therefore easier to see). Many saws will not produce accurate mitres straight from the blade, so you should be prepared to trim them with a sharp bench plane or block plane.

ANATOMY OF A SPLINED-MITRE JOINT

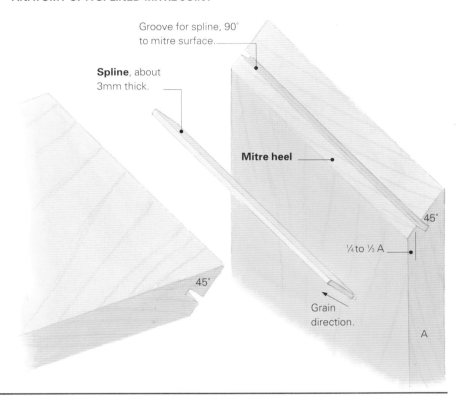

Groove for spline, 90° to mitre surface.

Spline, about 3mm thick.

Mitre heel

45°

¼ to ⅓ A

45°

Grain direction.

A

MITRING ON THE TABLE SAW

1–4 Keep the workpiece firmly in contact with the saw table and mitre fence (top left). Cut spline grooves against the rip fence (bottom left). Make a spline with a vertical then a horizontal cut (top right). Glue triangular blocks to the faces of the parts and apply quick-action cramps to draw the joint tight.

Assembled with glue alone, mitre joints have little strength. Grooving the surfaces and adding a thin 'spline' strengthens the joint and keeps it from slipping around during assembly. For maximum strength the grooves should be near the mitre heels and the grain should run across the width of the spline. You can make cross-grain splines easily on the tablesaw. Cut splines to fit the saw kerf groove by running a wide piece of scrap wood upright against the rip fence at the spline's thickness, then severing the thin spline using the mitre fence.

Assembling mitres can be frustrating. Even with splines to stop the surfaces from sliding and a welter of sash clamps to apply pressure from both directions, joints often will not close. Providing pressure at right angles to the mating surfaces usually produces good results. Glue triangular blocks to the faces of the parts, and apply quick-action clamps to draw the joint tight. Paper glued under the blocks makes it easier to separate them after assembly.

17

DOVETAIL BASICS

Of all the joints employed by wood-workers, dovetails have a special status. The joint is a marvel of low-tech engineering, unsurpassed in its combination of simple elegance, durability and strength. And, in a through dovetail at least, all of these qualities are on full display. What you see is what you get.

In the century since the Arts and Crafts revival of interest in handmade woodwork, dovetails have come to exemplify fine craftsmanship and quality construction. Despite the many varieties of durable machine-cut joints and strong adhesives, woodworkers continue to take the time to dovetail all sorts of case pieces, from tiny jewellery caskets to large bureaux, sideboards and desks. Dovetails, it seems, are as satisfying to cut as they are structurally sound to employ.

This chapter shows how to make the most basic form of this joint, the

Opposite: Dovetailing is precise work. The strength and look depend on a tight fit.

through dovetail. Dovetailing is a straightforward skill, but one that takes practice to master. After you've suffered misalignments, gaps and other frustrations on half a dozen scrap-wood samples, and feel prepared to tackle a project you hope to keep, consider building the dovetailed table in chapter 19. Then progress to a simple dovetailed box, like the showcase in chapter 20. When you are confident of your through-dovetail skills, try the half-blind dovetails in the carcass and drawers of the small chest in chapter 21.

To make the through-dovetail sample, you'll need two pieces of 20 to 25mm-thick stock, about 30cm long and 13 or 15cm wide. Take particular care preparing stock (even sample pieces) for dovetailing. Dovetails are harder to lay out, to cut, and to assemble if the parts are twisted or out of square.

TAIL LAYOUT

The strength and beauty of a dovetail joint resides in the fit of its two parts. The wedge-shaped tails and pins must

fit seamlessly. The best way to achieve a close fit is to lay out one member using the other as a template. Here we will show how to lay out and cut the tails, then use them to scribe the pins onto the end of the mating piece. Some woodworkers prefer to lay out the tails from the pins; after you have spent time working with the method shown here, give the other a try, and pick the one that works best for you.

Start by scribing shoulder lines around the ends of both pieces with a marking gauge. (This is why it is so important for the ends of the members to be square to their edges and faces.) Set the gauge to slightly more than the thickness of the mating pieces. It is more convenient to plane off protruding pins and tails than to plane the faces down to recessed pins and tails. Often both pieces are the same thickness and will require only one gauge setting. A chisel-point gauge makes a cleaner line than one sharpened to a pin point. Scribe all around each part, on both faces and both edges, making a light

LAYING OUT THE TAILS

1–3 Begin layout by setting a marking gauge slightly wider than the thickness of the parts (left). Scribe shoulder lines on the faces and edges of both pieces (centre).

Reset the gauge if the pieces are different thicknesses. After setting out the pin and tail spacing, measure to establish the width of the pins, then mark the tails using

a sharp pencil and a sliding bevel (right). Working from the angled lines, square lines across the end. (These are shown here already in place.)

THROUGH-DOVETAIL ANATOMY

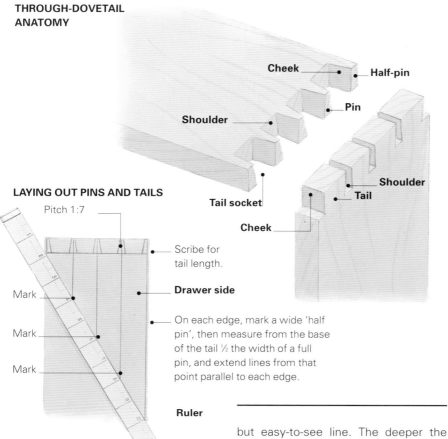

Cheek
Half-pin
Pin
Shoulder
Shoulder
Tail
Tail socket
Cheek

LAYING OUT PINS AND TAILS

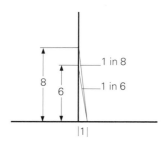

Pitch 1:7

Mark

Mark

Mark

Ruler

Scribe for tail length.

Drawer side

On each edge, mark a wide 'half pin', then measure from the base of the tail ½ the width of a full pin, and extend lines from that point parallel to each edge.

To find the centrelines of three full pins (for four tails), line up the ruler to divide the board into four equal parts, as shown. Extend the divisions to create pin centerlines. For more pins, divide the board into more parts.

Establishing pitch

1 in 8

1 in 6

8

6

|1|

Square a line to the edge of the workbench, measure to the layout the desired pitch as shown, set the sliding bevel to the line.

pins are 8mm in the sample.) To make the tails exactly equal in width, you need take into account this extra thickness on the edge when laying out.

Measure from the marked centre points to establish the width of each full pin (10mm in the sample), then pencil in the angled pin/tail lines against a sliding bevel set to the correct pitch. It will be easier to clean up the pin sockets if the pin width is slightly more than that of a bevel-edge chisel in your set. Next, square the lines across the end of the piece and extend them down the other face with the bevel. (Experienced dovetailers often omit drawing them on the second face.) You might want to darken the waste portions (the pin sockets) with a pencil to remind you on which side of the layout lines to saw.

CUTTING THE TAILS

You will need a sharp dovetail saw to cut the tails, a coping saw to remove the waste from the pin sockets, and a chisel to clean up the shoulder of the pin socket. The key to good dovetailing is developing skill with the saw. Master the deceptively simple task of cutting unerringly along a straight line and you are home free. When cutting the tails, the task is complicated by having to keep the saw perpendicular to the face of the board (that's why you pencil the lines across the end grain) while you follow the angled outline of the tail. Some woodworkers tilt the board in the vice so they are sawing straight up and down. Others prefer to tilt the saw and make all the cuts at that angle, then tilt it the other way for the cuts at the second angle.

Whether you tilt the saw or the board, start the cut at an angle to the arris at the intersection of the end and the face, then drop the blade gradually until it is horizontal. This allows you to make incremental adjustments as the cut proceeds along the end-grain layout line. It is easier to track your progress if you cut right up to the line, but don't remove it.

With the angled cuts made, clear the waste from the full-pin sockets with a coping saw. Cut quickly and away from the gauged scribe line; a sharp chisel makes a far neater job of the shoulders

but easy-to-see line. The deeper the marks, the more shavings you will have to take after assembly to remove them, though some people leave the scribe marks as a decorative feature.

Next come the tails themselves. You can figure out the number, pitch (the angle of the wedge), and spacing full size on a sheet of paper, or do it right on the part. An easy method for spacing any number of tails and pins, and for establishing pitch, is shown below left. Most dovetails are pitched between about 1 in 6 and 1 in 8. The former makes a more noticeable wedge shape, the latter is more 'refined.' (Pitch in the sample is 1 in 7.) For purely visual reasons, many makers prefer tails to be considerably wider than the pins; joints with very thin pins seem to be as strong as those with hefty pins.

The spacing method shown finds the centre of each pin. Note that the half-pins at each edge are slightly wider than half the width of a full pin; a tight-fitting tail can split the edge of a pin-piece if the half-pin is too thin. (Half-

than a coping saw. Reposition the part horizontally in the vice to cut the shoulders of the half pins on each edge. Try to cut the scribed line in half.

To trim the full-pin sockets, slip a chisel's cutting edge into the scribed shoulder line and slice down with even pressure about half-way through the wood's thickness. Flip the piece over and do the same thing to clear the waste, then clean out the socket's corners as needed; the chisel's bevelled edges make it possible to do so. Pare a shaving or two from the centre of the shoulder socket, so the surface is slightly concave and will not hold the joint apart. Trim the half-pin shoulders with a wide chisel if necessary.

LAYING OUT THE PINS

Tracing the outline of the actual tails directly onto the end grain of the pin piece helps ensure snug-fitting joints (see photos p.138). A sharp thin-bladed knife (a chip-carving knife works very well) makes a fine, accurate line. A knifed line is harder to see, but a task light set at a low-angle to create shadows in the lines can solve this problem.

Fix the pin piece end-up in a bench vice and position the tail piece on it, supporting its other end on scrap wood. It may take a bit of adjustment to get the tail piece to lie perfectly flat on the end of the pin piece.

To ensure a square joint, it is important to position the edges of the tail piece square to the face of the pin piece. The shoulders of the pin sockets in the tail piece should be flush with the inside face of the pin piece. Look down on the tail piece and move it until there are just the tiniest slivers of light visible in the sockets. This method usually works, but it is a good idea to check the alignment with a square

Pressing down on the tail piece firmly with one hand, scribe along the tails with the knife. Make sure that the blade is flush with the tail so the scribed pin exactly matches the outline of the socket: the smallest discrepancy will show up as an irritating gap in the joint. It may take two passes to deepen a line enough to see clearly. Then, with a pencil and square, extend the knifed lines down both faces of the pin piece

CUTTING THE TAILS

1 Following the lines closely, cut the tails with a sharp backsaw. For speed and accuracy, try making all the cuts at one angle first, then all the cuts at the other.

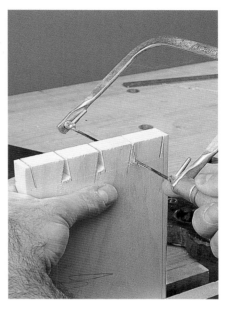

2 Clear the waste material between the tails with a coping saw. Try to remember to cut well away from the scribed shoulder line.

3 Cutting right to the scribed line, remove the waste from the half-pin sockets on the edges of the board. Clean up with the chisel if necessary.

4 Working to the scribed shoulder line, square the bottoms of the sockets with a sharp chisel. (Hardboard placed underneath protects the benchtop.)

SAWING THE PINS

1 With the tail piece resting squarely on the pin piece, carefully mark the position of the tails using a sharp, thin-bladed marking knife.

2 Try to cut to the centre of the knifed lines, as shown in the cut on the far left. If you do not quite manage this, it is easy to trim to the line with a chisel.

to the shoulder scribe. You may want to scribble on the waste here too, to remind you to cut on the right side of the lines.

CUTTING THE PINS AND SOCKETS

While this is much the same sort of job as cutting the tails, here the sawing must be more precise. The pins and sockets must conform exactly to the knifed scribe lines (the actual shape of the tails) or the joint will not be gap-free. Try to cut to the centre of the thin knifed line, but be sure to err on the waste side. It is much easier to pare away a sliver of wood to get down to the knife line than it is to add a sliver to patch a gap.

The sawing technique is the same as before: an angled start, gradually lowering to horizontal with minute adjustments along the knifed line. The thicker pencil lines running down the faces will help you maintain the cut at right angles to the end of the piece. After you get the hang of cutting accurately, the biggest problem you will

have is keeping those tiny knife lines in focus. Raking light helps a lot. As before, clear the waste from each tail socket with the coping saw. Now chisel to the gauge line. First, deepen the scribe lines slightly on both faces with a gentle mallet tap on the widest chisel that will fit between the pins. If the waste extends more than 2mm or so beyond the scribe line, take it out in several cuts with a mallet-driven chisel. Holding the part in the vice, clean out the socket corners, and take a few thin shavings off the bottom of the socket (the shoulder) to ensure that it is flat or even slightly concave so the tail will seat properly. Trim the socket cheeks to the knife lines if necessary, then pare away a very fine shaving or two from the centre of each pin cheek, not touching the periphery where gaps could show. This slight concavity eases the fit, while producing no gaps on the surfaces.

FITTING

Old-timers say that a dovetail goes together perfectly only once. A joint

driven home to check the fit then disassembled will not be as tight the second time around, even less so the third. Pushing the joint not more than a quarter or third of the way home will alert you to most significant problems. Before trying the joint, chamfer the inside arrises of the tails. If the fit seems too tight, pare a bit off the cheek of this or that pin with a very sharp chisel.

If the joint is too loose, there is not much you can do but resort to filling the gaps with little slivers of wood. Of course, there is no point with a sample joint, but this can salvage a project joint with just a few gaps. If there are many gaps, it is a tedious process and the results are not always satisfying; remaking the part may be the better choice in the long run.

FINAL ASSEMBLY

Assembly varies according to the number of tails and the complexity of the piece being built. The projects in subsequent chapters cover several situations. Here general procedures are outlined. Well-cut dovetails can be pushed part way home by hand and driven the final distance with a hammer and block of wood. For the tightest fit, however, it is best to pull the tails tight to the socket bottoms with a sash clamp, which will squeeze out glue and eliminate tiny gaps the hammer cannot close. Once the joints are tight, they will often stay put and will not need clamping while the glue sets.

There are several different methods of using a clamp on dovetails. Because the pins protrude slightly beyond the tails, you need a clamping block that fits between pins to bring pressure on the tail. Often you can work with a single clamp and one block of wood, narrower than the narrow waist of a tail, moving block and clamp from tail to tail. Where speed is a concern (lots of tails or a tricky assembly), you might prepare one or more special clamping blocks that allow you to move the clamp down a row of tails without moving the block each time.

No matter how simple the project, it pays to be well organized when gluing up. Before spreading any glue, make sure you have a hammer, a hardwood

TRIMMING THE TAIL SOCKETS

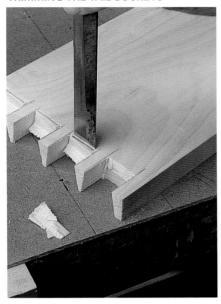

1 After cutting out the bulk of the waste with a coping saw, establish the bottom of the tail sockets by making a series of mallet-driven cuts with a wide chisel.

2 Clean up the corners of the tail sockets and slice a few shavings from the bottom of the socket to make it slightly concave.

3 If necessary, trim the pin cheeks to the knife lines. Taking a very fine shaving or two to make the centre of the cheek slightly concave will ease assembly.

driving block (to use with the hammer), a clamp of the right length and a clamping block of some sort. In addition, have a small brush or thin piece of wood handy for spreading the glue.

Begin by spreading a thin glue film on all the mating surfaces of the joint – both cheeks of each tail and pin and the socket shoulders. Old-timers brushed a bit of hide glue only on the pin cheeks, which seems to have been enough to keep tightly fitting joints together and certainly cut down on mess from squeezed-out glue.

Push on the tails as far as you can by hand, then drive them with the hammer and block until glue squeezes out of the socket shoulders. Use the clamp and block to draw the tails tight to the sockets. Move from tail to tail, working as quickly as possible. After the glue has cured, plane off the protruding tails and pins, and excess glue. Even after years of dovetailing, revealing the pattern of tightly fitting tails and pins with a few strokes of the plane is a satisfying moment.

FINAL FITTING

1 To ease assembly, chamfer the inside arrises of the tails. Stop the chamfers before the end of the piece, otherwise gaps will show after assembly.

2 Dry-fit the joint before gluing up. Pushing the pieces no more than about halfway home will reveal most problems in the joint's fit.

Below
JOHN COLEMAN
Veneered in Macassar ebony, John Coleman's desk could also serve as a dressing table.

Middle
PAUL GOWER
The curving sides of this desk were assembled of maple veneer on a curved form.

Above
TONY McCULLEN
This unusual writing cabinet combines a mahogany carcass, laminated legs of blistered maple, and a tambour roll top (retracted in photo).

Right
ROBERT WILLIAMS
Stacked without a case, the finger-jointed drawers in this desk pivot at a corner to open.

Left
**ROY TAM AND DAVID
COLWELL**
Spreading the doubled
legs to join a flat rail under
the top provides physical
and visual stability to a
simple desk design.

Right
ANDREW LAWTON
Folding the ends like
paper adds interest and
stability to an otherwise
staightforward plank
construction. Note the
through wedged tenons
connecting the legs to
the drawer rail. This piece
is made of rippled
sycamore with mahogany
drawer sides.

18

A SIMPLE BOOKCASE

Woodworkers spend a lot of time making boxes of one sort or another. The ones we tend to remember are the show pieces: handsome pedestal desks, chests of drawers, or jewellery cases displaying beautiful wood, elegant proportions, and meticulously cut decorative joints.

The ones we most often make are rather more humble, produced to fill an immediate need on limited budgets of time and money. Certainly, these projects can also be well proportioned and well made, but their designs should above all be utilitarian, their joinery sound and uncomplicated.

The simple bookcase made in this chapter is functional, sturdy and can be made quickly (in a day, if you substitute a sheet of plywood for the frame-and-panel back). Using the same joinery, but varying the sizes of the parts, you can make a simple version of virtually any case piece: kitchen cabinets, night stands, chests of drawers, blanket chests. And you can make lots of them. Having set up the machines to cut a joint, it is just as easy to run off parts for half a dozen bookcases or kitchen cabinets as for one.

You can alter the joinery (which is also well-suited to plywood construction) to suit your preferences. Cutting the tongues on the top, rather than on the sides, makes assembly easier (all clamps run the same direction) and moves the exposed end grain to the top surface, ideal for tall bookcases. The bottom dados into the sides, which run by to form the feet. By running the sides of the case several inches beyond the top, the bookcase could be constructed entirely of identical dado joints, making the job even quicker.

The back helps to strengthen the case considerably; if you do not want a back, substitute two back rails running below the top and bottom boards to provide stiffness. If you do not want adjustable shelves and decide instead to house them permanently in dados, the case will be sufficiently strong without rails or back.

Opposite: Nicholas Below's bookcase provides shelving and a bit of fun.

CONSTRUCTING THE CASE

To ensure a square carcass, take care during stock preparation to make the paired parts (top and bottom, two sides) equal length, with ends square to their edges.

The joints differ from those described in chapter 16 only in that the dados stop short of the front edge, so the joints are hidden. It is much easier to make stopped dados with a router than a tablesaw. For control and safety, it is important to feed the router so the rotation of the bit pulls the tool toward the fence; if the fence is attached to the router base, the bit should pull the fence against the wood. (The easiest way to figure out the right direction is to rout a piece of scrap.) Because of this, only one of each pair of stopped dados can be made starting the cut at the back edge of the board. To feed the router correctly for the other dado, you must begin the cut at the stopped end by lowering the bit into the wood.

A plunge router is designed for such cuts, but you can do the job with a

---

TOP TO SIDE TONGUE DETAIL

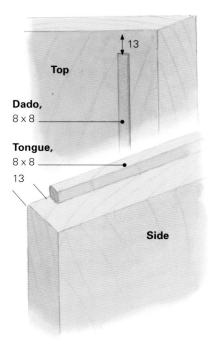

Top

13

Dado,
8 x 8

Tongue,
8 x 8

13

Side

standard router, too. (See photos on p.144). To cut the bottom dados against a straightedge fence clamped to the work, start by tilting the tool so the bit clears the surface while the router base remains firmly in contact with the fence. As you carefully lower the spinning bit into the wood, move the router slowly in the direction of the cut until the base rests flat on the face of the board. Carefully back the router up to extend this first 25mm or so of the dado to full depth, then complete the cut. For cutting the narrow dados in the top, use a fence attached to the router. Tilt the router, then keep the fence firmly in contact with the end of the board as you lower the bit into the cut. Use a sharp chisel to square up the stopped ends of the dados.

After you cut these dados, rout a groove in each side to house the bottom 'plinth' rail. You can also use the router to make the 'feet' on the sides. The bookcase back is housed in rebates cut in the sides and top; it runs by the bottom. It is easiest to rebate the full length of the back edge of each side on the tablesaw now, but rout the stopped rebate in the top after assembly (as described below). Adjust the depth of the rebate if you use a 13mm or 10mm piece of plywood instead of the frame-and-panelled back. Once the sides are rebated, cut the case bottom to final width. Its rear edge must finish flush with the rebate so that the case back can extend over it.

It is best to add a tall auxiliary fence to the tablesaw rip fence for cutting the tongues on the sides. (See photos on p.146). Create a short shoulder at the front edge to fit the stopped dado. Lightly chamfering the top arrises of the tongues will ease assembly; because the dado is stopped, the chamfers will not create gaps on the front edge of the case.

Shelf supports

The bookcase's adjustable shelves are supported on commercially made 'pegs' that fit in 6mm holes. The most efficient and accurate way to ensure that the holes on both sides will align and the shelves be level is to lay out the holes with a template. The template

CUTTING STOPPED DADOS

1 Keep the router base in firm contact with the straightedge fence as you lower the bit to begin a stopped dado.

2 The procedure is much the same when the fence is attached to the router, as shown here for the dado cut in the top.

shown on p.147 is a piece of 3mm hardboard whose ends have been carefully squared to its front edge. Lay out a grid of holes positioned to fall about 50mm in from the front edge and back rebate and spaced 50mm on centre. With a drill bit the size of your bradawl (or other pointed marking tool), bore small pilot holes on the grid.

On each bookcase side, make a mark 20cm from the bottom dado (mark one side from the other for greatest accuracy) and position the template with the first row of holes at the mark. Poke the bradawl through the template to mark the centres of the shelf-peg holes. Move the templates as necessary to mark all the holes on one side, then do the same on the other.

A drill press will ensure holes that are square to the sides and uniformly deep, but careful hand drilling will work, too. Countersink the holes to produce a light chamfer, which eases insertion of the pegs and cleans up the sometimes ragged edges left by the drill bit.

ROUTING 'FEET'

3 Square up the stopped ends of the dados with a sharp chisel. Note the short groove that houses the 'plinth' rail beneath the bottom of the bookcase.

Routing against a fence with a long straight bit, you can create 'feet' on the bottom end of each side. Make several passes instead of one heavy cut.

CUTTING LIST
(Overall dimensions of finished parts.)

Part	Quantity	Dimensions
		(L x W x Th in millimetres)
Case		
Side	2	1127 x 241 x 22
Top	1	889 x 241 x 22
Bottom	1	854 x 222 x 22
Plinth rail	1	854 x 51 x 22
Shelves	2 or more	841 x 219 x 22
Back		
Stile	2	980 x 76 x 16
Top rail	1	867 x 76 x 16
Bottom rail	1	867 x 102 x 16
Panels	as needed	821 x random x 10

A SIMPLE BOOKCASE

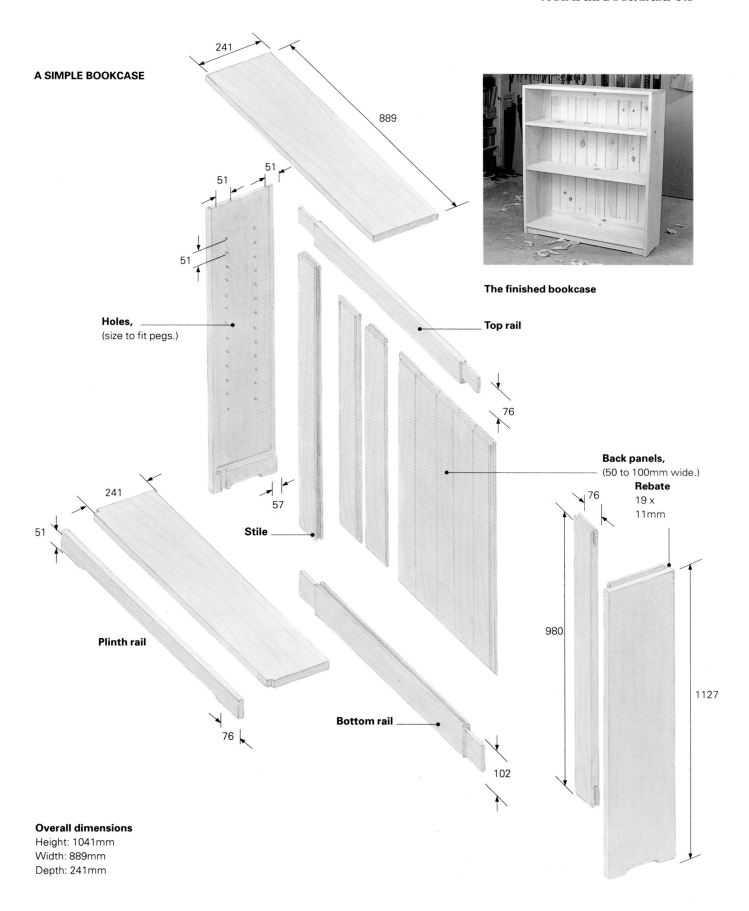

241

889

51

51

51

51

Holes,
(size to fit pegs.)

Top rail

The finished bookcase

76

Back panels,
(50 to 100mm wide.)

Rebate
19 x
11mm

76

241

51

57

Stile

980

Plinth rail

1127

Bottom rail

76

102

Overall dimensions
Height: 1041mm
Width: 889mm
Depth: 241mm

CUTTING THE TONGUES

1–2 A tall auxilary fence stabilizes the long sides when cutting the tongues. Make sure the fence is perfectly square to the saw table; even a slight error is **magnified by the fence's height. With tenon saw and chisel, cut and trim a short shoulder to accommodate the stopped dado in the top.**

PLINTH DETAIL

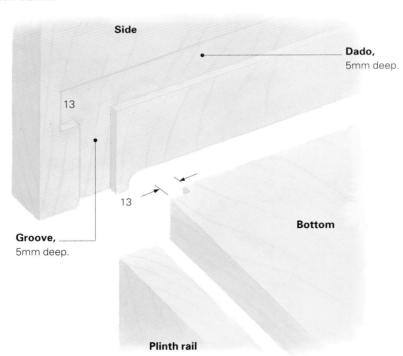

Side

Dado, 5mm deep.

13

13

Groove, 5mm deep.

Bottom

Plinth rail

ASSEMBLY

Assemble and clamp the case without glue as a final check on the joints and clamping sequence. You may wish to sand interior surfaces now (sand up to, but not across, those areas that fit in the dados). If you are chamfering arrises, it is easiest to rout or plane before assembly those that will fall inside the box. Chamfer nearly the full length of the parts but stop short of the dados on the top and sides. (After assembly finish the job with a mason's mitre, as described on page 148.)

The joints are assembled with sash clamps and bearers as described in chapter 17. The clamping set up shown on p.148 is complicated by the need to pull the joints together in two different directions. Long bearers allow the horizontal clamps drawing the bottom and sides together to clear the vertical clamps. To simplify assembly, you could reverse the positions of the tongues and dados joining sides and top (tongues on top, dados in sides) so that all the clamps could run horizontally. This would, however, expose end grain on the top, rather than the sides, and may not be the look you want.

Often the biggest challenge in assembling a large, but simple carcass, is making sure it is square. When the clamps obstruct the use of a tape measure to check the lengths of the diagonals, you can do the job with two thin pieces of wood. Holding the two side by side, extend one end of each into diagonal corners, then mark across the two somewhere in the centre (it does not matter where). Now span the other diagonal in the same way. If the pencil marks align again, the case is square; if not, it is out of square by the amount of the distance between them.

You can adjust an out-of-square case by repositioning the clamps to force diagonals closer or farther apart. Notice that in the photo on p.148 the vertical clamps are angled from top to bottom, not centred on the side. This was done to shorten the diagonal between the top left and bottom right corners and square the case. When adjusting clamps in this way, make sure any paired clamps, like the two on the left side here, are angled in the same way.

Instead of the typical dresser arrangement of storage below and display above, David Field split the enclosed storage areas at each end of his dresser with open shelving. The solid sycamore case incorporates sliding dovetails (a dovetail-shaped tongue-and-dado joint) to accommodate wood expansion and contraction.

SHELF SUPPORT HOLES

1 Mark the centres of the support-peg holes using an accurate template and bradawl. Spring clamps keep the template in place.

2 A piece of masking tape serves as a depth stop when boring the holes. Take care to keep the drill bit perpendicular to the side.

3 Countersinking the holes improves their appearance, makes it easier to insert the shelf pegs and cleans up any ragged edges left by the drill bit.

PANELS

Back panel (face inside case). _____

→ **Stile**

BACK FRAME BRIDLE JOINTS

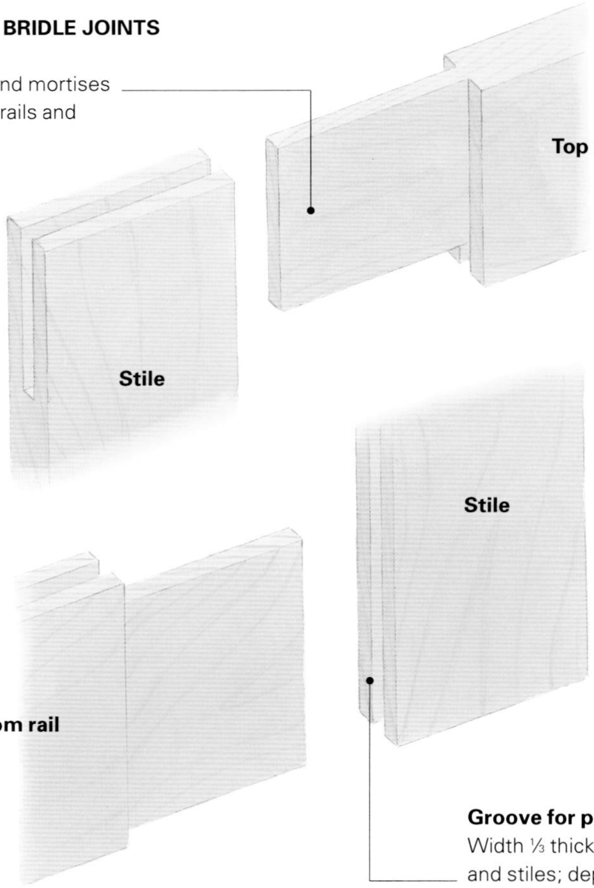

Make tenons and mortises _____
⅓ thickness of rails and
stiles, centred.

Top rail

Stile

Stile

Bottom rail

Groove for panels:
Width ⅓ thickness of rails
and stiles; depth 13mm.

BACK TOP CORNER DETAIL

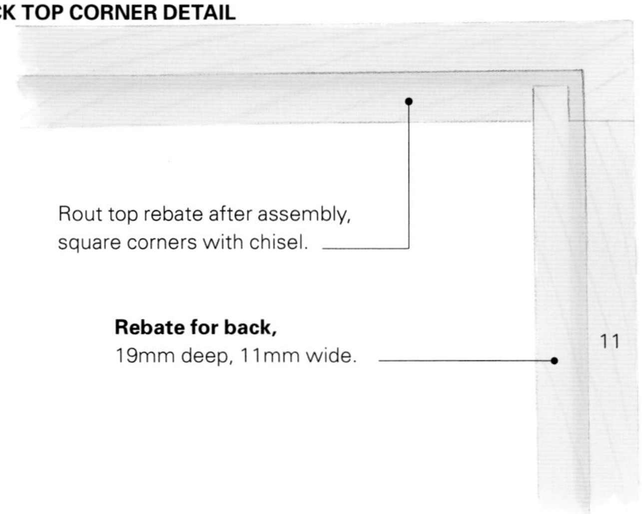

Top

Rout top rebate after assembly,
square corners with chisel. _____

Side

Rebate for back,
19mm deep, 11mm wide. _____

11

ASSEMBLY

**1 Angled clamps (vertical on the left)
bring the bookcase square, as checked by
comparing the extension of two thin
sticks across opposite diagonals.**

Otherwise you may end up with a
square, but twisted case. Check for
twist by sighting across the front or
back edges of the case to make sure
they are in the same plane, as for winding sticks.

When the glue has cured, clean up
the joints and exterior surfaces with a
sharp handplane. Supporting the case
as shown in the photo subjects the
joints to far less racking force than placing one side on the floor while planing
the other unsupported side. Flush the
front edges of the case, then complete
the chamfers with a mason's mitre, as
shown in the photo. The technique is
borrowed from stonemasons. Two
pieces of stone cannot be cut on an
angle and joined to produce a mitre, so
the 'mitre' must be carved. When the
chamfers are finished, fit the plinth rail
to its grooves and glue it in place.

Turn the case over and complete the
rebate for the case back by running a
ball-bearing-piloted bit along the back
edge of the top. Clamp a wide bearer to
the top to provide stability for the router

MASON'S MITRE

PLINTH RAIL

2 Boards cantilevered from the bench help to support the case while the joints and exterior surfaces are cleaned up after assembly.

A sharp chisel forms a mason's mitre to complete the chamfers routed before assembly. Avoid splits due to awkward grain by nibbling the wood away.

Fit the plinth rail snugly into its grooves and glue it in place. Glue it to the bottom as well to further stiffen the case.

base and set the depth to match the rebates cut earlier on the sides. Form the rebate by making several shallow passes rather than a single deep one.

The back is a simple bridle-jointed frame (see chapter 14), grooved to accommodate the rebated ends of about 10 narrow slats of varying width. The edges of the slats are also rebated so they overlap (as described in chapter 15) and lightly chamfered. A panelled back improves the looks of a basic bookshelf like this a great deal, but takes about as long as the case itself to make. A plywood back, perhaps painted to contrast with a natural wood case, takes a fraction of the time.

After assemblying the back, plane it to fit the case. With a sharp chisel, square the round routed corners of the rebate at the top, then screw the back to the rebate and back edge of the case bottom. Because the rebates are a bit narrow, slightly angle the screws toward the corner of the rebates to make sure they do not break through the inside faces of the sides.

THE CASE BACK

1 Rebate the top with a ball-bearing-piloted rebate bit. A piece clamped to the top provides bearing surface for the router base.

2 Trim the routed corners of the rebate square when you fit the back to the case. Screw the back to the rebates and edge of the case bottom.

GALLERY
SHELVES

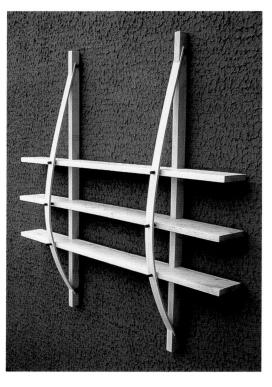

Above
STEMMER & SHARP
A whimsical plywood construction is as much an object of interest as the items placed upon it. Shelves are dadoed and glued to the sides; joints are reinforced with screws.

Top right
ROY TAM
Made from small-diameter coppiced ash, these hanging shelves are a neat piece of engineering, making good use of the strength of ash and its capacity for bending.

Right
PETER SOUTHALL
Standing over 2m tall, this hall seat and coat-rack gives a twist to a traditional form of furniture. The solid oak uprights were steamed then twisted to shape.

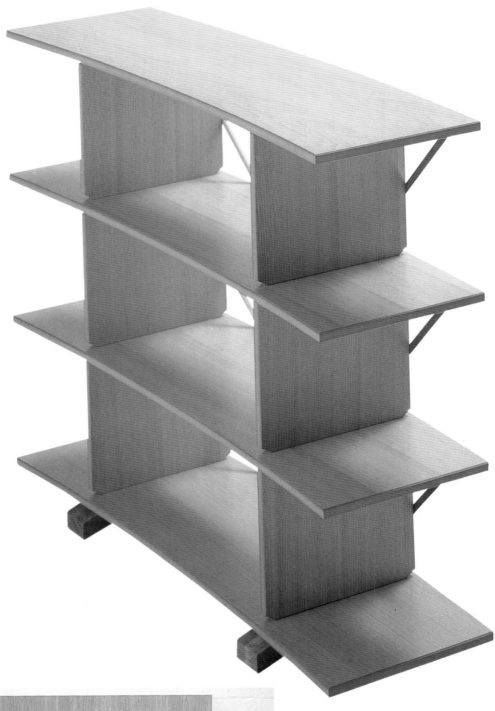

Right
ROBERT WILLIAMS
Made of oak veneer on medium-density fibreboard, these shelves and uprights appear to be stacked like a house of cards. Biscuit-like splines position the uprights on the shelves, diagonal braces at the back provide stability.

Left
JOHN COLEMAN
These cherry-veneered shelves are designed to lean against a wall at an angle of 10° so they require no fastenings.

MAKING THE PINS

1–3 In order to scribe the position of the pins from the cut tails, it will be necessary to support the leg at right angles to the top. At left, a framing square is used to

check squareness of the leg to the width of the table. Saw the outer cheek of the mitre pin at a 45° angle (centre), making sure you do not saw through the top face

of the tabletop. Clean up the pins and tail sockets using a sharp chisel (right). A piece of hardboard placed underneath your work protects the benchtop.

MITRED DOVETAIL JOINT

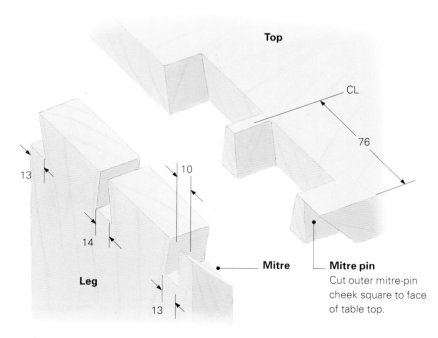

Top

CL

76

13

10

14

13

Mitre

Leg

Mitre pin

Cut outer mitre-pin cheek square to face of table top.

aid for fine-tuning mitres like these. To make one, cut accurate mitres on both ends of a thick hardwood block, then rebate out all but about 13mm on two adjacent faces of the block so it fits over the edge of the workpiece as shown in the photo on p.156.

When all the joints fit satisfactorily, glue the legs to the top. A clamping block can be made by gluing thin band-sawn spacers slightly narrower than the actual tails to the edge of a scrap block, as shown on p.156. A straight piece on one end applies pressure to the mitred strip. There is not much to worry about in this glue-up. When you have pulled the joints tight, check with a framing square to make sure that the legs are at right angles to the underside of the top. You can alter the angle if necessary by changing the position and pressure of the clamps.

When the glue has cured, clean up the joints and adjacent surfaces of the top and legs. Plane the outside edges of the top and legs flush, then chamfer them and the table's other arrises with

DOVETAILED TABLE

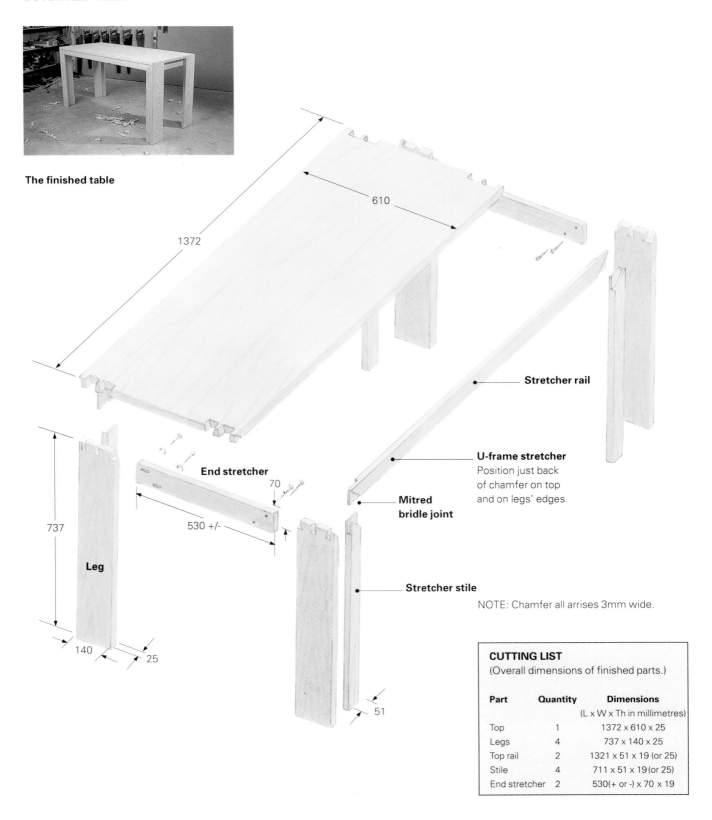

The finished table

Stretcher rail

U-frame stretcher
Position just back
of chamfer on top
and on legs' edges.

End stretcher

70

530 +/-

**Mitred
bridle joint**

1372

610

737

Leg

140   25

Stretcher stile

51

NOTE: Chamfer all arrises 3mm wide.

CUTTING LIST
(Overall dimensions of finished parts.)

Part	Quantity	Dimensions
		(L x W x Th in millimetres)
Top	1	1372 x 610 x 25
Legs	4	737 x 140 x 25
Top rail	2	1321 x 51 x 19 (or 25)
Stile	4	711 x 51 x 19 (or 25)
End stretcher	2	530 (+ or -) x 70 x 19

MITRING THE EDGES

1 Cut the mitres with a backsaw on the knifed lines. Here, the mitre pin on the top is being sawn. Cut as close to the knifed scribe line as possible.

2 To check the fit of the mitres, you will need to drive the joint completely home. A rubber mallet protects the surfaces from damage.

3 A mitre template and sharp chisel trim a leg mitre. Rest the back of the chisel flat on the template and slice thin shavings off the mitre.

ASSEMBLY

1–2 Draw the tails and mitres tight with sash clamps. A bearer block distributes pressure to the tails and mitre strip; the joint's slightly protruding pins fit

between the glued-on wedges. To clean up the joints, secure the assembled table firmly to the bench. The blanket protects the legs from damage on the floor.

a router. Extend the chamfers into the mitres with a chisel and cut mason's mitres where the inner edge of the leg meets the end of the table. (If you chamfer by hand, do so before gluing-up the table.)

Stretchers

The U-frame stretchers are joined with mitred bridle joints. Make the frames just slightly larger than the distance between the legs, so you can plane their edges for a tight fit. A mitred bridle joint is not a lot more difficult to cut than the basic bridle joint. If you band-saw the cheeks, note that the mitred cheek of the tenoned piece must be sawn at a 45° angle with a tenon saw. You can cut the mitred shoulders on the tablesaw or with a tenon saw. The mitred cheeks have enough bearing surface to fit by trimming freehand with a shoulder plane.

Like many bridle joints, mitred bridles may need to be clamped in three directions to pull the joint tight. The one made here required only one sash

MITRED BRIDLE JOINT FOR U-FRAME STRETCHER

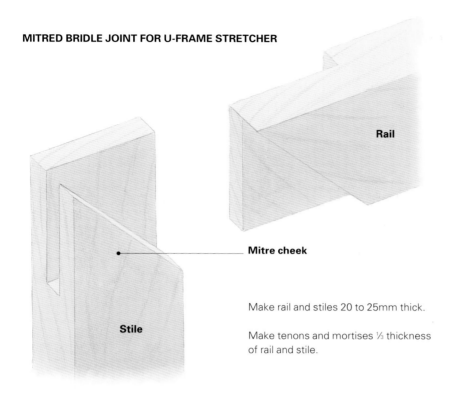

Rail

Mitre cheek

Stile

Make rail and stiles 20 to 25mm thick.

Make tenons and mortises ⅓ thickness of rail and stile.

clamp to tighten the shoulders and mitre. The waste from the mitred cheeks comes in handy as pads for the quick-action clamp that draws the cheeks tight. Fortunately, on an open frame like this you can assemble the joints one at a time so you do not have to hurry so much.

When the frames are cleaned up, plane them to fit tightly against the top and legs. Because the mating surfaces are all long grain, a glue joint is more than adequate between frame and table. To position the frames for gluing, gauge a light pencil line about 1mm in from the chamfer on the edge of the top and legs. It is least messy to apply glue to the table not the frame; keep the glue back slightly from the positioning line and you will have less squeeze-out to clean up. Clamp the frame in place. Complete assembly by screwing the rails across each end. The grain direction of rails and top cross each other, so slot-screw the rails to one leg to allow movement with changes in humidity.

STRETCHERS

1–5 Cut the mitred shoulders with a tenon saw and bench hook (top left). A sash clamp draws the shoulders tight while clamp pads for the quick-action clamp are positioned on the mitred cheeks (bottom left). Note the 'forked' clamp pad that keeps the projecting tenon from interfering with the sash clamp. Quick- action clamps draw the U-frame tight to the legs and top (top centre). Screw the end rails to the legs. Slot screws at the back allow movement (bottom centre).

20

HANGING CABINET

Part of the fun of woodworking is stretching your skills on challenging pieces. Just as the bookcase in chapter 18 provides a basic model for making a range of simple casework, the display cabinet in this chapter is intended to serve a similar role for 'finer' pieces.

The through dovetails joining the case corners and through-wedged stub tenons that fix the internal divisions are mainstays of traditional cabinetmaking valued today as much for their decorative qualities as for their strength and durability. The bridle-jointed door is also a more refined frame than we have met previously. The front shoulders of the mortised rail have been relieved slightly to accommodate a neat mitre on the bevelled inner edge.

Like the joinery, the design is more sophisticated than that of the rough-and-ready bookcase. The overall proportions and the relationships

Opposite: Mathew Burt used English sycamore for this small display cabinet.

between the parts, are more coherent and eye-pleasing, and details receive more attention. For example, the rails and stiles of the back appear to the viewer to be the same size as those of the door frame. By running the horizontal rails the full width of the door, they blend nicely into the lines of the back. Book-matched panels in the back catch the eye from a distance, while neatly mitred chamfers on the case's front edge provide close-up interest.

MAKING THE CASE

The through dovetails joining the case at the corners are similar to the sample set cut in chapter 17. The front edges are mitred, as described in chapter 16, while the back edges are rebated for the panelled back. Rather than cutting a stopped rebate on the case top and bottom, as for the bookcase, these rebates extend the full length of all four parts, which makes them easier to cut. A simple butt joint or mitre across the ends of the rebates would hide them from view, but the unreinforced end-grain glue joint

would eventually fail, opening an unsightly gap. Adding a small dovetail to the butt joint takes a few extra minutes to lay out and cut, but ensures that the joint will never open.

Through-wedged tenons are without doubt the strongest method of fastening the internal dividers in a carcass. But given the strength modern glues bring to a divider housed in a simple dado, the decision to use them usually has more to do with their looks than their indestructability. Note that these dividers are also set in shallow dados so that the chamfered edges of divider and top (or bottom) can meet in a mitre.

The steps for making the through-wedged tenons are shown on p.162. In cutting the joint the stub tenons are laid out and cut rather like square dovetails. The dividers are the same length as the case sides, but when you scribe the tenon length, remember to allow for the depth of the dado. Cut the cheeks with a backsaw, clear the waste with a coping saw and clean out the sockets with a chisel, as for dovetails.

DOVETAIL DETAIL AT REBATE

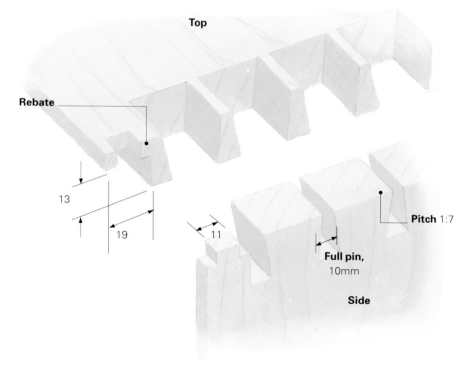

Top

Rebate

13

19

11

Full pin, 10mm

Side

Pitch 1:7

JOINING CORNERS

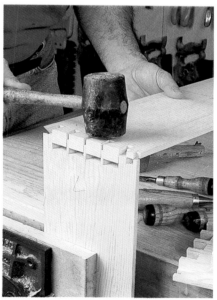

Through dovetails join the case corners. To fit the mitred front edges, drive the joint home dry. A small dovetail secures the rebated back edge.

DOOR HANDLE

(Lightly chamfer arrises.)

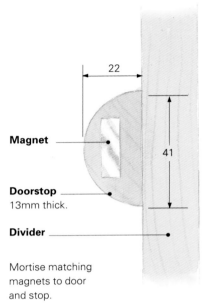

Tenon, 10L x 13W x 6Th

DOOR STOP

Magnet

Doorstop
13mm thick.

Divider

Mortise matching
magnets to door
and stop.

PANEL DETAIL

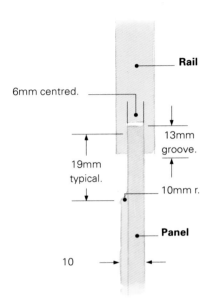

Rail

6mm centred.

13mm
groove.

19mm
typical.

10mm r.

Panel

10

Lay out and cut stopped dados in the top and bottom. For the mitres to meet properly, they must be the same depth as the chamfer on the edges. With only four dados to cut, it can be quicker to knife the shoulder lines, clear most of the waste between them with a router, then cut to the knife lines with a sharp chisel. A crank-neck paring chisel comes in handy for cleaning up the dado bottom. At the front of the joint, the dado is mitred. On the front edge of the top (or bottom) scribe the depth of the dado, then extend 45° knife lines from the lines marking the full-width dado shoulders down to the scribe line. With a small bit, rout between the mitres to establish the depth of the mitred dado. (You will cut the mitres with a chisel a little later.)

For a gap-free joint, the mortises must be very carefully laid out on both faces of the top. The best way to do this is to mark the position of the mortises directly from the tails (again, similar to dovetailing), aligning the front edges of the pieces carefully each time. Extend these lines with a knife and straight-edge or a chisel-point marking gauge. Bore in from both sides to clear most of the waste, then chisel to the knife lines on both faces. Do not be too concerned

CUTTING LIST
(Overall dimensions of finished parts.)

Part	Quantity	Dimensions
		(L x W x Th in millimetres)
Case		
Sides	2	559 x 152 x 19
Top	1	914 x 152 x 19
Bottom	1	914 x 152 x 19
Dividers	2	559 x 133 x 19
Glass shelves, outside	As required	251 x 127 x 6
Glass shelves, center	As required	327 x 108 x 6
Door		
Stiles	2	521 x 44 x 19
Top rail	1	330 x 44 x 19
Bottom rail	1	330 x 70 x 19
Top and bottom fillet	2	241 x 16 x 6
(for glass)		
Side fillets	2	406 x 16 x 6
Handle	1	32 x 22 x 16
Door stop	1	41 x 22 x 13
Hinges (brass butts)	2	44 (L) x 25 (W, open)
Back		
Stiles	2	546 x 57 x 16
Top rail	1	902 x 57 x 16
Bottom rail	1	902 x 83 x 16
Intermediate stiles	2	430 x 108 x 16
Outside panels	2	425 x 184 (+or-) x 10
Centre panel	1	425 x 260 (+or-) x 10

HANGING CABINET

Overall dimensions
914mm wide
559mm high
152mm deep

The finished cabinet

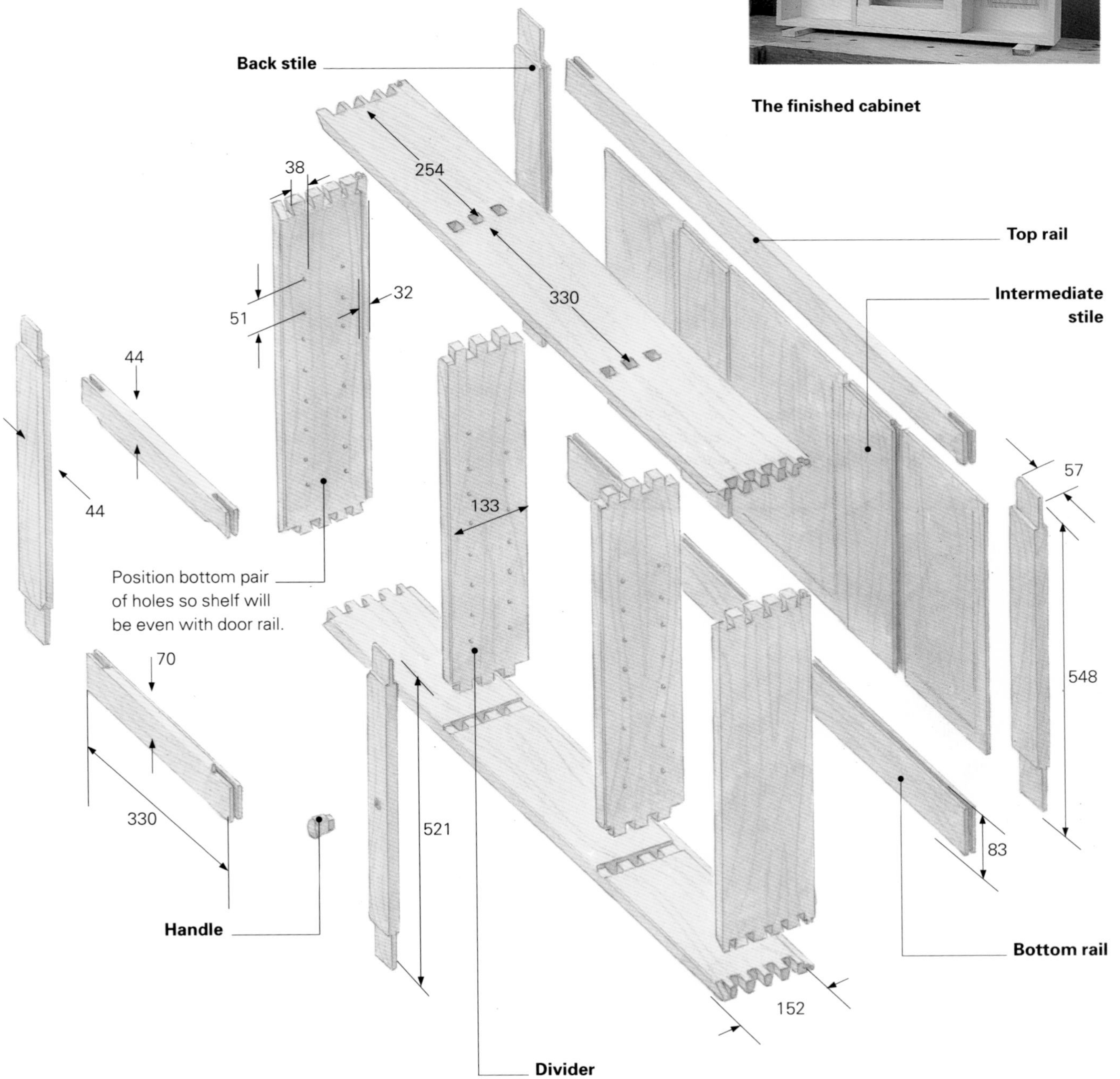

Back stile

38

254

32

51

330

44

44

Top rail

Intermediate
stile

57

133

Position bottom pair
of holes so shelf will
be even with door rail.

70

548

330

521

83

Handle

152

Bottom rail

Divider

MAKING THE THROUGH-WEDGED TENONS

1 Cut shallow grooves to house the dividers. Note the narrow extension of the groove at the front; mitres will extend its width to match the thickness of the divider.

2–3 Lay out the position of the mortises very carefully on both faces of the case top (and bottom). Set the divider in the groove on one face; a square aligns the front

edges. Lay the divider in place on the other face, aligning the front edges by feel. Extend the knife lines with a straight edge or marking gauge if necessary.

4 After boring holes to clear waste, square up the mortises by chiselling carefully from both sides.

5 Trim the mitres against a template. Clamp the template and take thin shavings until the chisel rests flat on the template.

6 The completed mitre. Just before assembly, chamfer the arrises, making the chamfers as wide as the depth of the dado.

if the joint does not dry fit as tightly as a dovetail; the wedges will spread the tenons and close small gaps.

Use a template to chisel the small mitres on the divider and top, as shown in the photo on the facing page. Start by cutting close to but not on the knifed lay-out lines, then try the joint and adjust the depth and angle of the mitres as necessary to get a snug fit.

Before assembling the case, cut the dividers to width (flush with the rebate) and chamfer their front edges and the inner arrises of the top, bottom and sides. Cut saw kerfs diagonally across the tenons for the wedges.

Bore holes for shelf pegs, using a template as described in chapter 18. Short lengths of thin brass rod, polished and chamfered on their ends make handsome pegs. Sand and, if you wish, finish the interior surfaces of the case.

Assembly is less nerve-wracking if done in two stages, as shown on p.164. First glue the dividers in place. If you draw the joints together with clamps, you will need to place them (and a

MITRED AND REBATED BRIDLE JOINT FOR DOOR

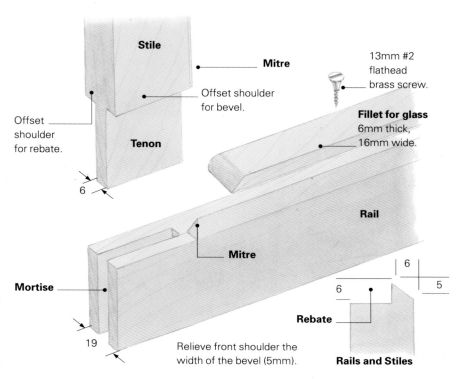

THROUGH-WEDGED JOINT FOR DIVIDERS

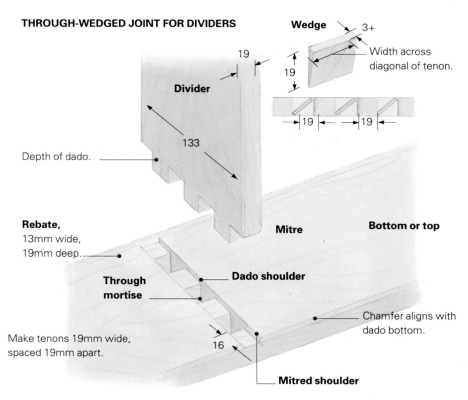

batten to distribute the pressure) to one side of the protruding tenons or you will not be able to drive in the wedges. Offset clamps like these can easily distort the case, forcing it out of square. Driving the dovetailed ends part way on will counter this tendency, but try to use the least amount of clamping pressure possible, and measure diagonals frequently to check for squareness. Make the wedges as wide as the diagonal measurement of the tenons. Taper them on a bandsaw or with a chisel so they are two to four times as thick as the saw kerf.

After the glue has cured on the divisions, add the ends. You can make four full-width clamping pads with narrow shallow tails or draw the tails down individually with a single block. Although the fixed divisions will have stiffened the carcass, you can still make some adjustments for squareness by altering the clamp positions. Check the diagonals with a tape measure to see whether or not the case is square.

CARCASS ASSEMBLY

1 Glue the dividers in place first. Drive the carcass ends part way on to keep the case square. Draw the dividers tight, then drive the wedges in the tenons.

2 Add case ends after the clamps are off the dividers. This clamp block's edge has been chiselled out to straddle the dovetail pins and apply pressure to the tails.

3 Four clamps draw the joints together tightly, while a tape measure is used to check the diagonals to see whether the case is square.

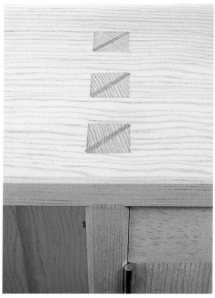

4 Clean up the joints and exterior surfaces of the carcass with a sharp handplane. Boards cantilevered off the bench support the top.

Once cleaned up, the dovetails and through tenons are eye-catching; a coat of oil or varnish will darken the end grain even more than shown here. Note how

the door is recessed behind the chamfers on the edge of the cabinet (centre). Wedging the tenons diagonally closes any small gaps in the joints.

THE FRAME-AND-PANEL BACK

1–2 The frame's wide intermediate stiles are stub-tenoned into the groove cut in the rails for the panels. The corners are joined with bridle joints.

Mark the position of the intermediate stiles carefully before assembly. Screw the back to the rebate and the rear edges of the dividers.

THE BACK

Like the case, the back is divided into three sections. The top and bottom rails are joined to the two end stiles by simple bridle joints, and grooved to take the panels. The wide internal stiles are stub-tenoned (easily cut on the tablesaw) into the panel grooves. See chapter 14 for detailed discussion of the construction techniques. The width of the rails and stiles are set so that the portions of them visible inside each 'bay' of the carcass will match the width of the door rails and stiles.

These panels were made by bookmatching pieces resawn from 38mm thick boards, and fielding them on the tablesaw and router. (Bookmatched boards are edge-joined so the figure forms a symmetrical pattern.) Chamfer inner edges of the rails and stiles before assembly, stopping short of the joints. After assembly, finish them with neat mason's mitres. Fit the back into the rebate and screw it in place, angling the screws slightly into the corner of the rebate.

DOOR JOINERY

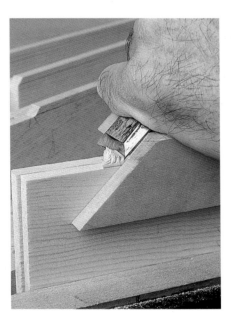

1 To mitre the door's inner bevel, relieve the shoulder on the rail on the tablesaw. Aligned pencil marks on the stile and rip fence indicate where to stop the cut.

2 Cut the mitre at the end of the new shoulder with a sharp chisel and template. Clean up the remaining waste on the shoulder with paring cuts.

3 The partially assembled joint on top shows the rebated face, the one on the bottom the mitred front face, before the bevel is worked on the inner edge.

DOOR FITTINGS

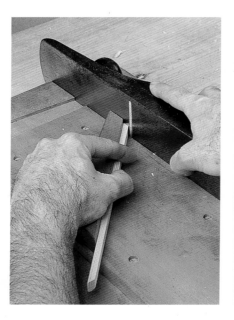

1 Hang the door with small brass butt hinges mortised into the door stile and divider. Position the door just inside the chamfer on the cabinet's front edge.

2 A shooting board with mitre stop helps when fitting the small fillets for the glass. For small pieces like these, you need not saw the mitres first.

3 Screw the fillets to the rebate so they can be easily removed in case of damage to the glass. Note how the rounded edge of the fillet stands proud of the frame.

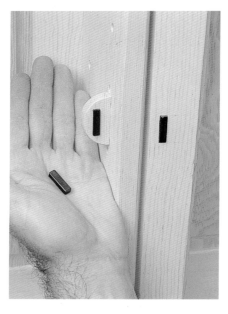

4 To make the handle, dado tenons across the handle blank, then carefully work the tapered oval cross section with a sharp chisel and fine files.

5 By mortising the handle to the stile of the door you can ensure a much more permanent attachment than fixing it with a screw.

6 You can make a simple door catch with two small magnets. Mortise one into the door stile (right) and the other into a small block which you then glue to the divider.

Thomas Loeser's painted cabinet frames an asymmetrical white oak door.

THE DOOR

To provide a view of as much of the contents of the centre bay as possible, the rails and stiles of the door are quite narrow. (The bottom rail, however, is wider than the other parts, to make the proportions more pleasing.) For maximum gluing surface in pieces with such narrow dimensions, the door is assembled with bridle joints, rebated with offset shoulders to take the glass. See chapter 14 again for details of the basic construction.

The inside edges of the door are bevelled and meet in mitres at the corners. Mason's mitres expose small portions of end grain, which darken more than the surrounding wood when finished, a drawback in work of the best quality. To make the 'true' mitres shown here, the front shoulder of the mortised rails must be cut away to the depth of the bevel for the nearly the width of the mating stile, then mitred. Because the rails are rebated, most of the waste can be removed on the tablesaw, as shown on p.165.

When setting up the cut, remember that the arc of the saw will produce a deeper cut on the bottom face of the rebate. Mark the saw's cutting arc on the rip fence and the position of the mitre on the rail and stop feeding the rail into the saw when the two marks draw together. Clear the rest of the waste when you trim the mitre with a chisel and template. If the saw blade is sharp and the setting accurate, the sawn shoulder should fit snugly against the tenon shoulder without trimming. Work the bevel with a sharp bench plane or block plane; the bevel must align with the mitre.

Two small brass butt hinges mount the lightweight door to the divider. The hingeing procedure is the same as that shown in chapter 15. Mortise the hinges to the door stile first, then mark their position on the divider. When scribing the width of the mortises on the door stile and the divider, remember to take two things into account: the door is set into the cabinet just slightly

HANDLE AND SHELF SUPPORTS

The little handle fits well with the clean lines of the cabinet. Note the glass shelf and shop-made peg, cut from a length of brass rod.

behind the chamfer on the front edge. For the door to fully open, the center-line of the hinge pin must be even with the cabinet's front edge.

Once hinged, the door should be planed to show a small, uniform gap all around. If fitted in a dry season, size the gap to allow the rails and stiles to expand when the weather turns humid. If you are fitting to very close tolerances, the weight of the glass could make a difference, so install it before fitting. Thin wooden fillets, mitred in the corners and screwed to the rebates hold the glass in place. The outer edges of the fillets extend just beyond the rails and stiles, and are slightly rounded.

The wooden handle and magnetic catch shown on the facing page are relatively simple to make. You can hang the cabinet by screwing through the top rail of the panelled back into the wall. Alternatively, use a special 'key-hole' router bit to cut blind pockets in the back face of the top rail to take the heads of large screws fixed to the wall.

GALLERY
CHESTS OF DRAWERS

Right

NICHOLAS PRYKE
Veneered in burr ash to
form laminated carcass
components and drawer
fronts, the chest is a
good example of some
of the most complicated
cabinet making
techniques. The painted
aluminium handles have
walnut inserts.

Left
MATHEW HILTON
This chest of drawers is
made of solid maple and
maple veneer on plywood.
Thin veneered panels form
the sides, attached to solid
maple 'wings' either side
of the drawers.

Above
ANDREW VARAH
This small CD storage
cabinet features solid
American cherry,
decorative through
dovetails, and Indian
rosewood handles.

Right
JOHN COLEMAN
Case and drawer fronts of
John Coleman's cabinet
are veneered in makore,
the legs and handles are
bronze. The case is mitred
at the corners.

21

A SMALL CHEST OF DRAWERS

Drawers seem to bring out the curious child in all of us — it is difficult to resist the urge to open them. Woodworkers are especially susceptible to this temptation as drawers provide a quick and reliable indication of the quality of a piece. A drawer gliding effortlessly in a carcass like a piston in its sleeve, handsome rows of precise dovetails at the corners, epitomizes fine workmanship.

This chapter shows how to make a traditional lap-dovetailed drawer and how to fit it into a simple carcass. Though most of the chapter is devoted to the drawers, the carcass, like the cabinet in the previous chapter, demonstrates constructions found in better-quality work. This small two-drawer chest fits nicely under the dovetailed table in chapter 19 or it can stand alone as a bedside table. It is not a big step to imagine a pair of them serving as the pedestals for a desk. Enlarge the case, add more drawers, and you have a bedroom bureau.

Traditional drawer joinery is not easy and takes time to master; do not worry if you have not got the hang of it until you have made a half dozen drawers. Why bother, you may ask, when machine joints and high-quality ball-bearing drawer slides produce perfectly serviceable results? If you are like many woodworkers, the answer lies in the personal satisfaction of mastering exacting technical skills, and in the compliments of family and friends on the handsome results. Of course, you cannot lavish time and effort on all the drawers you make, so we show a serviceable machine-cut drawer joint, too.

MAKING THE CARCASS

For obvious reasons a drawer carcass is usually a simple box: two sides, top, bottom, and back. Here, a loose top is screwed to three lap-dovetailed rails that join the sides. This construction is often used for desk pedestals and other situations where something is 'planted' on top of the case. (Omit the top if you intend to slide the chest under the desk.) Tongue-and-dado joints join the

bottom to the sides. As it is difficult to mitre the front edges of a carcass assembled with tongue-and-groove and lap-dovetail joints, mitred strips were added after the carcass was assembled. The case parts are heftier than usual, at 25mm thick. (Plane them to size from 32mm roughsawn stock.) This is a purely visual consideration; thicker sides seemed to look good with the proportions of the case and drawers.

The drawers are supported by rails and runners housed in full dados and slot-screwed to accommodate movement in the carcass sides. Double stub tenons strengthen the rail-to-side joint. Housing the runners ensures accurate alignment that will not alter with wear and tear over the years. To create interesting shadow lines, the rails are set just behind a small chamfer on the front edge of the case, and the drawers are stopped just short of the edges of the rails. To keep the top drawer from dropping as it is withdrawn, 'top kickers' are screwed between the top carcass rails. Grooves in the sides and top back rail

house the fielded solid-wood back, which slides by the case bottom. A separate plinth raises the case off the floor. Its front corners are spline-mitred, a full dado houses a back rail. (If the case is meant to be seen from the back, mitre that side like the front.)

The techniques for laying out and cutting the joints and assembling the carcass are all covered in previous chapters. (The photos on p.175 summarize the process.) The lap dovetails are made using the same techniques covered below for the drawers.

THE DRAWERS: PREPARATION

The most important attribute of a carcass for drawers is squareness. It is impossible to achieve anything but a rattling fit of drawer to opening in an unsquare or twisted carcass. At every stage of construction — gluing up the sides and bottom from narrower stock, cutting the joints, and final assembly, pay particular attention to squareness.

Drawer fronts are generally made of the same material as the case in which

CARCASS DETAILS

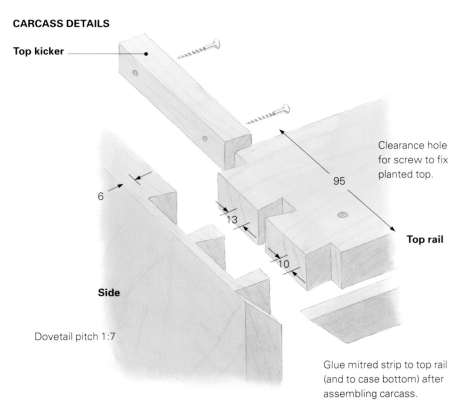

Top kicker

Clearance hole for screw to fix planted top.

95

6

13

10

Top rail

Side

Dovetail pitch 1:7

Glue mitred strip to top rail (and to case bottom) after assembling carcass.

CUTTING LIST
(Overall dimensions of finished parts.)

Part	Quantity	Dimensions
		(L x W x Th in millimetres)
Case		
Sides	2	584 x 492 x 25
Bottom	1	381 x 464 x 25
Mitred strips	2	419 x 10 x 25
Top rails, front and back	2	406 x 95 x 25
Top rail, centre	1	406 x 76 x 25
Drawer rails	2	394 x 64 x 19
Drawer runners	4	394 (+ or -) x 38 x 19
Top kickers	4	95 (+ or -) x 19 x 19
Back	1	568 x 381 (+ or -) x 13
Planted top (optional)	1	419 x 492 x 25
Plinth		
Sides	2	499 x 76 x 25
Front	1	432 x 76 x 25
Back	1	394 x 70 x 25
Corner blocks	2	102 (+ or -) x 38 x 19
Buttons	4	32 x 29 x 19
Drawers		
Top drawer		
Front	1	367 x 76 x 19
Sides	2	457 x 76 x 11
Back	1	367 x 60 x 11
Bottom	1	352 x 457 (+or-) x 10
Bottom drawer		
Front	1	367 x 108 x 19
Sides	2	457 x 108 x 11
Back	1	367 x 92 x 11
Bottom	1	352 x 457 (+or-) x 10
Drawer fittings		
Handles	2	46 x 40 x 16
Drawer stops	2	25 x 41 x 3 (+or-)

they reside. Durability and stability are more important than appearance when selecting wood for drawer sides as you do not want them to wear out, or swell and shrink with changes in humidity.

A surprising number of woods are durable enough. Mahogany and English oak are among the finest, but certain dense, hardwearing softwoods, such as Ponderosa pine, stand up well. As discussed in chapter 2, in any species, the boards least prone to shrinkage across their width are those cut so that their growth rings are nearly perpendicular to their faces. Sometimes you can buy specially cut or selected boards like this,

DRAWER BOTTOM

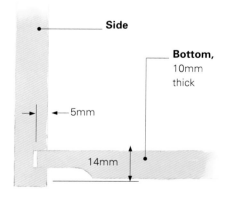

usually sold as 'quartersawn' or 'rift sawn.' Otherwise, picking through a pile of ordinary boards often yields several with the desired ring-orientation.

Flat, square stock is critical for success, so carefully machine the drawer fronts, sides, and backs on the table-saw, surfacer, and thicknesser. Novices frequently make drawer sides too thick; these 11mm thick sides are plenty robust. When the parts are roughly to size, fit the drawer fronts to their openings. Take fine shavings off the ends and top edge, until the front just slips about 10mm into the opening with no gaps visible around the perimeter. (The slightest of bevels back from the face on the top edge and ends eases this task considerably.) Next, cut the drawer back to the same length as the inside face of the drawer front; just use the front as a template.

Square the ends of the drawer sides to the bottom edge freehand with a benchplane or with the aid of a shooting board. Then plane the top edges so the sides can be pushed about half way into their openings with as little play up and down as possible.

DOVETAILING THE DRAWERS
The drawers are lap-dovetailed at the front and through-dovetailed at the back. The drawer back is set below the sides (to make it easy to insert the drawer in the opening) and on top of the bottom. The drawings and photos on pp.176 and 177 detail the process of making one of the chest drawers. Consult them as you read the following discussion.

Lap dovetails (also called 'half-blind' dovetails) are laid out much the same as their through cousins, with marking gauge, square and sliding bevel. Make the length of the tails about three-quarters of the thickness of the drawer front. Note also that the groove for the drawer bottom falls within the width of the bottom tail. The tail hides the groove in the drawer front and the blind socket in the front hides the groove in the side. (Layout is easier if you cut the groove in the sides and front first.) Size and spacing of tails and pins is a matter of taste. Traditionally, fine drawer work had wide tails and narrow pins, with a pitch of 1 in 7 or 1 in 8.

CHEST OF DRAWERS

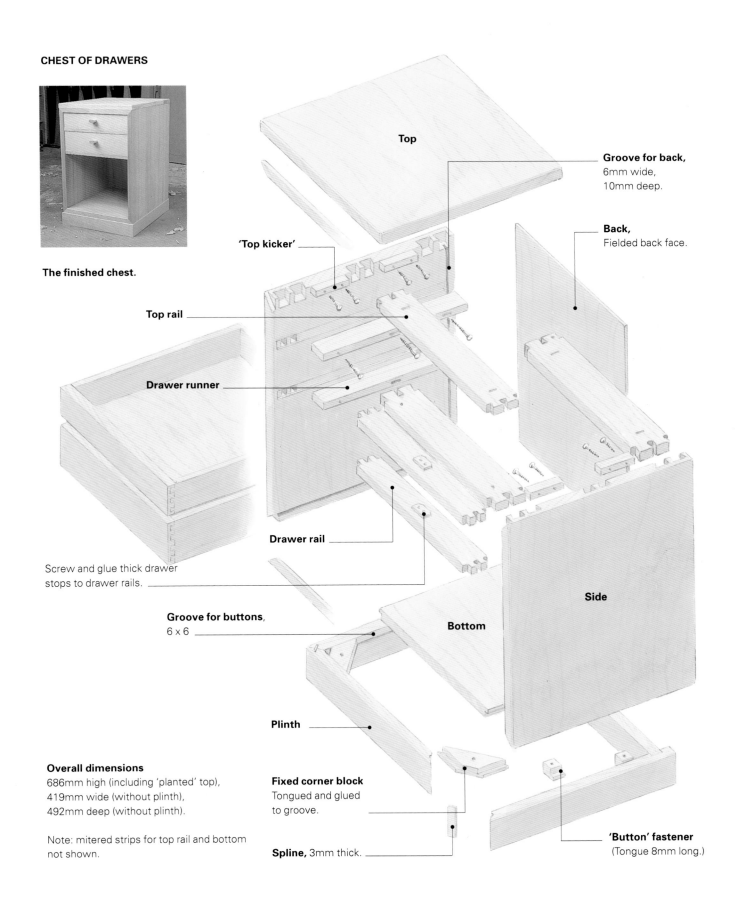

The finished chest.

Top

Groove for back,
6mm wide,
10mm deep.

'Top kicker'

Back,
Fielded back face.

Top rail

Drawer runner

Drawer rail

Screw and glue thick drawer
stops to drawer rails.

Groove for buttons,
6 x 6

Side

Bottom

Plinth

Overall dimensions
686mm high (including 'planted' top),
419mm wide (without plinth),
492mm deep (without plinth).

Note: mitered strips for top rail and bottom
not shown.

Fixed corner block
Tongued and glued
to groove.

Spline, 3mm thick.

'Button' fastener
(Tongue 8mm long.)

The clean lines of Paul Newman's mitred cherry veneered carcass contrast with the irregular edge of the door, which serves as a handle.

Dovetails on thin sides are easy to cut in pairs, which speeds the work. Lay out the tails on one side, then clamp the pair together in the vice, making sure the ends and edges are exactly flush. Extend the layout lines on the end across the end of the unmarked side, then cut along them with a backsaw. Cut the tails for the back in the same way. Clear the waste with a coping saw and clean up the sockets and tails with sharp chisels.

The pins

As for through dovetails, the most accurate way to lay out half-blind pins is to use the mating tails as the template. To help align the pieces, cut a small strip of scrapwood to fit snugly in the drawer-bottom groove, and slip it into the grooves of the side and front.

Position the side by eye so its end barely covers the scribe mark on the end of the drawer front. This should square the side and front, but a quick check with a square is prudent. Carefully pressing the side to hold it in place, scribe along the edge of each tail with a sharp, thin-bladed knife. With a pencil, extend the knife lines down the inside face of the drawer front.

Cutting to the knife lines is the hardest part of making this joint. Not only must you try to saw right to the line, but you must do it at an angle because the socket is 'blind'. You are doing well if you are close enough to the knife line to see fibres breaking away from it as the cut progresses. Stop the cut just short of the scribe marks on the end and back face of the drawer front.

Next, clear the waste from the sockets with chisels. Working 1mm or so in from the scribe for the bottom, or shoulder, of the socket, remove the bulk of the waste by chopping perpendicular to the back face, then popping the waste out from the end.

Complete each socket by carefully trimming to the scribed and knifed lines, striving to split the lines in half. A skew chisel is handy for working into the acute-angled corners. The shoulder, end and cheeks of the finished socket can be very slightly undercut (about the thickness of one or two fine shavings) to ease assembly.

When the sockets are clean, check the fit by gently tapping the tails no more than half of the way into the sockets. Working a slight chamfer on the end and cheeks of the tails (inner face of the side only) will aid insertion.

Assembly

If you have cut and fitted the joints well, assembly is easy. Many woodworkers finish the inside surfaces before assembly; the surfaces are more accessible now and glue will not adhere to finish or wax, making clean up easier. Sand and apply finish only up to the scribe lines, not on any of the joints' mating surfaces. A single coat of sanding sealer (followed by paste wax after the drawer is finally fitted) will provide sufficient protection for the insides of most drawers.

DRAWERS RAIL DETAILS

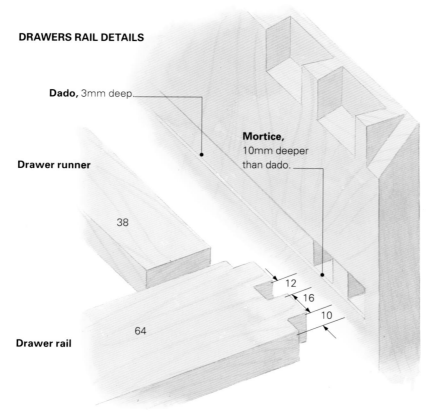

Dado, 3mm deep

Drawer runner

Mortice, 10mm deeper than dado.

38

12

16

10

64

Drawer rail

CARCASS CONSTRUCTION

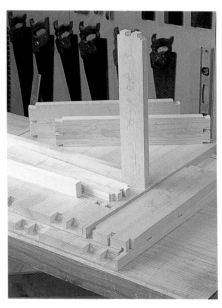

1 Dados for the drawer runners and case bottom intersect the groove for the fielded back panel. All dados stop short of the front edge of the side.

2 Joints are cut, prior to assembly. Top rails are lap dovetailed to the sides; drawer rails stub-tenoned and, with the runners, housed in full dados.

3 Glue up the sides, bottom, and drawer rails with the top rails (unglued) in place keeping the case square. Glue and drive the top rails home next.

4 When cutting tongues or fielding a wide panel, flatten cupping across the panel's width by clamping on a sturdy straight-edged piece of wood.

5 To attach the plinth, screw through front corner blocks glued to the plinth so the front edge of plinth and case will remain aligned. Buttons farther back permit movement.

6 A cranked screwdriver negotiates a narrow space to attach the case top. Countersink the screws so they will not interfere with the drawer front.

DRAWER: HALF-BLIND DOVETAILS

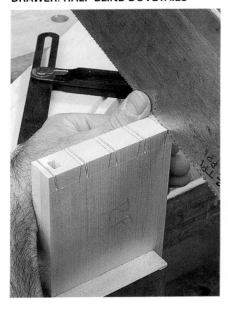

1 It is efficient to cut dovetails on pairs of thin drawer sides. Make sure the edges and ends of the pair are exactly aligned.

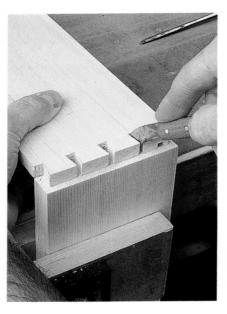

2 After carefully positioning the drawer side on the tail socket scribe line, knife the outline of the tails.

3 Cut the pin cheeks at an angle. Extend the cut up to the lines on the edge and back of the drawer front.

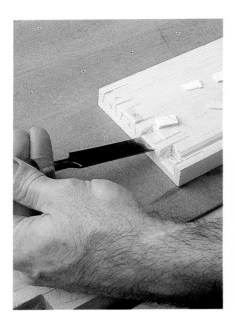

4 Clear the bulk of the waste from the sockets in increments. Chop down across the grain then lift the chip free by chopping with the grain as shown here.

5 With a wide chisel resting in the scribe line, carefully slice straight down in order to square up the end of the socket. You can undercut this surface slightly.

6 Clean up the pin cheeks by nibbling away at the waste in the corner with a chisel. Trim right up to the knifed lines, making careful slicing cuts.

DRAWER CONSTRUCTION

Overall drawer dimension
367mm wide,
76mm high (top),
108mm high (bottom),
457mm deep.

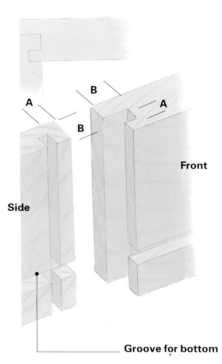

Side

5mm half pin.

Back

Slot screw
bottom to back.

Grain
direction

Front

6mm
full pin.

8mm
full pin.

6mm
half pin.

Bottom

Dovetail pitch 1:7

ALTERNATIVE DRAWER JOINT

A

B

B

A

Side

Front

Groove for bottom

DRAWER ASSEMBLY

Assemble the drawer on a flat surface. Drive the joints home by hand or with a rubber mallet. Draw individual tails tight with clamp and block.

Squareness is crucial for drawers. Apply gentle pressure across diagonals either by hand or with a clamp to equalize diagonal measurements.

Before gluing arrange all the materials and go over the sequence of events in your mind. Brush a thin coat of glue on all the mating surfaces. Laying one drawer side on a newspaper-covered benchtop, push home the drawer front and back as far as you can with hand pressure only, then quickly add the remaining side. A few raps on each tail with a hammer on a narrow hardwood block will seat the joint. A sash clamp and block will draw each tail tight. If the joints fit snugly, there will be no need to leave any clamps on while the glue cures. Push the drawer bottom in place. If the bottom is square, it can help square up the drawer.

Rest the bottom edges of the drawer on a flat surface (a tablesaw is ideal), check for squareness by measuring across the diagonals. Light clamping or hand pressure on appropriate corners is usually enough to even up the measurements. Tap down on each corner to see if the drawer rocks, indicating twist. Placing weight on a raised corner (and the one diagonal to it) usually cures this.

FITTING THE DRAWERS

1 Support the drawer on a piece of scrap wood that has been cantilevered off the bench edge to plane the sides during fitting to the carcass.

2 When fitting, try the drawer in the opening and mark where it hangs up, as shown here. Then take a few thin shavings and try it again.

DRAWER TOLERANCES

Close tolerances in the fit of the drawer sides to the case sides and rails make it a pleasure to open and close a drawer.

The drawer faces are shown with tolerances between the rails appropriate to the most humid time of year.

SIMPLER DRAWER JOINERY

If you want to make a drawer (or whole stack of them) quickly for a project that is not quite as special, you can join the front to the sides with a simple rebate, a tongue-and-dado, or the locking joint shown on p.177, a combination of a rebate and tongue-and-dado that hides end grain of the drawer side.

The joint can be cut entirely on the tablesaw, using the techniques covered in chapter 16. The trickiest part of the process is cutting the rebate and tongue on the drawer face so that the distance between them is exactly equal to the distance between the end of the drawer side and the dado. It helps to cut the rebate and tongue first, then size and position the dado to fit. A few attempts with scrap wood should sort out the method. Join the drawer back to the sides with simple dados, running the sides 25mm or so beyond the back to do so.

FITTING THE DRAWER

A well fitted drawer should slide easily in and out of the carcass. Because expansion and contraction of wood is almost nonexistent across its thickness or along its length, the drawer can be fitted with very little play from side to side in the opening. Wood movement across the grain is what causes problems. Drawers snugly fitted between runners when wood is bone dry from central heating will be immobile when humidity rises and the sides expand. Where humidity fluctuates significantly in a house from season to season, it is best to fit drawers during a period of highest humidity, or anticipate the consequences of that humidity if it is necessary to fit them at another time.

Start fitting by cleaning up the drawer sides, removing squeezed-out glue and protruding pins with a few passes of a sharp hand plane — don't take too much material off now, though. To plane the sides, rest the drawer on a piece of plywood or particle board clamped to the benchtop and protruding over the edge of the bench by the width of the drawer sides.

If you have not already done so, add the drawer bottom at this point, checking that it does not throw the drawer out of square. The grain of a solid-wood drawer bottom runs from side to side. Turned 90°, the bottom would alternately pull out of the grooves or push the sides apart with changes in humidity. To accommodate movement, the bottom is slot screwed to the back. Plywood works well for drawer bottoms, and although wood movement is not a problem, the grain is usually oriented as for a solid-wood drawer. Some makers glue the front edge of solid-wood or plywood bottoms to the drawer front. Do so only after you have finished fitting the drawer — you may need to remove the bottom to make planing easier.

Try the drawer to the opening. Slide it in as far as you can, then note where it seems not to fit —too wide, too high, or both. (Note the same things if it doesn't slip in at all.) As necessary, take a shaving off a side or top edge, then try it to the opening again. Avoid planing the bottom edges unless they're misaligned. Continue checking and planing until the drawer fits all the way. Do not overdo the planing after each trial; you cannot add wood you have planed off.

At the beginning of the process it is worth checking across the width of the bearing surfaces on the inside faces of the carcass sides with a straightedge. If they are bowed in, you can flatten them with a hand plane. (It's a good idea not to attach the runners permanently until after the drawers are fitted, though fastening wide runners in place can sometimes straighten a bowed side.)

Stop planing when the drawer slides all the way into the carcass with only a moderate amount of resistance. A few strokes on the drawer and carcass sides with fine sandpaper followed by a coat of paste wax on bearing surfaces usually reduces resistance to the point where the drawer can be opened and closed with almost no effort.

Now you can fix the drawer runners and carcass back in place. Because the grain of the runners is at right angles to that of the sides, you can glue the front ends while slot screwing them at the back. Slide the carcass back in its grooves, then fix it to the carcass bottom with two screws.

DRAWER STOPS

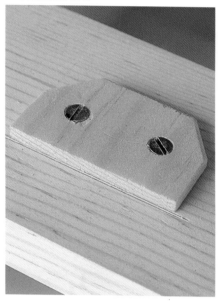

Thin drawer stops glued and screwed into the drawer rail engage the back face of the drawer front. Note that the contact surface is durable end grain.

Mortising the drawer handles into the front of the chest ensures a more permanent attachment than fixing them using screws.

DRAWER HANDLE

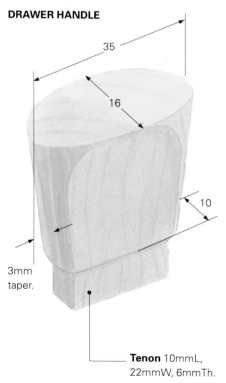

35

16

10

3mm taper.

Tenon 10mmL, 22mmW, 6mmTh.

FINAL DETAILS

Thin pieces of wood screwed and glued to the drawer rail stop the drawer from banging against the back of the case. The contact surface should be end grain, which is much more durable than side grain. Position them so the drawer front stops just behind the front edges of the rail. Err toward the front in placement, as it is easier to trim back a stop that is too far forward than to cut off and reglue one that is too far back.

The drawer handles are similar to those in chapter 20, and are made in similar fashion. Form tenons on a strip of handle blanks by cutting dados on the tablesaw. You can rough out the oval cross section with a series of passes over the tablesaw blade set at different heights. Shape and taper the oval with a chisel and flat file, then use a wide carving gouge (a round file will work, too) to relieve the top and bottom surfaces to produce the profile, which provides a grip for thumb and fingers. Or you can substitute a handle of your own design or one commercially made.

FINISHING TOUCHES

Woodworking is a craft of transformation. Rough timber turns into a neat pile of dimensioned stock; tenons, dados, and dovetails appear, then an assembled table, carcass, or drawers. While it can take weeks to effect these changes, one of woodworking's most dramatic transformations occurs almost instantly at the very end of the process. With a single stroke of a varnish-laden brush or oil-soaked rag, the pale surface of a tabletop, panel, or drawer front leaps to life, its figure shimmering, its colour vibrant. This final section outlines how to ensure the full satisfaction of this moment by careful surface preparation and choice of an appropriate finish.

Opposite: Colour, rubbed into the pores and outlining the chamfered edges, highlights the nature of the open-grained oak and the sinuous lines of the design in John Makepeace's tabletop

22

SURFACE PREPARATION AND FINISHING

Most wood finishes are only as attractive as the surfaces to which they are applied. Clear finishes magnify the effects of poor surface preparation, drawing our attention to flaws which overshadow impeccable joinery or subtle detail. Good preparation brings out the wood's beauty while maintaining the crispness of the design's details. Hand sanding, perhaps augmented by a steel scraper and random-orbit electric sander, can meet the needs of most non-professional woodworkers.

WHY SAND?

Sanding is most frequently done to improve the surface quality of previously dimensioned and shaped pieces in final preparation for applying a finish. Although there are sanding machines that can shape or thickness wood, hand sanding is just too inefficient and inexact for all but the smallest, simplest

Opposite: Sanding is a tedious task, but brings out the beauty in wood.

shaping tasks. Do not use sandpaper as a substitute for a cutting tool. The time you spend mastering the handplane or spokeshave will be a fraction of the time you would spend trying to do the jobs of these tools with sandpaper.

But edge tools have their limits. Even the sharpest handplane will tear some wood fibres as it slices along, particularly where the grain changes direction. These rough spots affect what we see in a wooden surface much like scratches on glass affect what we see through a window. A few scattered scratches go unnoticed; a dense swirl of them obscures part of the view and draws our attention to the scratches themselves. The process of sanding wood, like that of polishing glass, involves grinding away at the surface with a series of increasingly fine abrasives. Large, deep scratches are worn down, replaced by smaller, shallower scratches. As the abrasives become finer, the scratches become so small they no longer obscure the colour, grain and figure of the wood.

Most sanding for furniture work falls into three categories. Large flat surfaces include tabletops, drawer fronts and carcass sides. Narrow flat surfaces include the faces of rails and stiles and the edges and ends of parts. Finally there are shaped surfaces.

SANDING EQUIPMENT

A piece of sandpaper, a sanding block and a dust mask are all you need for hand sanding. There is a surprisingly large range of sandpapers in a confusing array of abrasives, backing materials and adhesives. Fortunately, the 23 by 28cm sheets of paper-backed aluminium-oxide sandpaper carried by most woodworking suppliers will do for most work. Garnet papers are also common; they are less expensive but wear out faster than aluminium oxide.

Sandpapers are rated by 'grit', the number of abrasive particles per square inch of the paper's surface. The higher the number, the finer the sandpaper. (Instead of grit numbers, some papers are labelled Fine, Medium, Coarse and

A SANDING PROGRESSION

Even sharp edge tools can tear wood, particularly where the grain changes direction, as shown here on a piece of curly cherry.

Sanding with 100-grit paper removes the tears, but the scratches created by the coarse grit of the sandpaper now obscure the grain.

Further sanding with 150-grit paper then 220-grit paper produces a 'clear' surface, which a thin coat of paste wax brings to shimmering life.

so on.) For furniture and cabinet work, keep a supply of 100, 120, 150, 180 and 220 grit paper. Grits higher than 220 make sense only for highly figured woods or for sanding out film finishes.

A sanding block makes it easier to hold the sandpaper, helps maintain the flatness of the surface you are sanding and prolongs the life of the paper. The block should be firm but resilient; solid cork or a wooden block faced with a piece of rubber work well. Cut the block to fit your hand comfortably. A block about 6cm wide, 12cm long and 25mm thick accommodates a quarter sheet of sandpaper nicely.

The random-orbit sander is a relatively recent addition to the range of electric-powered hand-held sanding-tools, and the only one of particular value to amateur craftsmens as a surface preparation tool. Belt sanders remove lots of wood quickly, but are difficult to control; far better to plane the surface. Old-fashioned pad sanders with eccentric-cam mechanisms that cause the sandpaper-covered pad to

EQUIPMENT FOR SANDING

Shown here are a shop-made rubber-backed sanding block (top) and cork block with sheets of aluminium-oxide (dark) and garnet (orange) paper.

jiggle around are only marginally more efficient than a sanding block, and they produce unsightly swirling scratches on the surface. The random-orbit sander removes wood efficiently, is easy to control, and leaves only mild scratches. You will need to buy special sandpaper (some models require a Velcro-like backing, others are glued in place on the head), but it is not expensive. The following sanding technique also applies to random-orbit sanding, except that sandpaper grits on the machine cut faster. Where you would use 100 grit by hand, for example, use 120 on the machine. To fully remove the small scratches left by a random-orbit sander, the last grit should be hand-sanded.

SANDING DUST AND YOUR HEALTH

A little sanding can raise a lot of dust, and a nose full of wood dust is uncomfortable and possibly unhealthy. Irritation of the skin and eyes by wood dust is common; some woodworkers suffer allergic respiratory effects, such as asthma. Non-allergenic and mucosal reactions include nasal dryness, irritation, bleeding, and obstruction; coughing, wheezing, and sneezing; sinusitis; and prolonged colds. Even more alarming, studies have established links between wood dust and nose cancer, with suspicions of connections to other cancers. To help protect yourself from discomfort or worse, wear a disposable particle mask for quick sanding jobs and a respirator with filters for prolonged bouts. Some woods seem more problematic than others; if you are concerned about a particular wood, consult public occupational health officials.

SANDING LARGE FLAT SURFACES

Tabletops, carcass sides, door panels – these are the surfaces most often employed to show off the variations in beautiful wood. Properly sanded, the figure, colour and grain of crotch walnut, curly maple, quilted cherry and other, more ordinary woods can be revealed with glowing clarity.

First, be sure that you have gone as far as you can with edge tools. Skim the surface with a finely set, razor-sharp handplane. Then, if you are adept with a cabinet scraper, scrape areas that are

SANDING WIDE SURFACES

A random-orbit sander speeds work on wide, flat surfaces. Work systematically across the surface. The weight of the sander supplies all the necessary pressure.

When sanding near the ends and edges with a block (or random-orbit sander), keep the block flat on the surface, do not allow it to roll over the arrises.

still blemished. Ideally, the surface should look – at a glance – almost good enough to finish before you begin to sand. But resist the temptation to wipe over a few rough spots with fine paper and be done. Begin with 100-grit paper. Work over the entire surface several times with even, overlapping strokes of a comfortable length. Always sand parallel to the direction of the grain, never across it, even at a slight angle. (It does not matter which direction you move a random-orbit sander.) Press hard enough to create some resistance, but do not struggle – additional pressure will not make a better job. Initially, the handsome sheen left by the edge tools will vanish, becoming uniformly dull and dusty. But as you work systematically through finer and finer grades of sandpaper, the sheen will return.

When working near the edges and ends of a surface, take care to keep the block flat on the surface. If you roll it off the edge, you can lose the satisfying crispness of the arris, as the intersection of two flat surfaces is called. Try not to push the block more than one quarter or one third of its length beyond the arris, while shifting pressure to the portion of the block still on the surface. If an area near an arris needs extra work, put pressure on the front of the block and work right up to the arris, but not over it.

Changing grits; changing paper

Knowing when to move on to the next grit is, by and large, a matter of experience. In general, when the whole surface has a uniform look and feel, it is time to change. A good test is to pick out the worst blemish and work on it with the new grit. The surface should quickly become clearer as finer scratches replace the coarser ones of the previous grade. If, however, sanding reveals some deeper scratches, go back to the previous grit, or an intermediate one, and work these scratches out. (Most of the time you will not need to work the entire surface again with the previous grit.)

As sandpaper wears, it cuts more slowly and finely and can even begin to burnish the wood. If you have a large surface or a lot of blemishes to root out,

REMOVING BLEMISHES

You can swell dented fibres back to the level of the surrounding surface with steam created by pressing a hot iron on a wet rag.

---

changing to fresh paper fairly regularly will save a lot of time. But when you are about ready to change grit, let the paper wear down. The slightly polished surface produced by the worn paper makes it easier to see remaining scratches and judge whether it is time to change to the next grit.

Removing blemishes

Torn grain or other blemished spots require additional strokes as you work through the coarser grits. Be sure to extend enough of these strokes into the surrounding area so you do not create a localized depression. (A glossy finish will make even small surface undulations noticeable.) As you work, examine the blemish frequently, up close. Move on when the only scratches remaining are those left by the sandpaper.

'Bruises', blemishes created by compacting or crushing the wood fibres rather than cutting or tearing them, can often be repaired by steaming, which swells the bruised fibres back to their

original level. Place a clean, fairly thick, and damp rag on the bruised area and heat it with an ordinary household iron. Hold the iron down to force the steam into the fibres. Take care not to leave the iron on too long, drying out the rag and possibly scorching the wood.

Glue stains show up as blemishes under most finishes (paint, of course being an exception). Prevention is the best policy for glue stains and squeeze out. When assembling pieces try to apply glue in a way that produces the least amount of squeeze out while not starving the joint. Wiping off squeezed out glue with a wet rag works well only where the surface can be easily sanded afterward. Diluted glue just soaks into the wood, and can be difficult to see until you have applied the first finish coat. Some woodworkers pare off squeeze-out when it has coagulated to a firm gel or when it is fully cured. This is easiest to do when the surfaces have been prefinished; the glue just lifts off the surface. The inside surfaces of carcases and drawers are good candidates for prefinishing.

The final surface

If you really want to show off everything the wood has to offer, the final sanded surface should almost shine, as though there were a subtle finish on it already. (Actually burnishing the wood might interfere with subsequent finishes, but you can get close.) Areas where the grain changes direction or rises obliquely to the surface, as around knots or a crotch figure, should be smooth as glass. Of course, only special surfaces require this lavish attention. For all secondary surfaces (door backs, for example) and even some show surfaces, you may not need to go beyond 180-grit, or even 150-grit paper.

NARROW SURFACES, FRAMES, AND SHAPED WORK

The only difference between sanding a narrow surface and a wide one is the extra care required to keep the surface flat. (It is difficult to keep a random-orbit sander from crowning narrow pieces; take the time to hand sand instead.) Because the block is usually wider than

SANDING TRICKY SURFACES

1–2 Skewing the block to a narrow surface (top) or applying pressure on the centre of an end or edge (bottom) keeps narrow surfaces flat.

3–4 To avoid cross-grain scratches, sand up to the line of a joint (top). Sand concave surfaces with a block shaped to the curve (bottom).

SHARPENING A SCRAPER

1–4 Flatten the scraper's edges with a fine file (top left). Polish the edges and faces with sharpening stones (bottom left, top right). Keep the edge and face square to each other and the arrises crisp. Turn the burr with a burnisher, such as the chisel shown here, held at about 85° to the scraper face (bottom right).

the workpiece, there is a tendency to remove more wood near the edges. So, instead of making contact with the entire block, work near its ends or edges or skew it to the surface and work with the front corner, applying pressure with your fingers to control where the sandpaper cuts. This is important for very narrow surfaces, such as the edges and ends of a table-top or door. Concentrate on cleaning up the centre of these surfaces, and the areas near the arrises will take care of themselves. Sanding end grain can take longer, but the extra effort can reveal lovely pattern and colour.

Sanding two or more assembled pieces that meet at an angle in the same plane requires a sensitive touch. There are two methods. Easiest is sanding across the joint for all but the final grit, for which you sand right up to the joint line. Each grit creates cross-grain scratches on one member of the joint, which must be removed by the next grit. Making new cross-grain scratches seems counter-productive to some, so they use the second method of sanding up to, but not across, the joint line with each grit. Apply pressure on the end or edge of the sanding block to make sure the paper cuts as near the joint as possible. The trick is to do so without creating a depression at the joint. A random-orbit sander creates no scratches when used over such joints, but the members must be wide enough to support the sander or you will end up with crowned surfaces.

Many curved surfaces can be sanded with a flat block – the flat edge of a round tabletop, for example. Some complex curves, like the seat of a Windsor chair, are best sanded with just paper and no block; this requires a deft touch to hold or enhance the shape. Shaped sanding blocks are best for mouldings whose curves are constant along a length of material; they make the sanding go faster, and they maintain the crispness of the details.

THE SCRAPER

Properly sharpened and skilfully employed, a scraper can save you from a great deal of dusty, tiring sanding. A scraper is just a thin sheet of hardened steel whose edge has been 'rolled' to produce a minute cutting edge capable of shearing feathery shavings off the most difficult surfaces. Both the production and use of this 'burr' or 'hook' take time to master, which is why there are a lot of unused scrapers to be found in toolboxes. But if you get the hang of it, a scraper can remove tears much faster than working through several grits of sandpaper.

Like chisels and plane irons, a scraper sharpens best when the surfaces that form the burr, the faces and edge, are flat and smooth. First, flatten the scraper's edges with a file. Then polish the tool's faces and edges with the same series of stones you use to sharpen chisels and plane irons. This will also remove the coarse wire edge left by the file. To turn the burr, hold the scraper in a vice or hang it over the edge of the bench and draw the burnisher (a chisel will do) along the arris at an angle of about 85°. Methods of producing the burr vary. Some woodworkers take just two very light strokes, one up and one back, applying just a little more pressure than that needed to keep the burnisher in contact with the arris. The burr is invisible to the eye, but can be felt. Others raise a more substantial burr with a series of heavier strokes. Experiment to see which method works best for you.

Using the scraper

Grasp the tool with both hands, thumbs in the middle toward the bottom edge. Flex the steel slightly with your thumbs as you put it on the wood, tipped forward at an angle of 70° or 80°. Push the tool away from you, parallel to the grain, adjusting the angle slightly if the edge does not bite immediately. As with a sharp handplane, you should not have to push very hard to raise good shavings.

Cover the surface you are working on in much the same way you would with sandpaper. Overlap strokes; work methodically. Unlike a plane, a scraper has no sole to ride over low spots, so it tends to follow and emphasize any surface contours, which can become quite noticeable under a glossy finish. To counter this tendency, every few

USING A SCRAPER

Flex the scraper and push it with the grain. Adjust the angle of the tool to the face until the burr catches and shears off feathery shavings.

passes alter the angle at which you hold the tool across the grain – skew the tool 30° to the right, then 30° degrees to the left for example. (Regardless of the angle of the tool to the grain, always scrape with the grain.) If you are removing a blemish, be sure to feather the spot very gently into the surrounding area. When the scraper begins to produce dust rather than shavings, it it time to renew the burr with a few more passes of the burnisher at a slightly greater angle. When renewal is no longer effective, return to the file and/or stones.

WOOD FINISHES

The protection, enhancement, and decoration of wood surfaces is a complex and fascinating craft, where practitioners employ millenia-old techniques and substances as routinely as tools and materials of the space age. With them, a finisher can draw out the shimmering figure of a walnut crotch, tint mundane maple any of a rainbow of colours, or impart the distinctive look of quarter-

sawn oak or Cuban mahogany to a piece of common pine.

Acquiring these diverse skills takes more time and more tolerance for the intricacies of modern chemistry than many of us possess. What many woodworkers, and particularly beginners, want is a small selection of clear finishes that can be applied simply and depended upon for consistent results. Here we will examine three such finishes for indoor use: polyurethane varnish applied with a brush, oil finishes applied with a brush or rag, and paste wax, also applied with a rag. To varying degrees, all these finishes enhance the colour and figure of the wood, but do not substantially alter it. All also protect the wood, though here the differences are pronounced and often determine the choice of one finish over the other.

Paint, which alters the appearance of the wood surface drastically, is once again becoming popular as a furniture finish, and painted finishes are commented on at the end of the chapter. Stain, which changes the colour of the wood while allowing the display of grain and figure, is a useful technique, but one that can cause considerable problems for a novice. If you are interested in staining, or any of the vast range of decorative and functional wood finishes, you will find sound guidance in the finishing book listed in 'Further Reading'.

Regardless of the finish you choose, a few basic rules will make your work easier and the results better. Remember that clear finishes (and even paint) usually highlight blemishes, rather than hide them; so do not skimp on surface preparation.

Panels of frame-and-panel doors, carcass backs, drawer bottoms, and the inside faces of carcases and drawers are often a great deal easier to finish before assembly. Just be careful not to get any finish on surfaces to be glued. It is generally a good idea to apply finish to both sides of project parts, so the amount of moisture gained and lost from each face will be in balance and the parts will remain flat. This is less important for case pieces where adequate joinery counters the tendency to warp.

Polyurethane varnish

Of our three finishes, this one is the most durable and offers the greatest protection from heat, water and various solvents and chemicals. Where toughness and easy care are of prime importance, as for tabletops and other surfaces subject to hard use, apply varnish rather than oil or wax. Like traditional shellac finishes (such as French polish) and modern lacquer finishes, varnish forms a film on the surface. Depending on the type of varnish and the 'polishing' you are willing to do, these films vary in reflectivity from matt to high gloss. Of the several different kinds of varnish, polyurethane varnishes, developed in the 1930s, are the ones you are most likely to find on the shelves of local suppliers. Buy a reputable brand and follow the directions on the label and you will find polyurethane a dependable finish.

Varnish flows easily from the brush and sets up slowly, allowing brush marks and air bubbles to dissipate and form a relatively smooth surface. Unfortunately, slow curing is also a disadvantage, as the tacky surface is a magnet for dust particles. If you have to apply finishes in your workshop (as most amateur woodworkers do), let the dust settle for a few hours. Applying varnish at the end of the day works well, minimizing dust problems and allowing the finish coat to cure overnight.

Before varnishing, clean dust off the surfaces to be coated. Vacuuming pulls dust out of the pores and does not raise a cloud of dust that will settle back into the finish. If you cannot vacuum, wipe the surface with a tack cloth, a rag (usually sold in paint stores) treated with a sticky dust-grabbing substance. At the least, just brush the surface carefully and cover it while the dust settles.

If possible, place the surfaces horizontal for varnishing, so the slow-curing liquid will not run. Start by brushing with or across the grain, working the finish into the pores with the first strokes, then brush with the grain to even out the surface with strokes taken with the tip of the brush. Inspect the surface closely for coverage; the finish sets up slowly enough that on all but very large surfaces you will have time

APPLYING A VARNISH FINISH

Work methodically across wide surfaces as you brush on the varnish. In a poorly ventilated room, it is a good idea to wear a respirator rated for organic solvents.

After a coat of varnish has cured, sand out brush marks, bubbles and other imperfections with a fine silicon-carbide paper (as here) or a wet-dry paper.

to even out overlapping areas with light and even tip strokes.

Varnish has a lot of 'body,' and forms a relatively thick film. Heavier use requires a thicker film; two to four coats will serve most purposes. Polyurethane is not difficult to sand, so you need not apply a separate sanding sealer as a first coat. (If you do, make sure it is one formulated for compatibility with the varnish.) If possible, let each coat cure overnight; the longer the finish cures the harder it is and the easier to sand and, if desired, polish.

Sand between coats to flatten brush marks and remove dust or other imperfections. A 220-grit silicon-carbide paper cuts fast and resists clogging and will suffice for many ordinary projects. For flawless 'show' surfaces, use 320-grit or finer wet-dry sandpaper lubricated with white mineral spirits. Regularly wipe off the surface and look at it in glancing light to see imperfections. When you are satisfied, thoroughly clean off dust or slurry and recoat. The final coat can be sanded

with very fine paper and buffed to a high sheen or rubbed with steel wool to produce a duller, 'satin' sheen. If your goal is a glass-smooth surface, you will need to fill the wood pores. The simplest, though not necessarily the most efficient, method is to fill them with finish by sanding the first few coats back almost to the wood.

The organic solvents that constitute a large percentage of any varnish, shellac or lacquer pose a variety of health, safety (fires), and pollution problems. When applying organic-solvent based finishes, work in a well-ventilated room or wear a respirator or mask with organic-solvent filters. Put solvent-soaked rags in airless containers.

In response to legal and consumer pressure to reduce these risks, more water-based finishes are appearing. These finishes are not solvent free, but they certainly reduce the amount you breathe and disperse into the air, and they are not fire hazards. Water-based finishes are tough, like polyurethane, but they are not as resistant to water, solvents or heat. They also pose a number of problems not found in polyurethane. They are less viscous so they do not flow as nicely (bubbles can be a nuisance) and are more prone to runs. Any particles of steel wool that float onto the wet surface will rust, leaving a black mark. Water raises the grain of the wood, resulting in a roughened surface that requires more sanding after the first coat than does polyurethane. While none of these problems is insurmountable, you may want to experiment with water- and solvent-based finishes to decide which you prefer.

Oil finishes

Oil finishes have gained enormous popularity in the past 30 years for two reasons. They produce a handsomely lustrous, silky surface that betrays little evidence of a 'finish' to either hand or eye. And they are truly simple to apply. Just wipe on and wipe off.

The 'oil' in an oil finish ranges from boiled linseed oil, straight from the can, to blends of various oils and varnish, to varnish thinned with a large dose of white spirit. Almost all the oil finishes sold commercially as 'teak' oil or 'tung' oil or 'Danish' oil are forms of the latter two. Boiled linseed oil (which, despite its name, is not refined by boiling) cures hard, but slowly, and offers little protection against water, solvents, or wear. It is cheap, it darkens the wood significantly (often imparting a yellowish cast with age), and three or four coats will rub up to a pleasant sheen. Other than cost and colouration, there is no reason to use linseed oil instead of one of the commercial oil finishes.

Oil-varnish mixes and thinned, or 'wiping' varnishes offer varying degrees of protection depending on their make-up. In general, more varnish and less oil produce a harder, more durable finish with greater resistance to water penetration and damage from solvents. It can be difficult or impossible to find out what is in a commercial 'oil' finish, so you may have to experiment with different brands to find the one that produces the combination of sheen and protection you are after. If you are not a workshop scientist, use

APPLYING AN OIL FINISH

Flood the surface with an oil finish, adding more to spots where the oil is quickly absorbed, then wipe off the excess. Several coats are usually necessary.

polyurethane varnish where you need assurance of protection and oil finishes where you want the oiled look and do not care so much about protection.

Apply oil finishes to well-prepared dust-free surfaces. (Dust will wipe off with the excess finish, so you need not be an overly fastidious duster.) Wipe it on with a rag or apply with a brush, keep adding oil to spots where it has soaked in. Follow manufacturer's instructions about when to wipe it off; those mixes with more varnish set up faster. Several coats are usually recommended for maximum protection (limited though it may be) and best appearance. High-varnish-content finishes can be sanded and buffed to a high sheen or steel-woolled to a satin surface.

Paste wax

Although it offers the least protection of any finish, paste wax is well worth having on your finishing shelf. If your wish is to display the texture as well as the natural colour of the wood, and the piece will be exposed to little wear or

handling, consider a good-quality commercial paste wax. Applied to raw wood, wax produces a slick, dustable surface but is otherwise invisible. Wax is also a good choice for carved or textured surfaces where the sanding required for varnish is impractical and the darkening caused by oil is unacceptable. Many woodworkers finish the face, edges, and ends of a drawer front with varnish or oil and wax all the other drawer surfaces inside and out, as well as the runners and sides of the carcass that contact the drawer. Paste wax can also be used on top of other finishes to add sheen.

Paint

More and more woodworkers are realizing that a 'natural' wood look is not the only choice for handmade furniture. This is in part due to interest in historical furnishing styles, particularly Shaker, early American, and the rustic or country furniture of North America and Europe, in which paint was common. High-style painted furniture, with sleek, flawless colourful surfaces, is also back in vogue. Finally, many woodworkers have discovered that creating different effects with paint can be fun.

Applying paint to furniture with a brush is not much different than applying varnish or painting the trim around your doors and windows or the side of the house. Using a good-quality paint, with appropriate primer on raw wood, you can produce results similar in surface quality to those of the Shaker or country pieces.

Ambitious finishers may want to try milk paints or other historical formulations, or experiment with the wide range of decorative effects that can be produced by manipulating paint and other finish materials with sponges, feathers and other special tools.

Achieving the glassy surfaces of high-style painted furniture is one of the most difficult finishing tasks. It requires good quality spray equipment, specially formulated paints hard enough to be sanded, and flawlessly prepared surfaces. Most importantly, it requires knowledge and sound technique obtained by special training or much trial and error experimentation.

SOURCES OF SUPPLY

Timber
To find your nearest timber merchant consult your local Yellow Pages. Alternatively contact one of the following:

Braemont Timber Ltd, Units A & B, Leith Walk Trading Estate, Leith Walk, Edinburgh EH6 5DX, 0131 554 8628

East End Sawmills Ltd, 367 Dalmarnock Road, Glasgow, G40 , 0141 554 7294

Lathams, Leeside Wharf, Mountpleasant Hill, London E5 9NG, 0181 806 3333

McCall, 16 Blackstaff Road, Clough, Downpatrick, Co. Down, BT30 8SN, 01396 811685

W. H. Newsons, Campaspe Trading Estate, Forbridge Road, Sunbury-on-Thames, Middlesex, TW16 6AT, 01932 780633

North Heigham Sawmills Ltd, Paddock Street, Off Barker Street, Norwich, NR2 4TW, 01603 622978

Timbmett, P.O.Box 39, Chawley Works, Cumnor Hill, Oxford, OX2 9PP, 01865 862223

Whitmores, Main Road, Claybrooke Magna, Lutterworth, Leicestershire, LE17 5AQ, 01455 209121

Boards
Eden Plc., Enterprise Close, Medway City Estate, Frinsbury, Rochester, Kent, ME2 4LY, 01634 291010

Richard Russell, Unit 4, The Ashworth Industrial Estate, 42 Beddington Lane, Croydon, Surrey, CR0 4TB, 0181 684 7575

Tools
Axminster Powertools, Chard Street, Axminster, Devon, EX13 5DZ, 01297 33656

Black and Decker, 210 Bath Road, Slough, Berkshire, SL1 1YD, 01753 511234

Robert Bosch Ltd, PO Box 98, Broadwater Park, North Orbital Road, Denham, Uxbridge, Middlesex, UB9 5HJ, 01895 834466

Grizard Tools, 84a, b & c Lillie Road, Fulham, London, SW6 1TL, 0171 385 5109

Mills Tools Ltd, Unit 14, Sovereign Park, Coronation Road, London, NW10 7QP, 0181 965 1000

Scott & Sargent, 1 Latchford Road, Horsham, Sussex, RH13 5QZ, 01403 273000

Tabwell Tools, Bridge Street, Bakewell, Derbyshire, DE45 1DS, 0162 981 3885

Tool Hire
There are many localized tool hire companies throughout the country, so it is best to consult your local Yellow Pages for those nearest to you. Below is a brief list of those companies which cover a wider area.

Countrywide
Jewson Hire Point, HSS Hire Shops,

Scotland
Hewden Tool Hire,

North-East
Lord Hire Centres

Birmingham area
A. Webbs Power Tools Ltd , 0121 459 9789

FURTHER READING

Woodworking is a vast field which no single book can hope to encompass. As you master the basic traditional woodworking skills in this book, other techniques and other aspects of woodworking will doubtless pique your interest. The following books are excellent reference books that can help you broaden your woodworking skills. Unfortunately, there isn't space to list even a sampling of the numerous books devoted to more specific technical topics or design, those that showcase contemporary and historical work, or those that examine the personal, rather than practical, side of the craft. Consult a book store or your library for such titles.

Encyclopedia of Furniture Making. Ernest Joyce, revised by Alan Peters. B.T. Batsford, London (UK); Sterling Publishing Co., New York (US). 1987. An excellent reference for construction, joinery, and techniques, though not a 'how-to' book.

Tage Frid Teaches Woodworking: Two Books in One, Unabridged. Tage Frid. The Taunton Press, Newtown CT (US). 1993. Book 1 (Joinery, tools and techniques) and Book 2 (Shaping, Veneering, and Finishing) in a single soft-cover volume. Step-by-step photo narrative by Danish-trained master craftsman.

Understanding Wood: A craftsman's guide to wood technology. R. Bruce Hoadley. The Taunton Press, Newtown CT (US). 1980. How wood behaves and why; essential reference for any woodworker.

The Workbench Book. Scott Landis. The Taunton Press, Newtown, CT (US). 1987. A wealth of practical and interesting information about work-holding devices; with numerous plans.

The Workshop Book. Scott Landis. The Taunton Press, Newtown CT (US). 1991. A detailed investigation of what shops need to do, with real-life examples.

Understanding Wood Finishing: How to select and apply the right finish. Bob Flexner. Rodale Press, Emmaus PA (US). 1994. A lucid and very practical examination of this complex subject.

Turning Wood with Richard Raffan. Richard Raffan. The Taunton Press, Newtown CT (US). 1985. Superb introduction to the wood lathe

Cabinetmaking, The Professional Approach. Alan Peters. Stobart & Son Ltd. London. 1984. A valuable guide for anyone considering craft woodworking as a profession.

INDEX

Page numbers in **bold** refer to the illustrations

AUTHOR'S ACKNOWLEDGEMENTS

There are a great many people that have made this book possible, and I regret that I can thank only a few of them by name here: Michael Farrell for his abundant energy, good humor, and fine photographs. Catriona Woodburn, Alistair Plumb, Janet Swarbrick, Helen Fickling, Clare Limpus and Helen Green at Conran Octopus for their hard work and forebearance. Rick Mastelli, Deb Fillion, Paul Bertorelli, Scott Landis, Deb Cannarella, Laura Tringali, and John Kelsey for years of stimulating talk about woodworking and what it takes to capture its essence on the page. Alan Peters for the privilege of working with a true master craftsman. Numerous woodworkers in Britain and the U.S. for sharing their work, their shops, and their thoughts over 25 years. The editors and publishers of the magazines *Fine Woodworking*, *Woodworker's Journal*, and *American Woodworker* in which versions of much of the material in this book first appeared. Finally, my father, Ralf Holmes for introducing me to woodworking; my mother, Helen Holmes for her encouragement; and my wife, Margaret, and children, Joseph, Zoe, and Benjamin, for keeping my spirits up during a very hectic year.

PUBLISHER'S ACKNOWLEDGEMENTS

The publisher would like to thank Jonathan Baulkwill for his assistance with the Anglicization, Trevor Semple and Paul Smith for their help, advice and use of their workshop facilities.

PICTURE CREDITS

The publisher thanks the following designers, photographers, makers and distributers for their kind permission to reproduce the photographs in this book:

Endpapers: Christine Osbourne Pictures; 2-3 Photo: Michael Freeman; 4 Design: Stemmer & Sharp; 6 Photo: Michael Freeman; 7 Photo: Sara Morris/Design: Erik de Graff/Craft Council; 8 Design: Stephen Hounslow/Pearl Dot; 9 above: Photo & Design: Illingworth & Partridge; 9 below: Photo: Silvio Posada/La Casa de Marie Claire; 10 Photo: Peter Martin & Liz Elders; 11 Photo: Ron Sutherland ; 12 Photo: Nick Brown/Design: Illingworth & Partridge; 13 Photo: David Barrett/Homes and Gardens Magazine/Robert Harding Syndication; 14 Photo: Michael Freeman; 15 Design: Robert Williams/Pearl Dot; 16 Photo: Andrew Watson/Design: Paul Gower; 17 Photo: Peter Martin & Liz Elders; 18 courtesy of Timbmet Ltd; 20 Christine Osbourne Pictures; 21 above left: Photo: David Cripps/Design: Adrian Swinstead; 21 above centre: Photo: David Gilliland/Design: Mathew Burt Splinter Group; 21 above right: Photo: Paul Lapsley/Design: Andrew Varah; 21 below left: courtesy of William Watts; 21 below right: Photo: Derry Robinson/Design: Wales & Wales; 22 Photo: Jon Stone/Design:Mathew Burt Splinter Group; 23 Photo: Jean Pierre Godeaut; 24 Photo: David Askham courtesy of Woody White (Fairground Woodcarver); 25 Ron Arad Studio, Italy; 26 Photo: Jean-Christophe Buggeai/Maison & Jardin; 27 Photo: Michael Freeman; 28 above: Photo: David Askham courtesy of Philip Hawkins; 31 Photo: Michael Freeman; 32 Photo: David Askham courtesy of Victor Hatherley; 40 Photo: Ken Adlard; 46 Photo: Angelo Hornak; 47 Photo: Tony McMullen; 48, 52, 58, 62 Photo: Ken Adlard; 67 above: Photo: John Tyler/Design: Robert Kilvington; 68 Photo: Ken Adlard; 74 Photo: Geoffrey Onyett/Design: Alison White; 75 Photo: Peter Martin & Liz Elders; 76 Photo: Ken Adlard; 84 left: Photo: Peter Hodsoll/Design: Samuel Chan/Fiell International Ltd; 84 above right: Photo: Robert Clifford/Homes & Gardens/Robert Harding Syndication; 84 below right: Design: Stemmer & Sharp; 85 above right: Design: Robert Williams/Pearl Dot; 85 below right: Photo: Dean Powell/Design: Rosanne Somerson/Peter Joseph Gallery; 85 left: Photo & Design: Rupert Williamson; 86 Photo: Steve Hall/Design: Howdle Bespoke Furniture Makers; 92 Photo: Alison Needler/Design: Nielson & Nielson; 96 above: Design: Robert Williams/Pearl Dot; 96 centre: Design: Stemmer & Sharp; 96 below: Design: Achille Castiglioni/Zanotta - Interior Marketing; 97 above left: Shaker Ltd; 97 above right: Photo: Graham Pearson/Design: Nicholas Pryke; 97 below: Photo: Ian Dobbie/Design: Mathew Hilton/SCP Ltd; 98 Photo: Jim Lowe/Design: Mathew Burt Splinter Group; 104 above: Design: Stemmer & Sharp; 104 below left: Design: Robert Williams/Pearl Dot; 104 below right: Photo: Jon Stone/Design: Mathew Burt Splinter Group; 105 above: Photo: Mann & Man/Design: John Callen; 105 below: Design: Andrew Lawton; 106 Design: Samuel Chan/Channels; 112 above right: Design: Nicholas Bentley; 114 Photo: Ian Skelton/Design: Alistair Fleming/AFD; 115 above left: Design: Robert Williams/Pearl Dot; 115 above right: Photo: David Barrett/Homes & Gardens/Robert Harding Syndication; 115 below left: Photo: Tim Imrie/Design: John Coleman; 115 below right: Design: Robert Williams/Pearl Dot; 116 Design: Oliver Morel/Bridgeman Art Library; 122 Design: Thomas Loeser/Peter Joseph Gallery; 124 Design: Robert Williams/Pearl Dot; 125 Ken Adlard; 126 above left: Photo: Ruth Davis/Design: Pat Booth/Studio Kew Bridge; 126 above right: Design: Hugh Scrivens/Crafts Council; 126 below: Photo: Mann & Man/Design: John Callen; 127 above: Design: Stephen Hounslow/Pearl Dot; 127 below: Photo: Peter Hodsoll/Design: Samuel Chan/Fiell International Ltd; 128 Photo: Ken Adlard; 134 Photo: Angelo Hornak; 140 left: Photo: Jack Evans/Design: Tony McCullen; 140 above right: Photo: Tim Imrie/Design: John Coleman; 140 centre right: Photo: Mike Murless/Design: Paul Gower; 140 below: Design: Robert Williams/ Pearl Dot; 141 above: Design: Roy Tam & David Colewell/Trannon Furniture/Craft Council ; 141 below: Design: Andrew Lawton; 142 Design: Nicholas Below/Aero Wholesale Ltd; 147 above: Design: David Field/Craft Council; 150 left: Design: Stemmer & Sharp; 150 above right: Design: Roy Tam/Trannon Furniture/Craft Council; 150 below right: Photo: Mike Muroess/Design: Petter Southall/I tre; 151 above: Robert Williams/Pearl Dot; 151 below: Photo: Tim Imrie/Design: John Coleman; 152 Photo: John Tyler/ Design: Robert Kilvington; 158 Photo: Jon Stone/Design: Mathew Burt Splinter Group; 167 Design: Thomas Loeser/Peter Joseph Gallery; 168 Photo: Graham Pearson/Design: Nicholas Pryke; 169 above left: Photo: Ian Dobbie/Design: Mathew Hilton/SCP Ltd 169 below left: Photo: Paul Lapsley/Design: Andrew Varah; 169 right: Photo: Tim Imrie/Design: John Coleman; 170 Design: Codrington Furniture; 174 Design: Paul Newman/Aero Wholesale Ltd; 180 Photo: Mike Murless/Design: John Makepeace; 181 Photo: Peter Martin & Liz Elders; 182 Photo: Ken Adlard

All other photography by Michael Farrell

Every effort has been made to trace the copyright holders and designers and we apologies in advance for any unintentional omission and would be pleased to insert the appropriate acknowledgement in any subsequent edition.